'Amanda's work and writing is a whole practice for artists seeking a greater connection through the creative expression of performance. My work with her has been invaluable and through her thinking and teaching I feel that my work as an artist can take on an importance to me and the people I connect with in a performative environment that transcends the simple act of regurgitating someone else's writing. She deals with a whole universe of connected energies – through qigong and her interest in the energy within the performer she empowers us as actors to do something pure, simple and revolutionary in its implications. The delicate balance and exchange of energy she talks about in this book will be eye-opening to anyone in the creative arts. Dancers, actors on stage and screen, and musicians can have a fire lit within them by her gentle wisdom. I am eternally grateful that I met her as a student and always seek her out to work on characters and to discuss the physical and inner life of the people I am trying to inhabit. She elevates the work of the artist to a spiritual level and I realised through working with her that there was nothing else I want to do through being an actor.'

— Johnny Flynn, actor and musician

'An insightful and brilliantly researched study of emotional awareness rooted in an in-depth understanding of the anatomy of the body. Offering both practical and holistic exploration to support and interpret character through imagination and perception, it is an inspiration for anyone involved in public speaking and communication and an absolute must on every actor's bookshelf. I shall treasure it on mine!'

— Sara Kestelman, actor and writer

of related interest

Breath in Action
The Art of Breath in Vocal and Holistic Practice
Edited by Jane Boston and Rena Cook
Foreword by Cicely Berry
ISBN 978 1 84310 942 6
eISBN 978 1 84642 948 4

You Are How You Move
Experiential Chi Kung
Ged Sumner
ISBN 978 1 84819 014 6
eISBN 978 0 85701 002 5

Meet Your Body
CORE Bodywork and Rolfing Tools to Release Bodymindcore Trauma
Noah Karrasch
Illustrated by Lovella Lindsey Norrell
ISBN 978 1 84819 016 0
eISBN 978 0 85701 000 1

Rhythm and Timing of Movement in Performance
Drama, Dance and Ceremony
Janet Goodridge
ISBN 978 1 85302 548 8
eISBN 978 0 85700 104 7

the Energetic Performer

An Integrated Approach to Acting for Stage and Screen

Amanda Brennan

SINGING
DRAGON
LONDON AND PHILADELPHIA

Figure 3.1 is taken from Henry Gray (1918) *Anatomy of the Human Body* (20th edn, thoroughly rev. and re-edited by Warren H. Lewis), Philadelphia, PA: Lea & Febiger, and is reproduced with kind permission of www.bartleby.com.

Figure 3.3 is taken from Jim Harter (ed.) (2005) *Old-Time Anatomical Illustrations*, New York, NY: Dover Publications, and is reproduced with kind permission of Dover Publications.

Figure 7.1 is reproduced with kind permission of Sensei Phil Perez of the Northern Crane Martial Arts Association.

The five-step exercise in Chapter 2 is taken from Stanley Keleman (1987) *Embodying Experience: Forming a Personal Life*, Berkeley, CA: Center Press, and is reproduced with kind permission of Center Press.

Extracts from the script of *The White Queen* are reproduced with kind permission of Emma Frost and Company Television Ltd.

First published in 2016
by Singing Dragon
an imprint of Jessica Kingsley Publishers
73 Collier Street
London N1 9BE, UK
and
400 Market Street, Suite 400
Philadelphia, PA 19106, USA

www.singingdragon.com

Library of Congress Cataloging in Publication Data
Names: Brennan, Amanda, author.
Title: The energetic performer : an integrated approach to acting for stage and screen / Amanda Brennan.
Description: London ; Philadelphia : Singing Dragon, [2016] | Includes index.
Identifiers: LCCN 2016006330 | ISBN 9781848190979 (alk. paper)
Subjects: LCSH: Acting.
Classification: LCC PN2061 .B725 2016 | DDC 792.02/8--dc23 LC record available at http://lccn.loc.gov/2016006330

British Library Cataloguing in Publication Data
A CIP catalogue record for this book is available from the British Library.

ISBN 978 1 84819 097 9
eISBN 978 0 85701 084 1

Printed and bound in Great Britain

MIX
Paper from responsible sources
FSC
www.fsc.org   FSC® C013056

For my mother

ACKNOWLEDGEMENTS

Along the way there are many people who have supported and encouraged me and without whom it is likely I would have fallen at the first hurdle. First, I thank all the many actors who I have taught and especially to those who have given their time to explore exercises and share in discussion. There are too many to mention, but these few have been pivotal: Fiona Graham, Antoinette Tagoe, Nicky Raby and Johnny Flynn. I also thank colleagues at Royal Central School of Speech and Drama, particularly Nick Wood, who read early drafts of the manuscript and made wise comments.

Armen Gregory and Miriam Lucia took many of my classes whilst I struggled with words, and for this I am very thankful. I am also grateful to Philippe and Annie Cherbonnier who let me stay in their house in France at one point in the journey, and to Janis Pugh who brought humour and immense support in times of despair and also provided a refuge by a lake in summer 2015.

My deep gratitude also goes to Naomi Waring with whom I first shared the idea to write this book and who freely contributed her ideas, time and brilliant imagination, as did the three artists – Daniel Hughes, Valentina Piras and Amy Stevens.

I give thanks to my dearest friends – Evelyn Gillan, who was a beautiful and inspiring woman, Sara Kestelman, Rose Rouse, Laura Blumenthal, Teresa Ward, Melanie Carrick, Jake Farr, Carolyn Fellus and Sarah Mair Thomas – who always said the right things, and to my son, Jacque, who prompted me to keep going by giving me love and encouragement. I thank Emily Gowers for guiding me through the editing process, as well as Jessica Kingsley for believing in me and being very patient.

CONTENTS

INTRODUCTION

Background

Teaching and coaching presents challenges. It involves finding solutions and being curious about 'why' and 'how'. As a result of reflections and musings on what seemed like repeated obstacles in my work, I felt the need to experiment and look further afield. These obstacles revolved around the body and what to do with it.

It seems to me that when I am working with an actor they want to know how to do one or more of the following:

- to summon feelings and emotions that are believable and creatively portray the imaginative situation

- to find depth, detail, originality and truth

- to discover a genuine connection with whom they are working.

There are many techniques that, with dedicated training, provide this. However, despite many years of experience, I felt something was missing in what I was doing.

My approach to working with actors is influenced by many sources. Rather than being a pure disciple of any one method, I have applied and adapted as I have grown as a practitioner. My initial training was at Darlington College of Arts, the location in which Michael Chekhov found himself in 1936, and, although I did not realise whilst studying, it was his techniques that were to have a profound impact on my later practice. How I teach has always been rooted in psycho-physical methods, primarily Stanislavsky and Chekhov, but I have also embraced the ideas of Jerzy Grotowski, Eugene Barba, Philip Zarrilli, Tadaski Suzuki and Lorna Marshall, to name a few. Providing and believing in the idea of the tool kit has been fundamental.

The discoveries

My solution to these ongoing challenges came by accident when due to an injury I was introduced to qigong and quickly discovered that as a result of a few weeks of practice my body felt different. I was aware of new sensations, and able to feel subtle inner movement, which despite tinkering with other bodywork practices, such as yoga and Alexander Technique, I had never experienced before. Over time, I observed how sensing and feeling was enhanced. I learned how to quieten my mind and adapt to situations where I may have previously become overwhelmed. I immediately realised that placed beside my existing actor-training practice, qigong would proffer interesting results. As the two languages can be quite alien to each other, it was with caution that I gradually introduced the key concept of qi and the principles of Traditional Chinese Medicine. Once I developed confidence in the approach, I trained to teach qigong at the Elemental School of Qigong in London and started to use it in my practice. The positive effects were instant.

Following this discovery, I found my knowledge on anatomy and physiology lacking and undertook a year's course in living anatomy with the Craniosacral Therapy Educational Trust. My direction shifted again towards biology, energy medicine and somatic psychology. Coming across research papers on topics such as anxiety and performance, self-talk and the role of mental imagery also stirred a curiosity in scientific studies. So began further interrogation on topics which, as an acting specialist, I had not considered relevant to my work.

It often seems like what is current is almost in the air, which would fit with Rupert Sheldrake's concept of morphic resonance. By this I mean that there are not only trends in fashion and style but in what seems important to us, what knowledge needs to surface to satisfy the condition of the world we live in at any one time. In the early twentieth century, the leaders in actor training were toying with concepts which reflected a world in transition in all aspects of life. The work of Stanislavsky and Chekhov incorporated the discoveries in social science, philosophy and even areas such as the occult and telepathy. Both embraced the philosophies of Eastern cultures and experimented with ideas, notably around energy, which can be seen to be ahead of their time. In different parts of the world there were pioneering inventions and studies, some of which were not quite linked up. It was not so common for disciplines, such as the pure sciences, to combine and provide shared knowledge. The continued incorporation of Eastern training methods into contemporary acting practice has been cultivated by practitioners such as Suzuki, Zarrilli, Marshall, Barba and Grotowski. But what has been in the air since the early 2000s is the growing interest in neuroscience and acting. Rick Kemp and Rhonda Blair are examples of trainers who have written excellent books that tackle this complicated territory and suggest how current studies can contribute to the pursuit of embodied performance.

The challenges

So I came to write this book and place the various topics that interest me and seem relevant side by side. It is an account of how I currently work. It is not necessarily anything totally brand new but builds on the practice of many actor trainers. The main difficulty over the last seven years has been how to make at times quite complex material accessible. I have struggled with the basic principles of physics, biology and chemistry, subjects that I steered well away from at school; got side-tracked by fascinating studies in areas like tensegrity, healing and cures for disease, earthing as a solution for jet lag. (The list goes on but I arrived at this particular compilation.)

The goal

I set out to find strategies that would support my work as an acting teacher/coach. I wanted primarily to extend my knowledge and experiment, to see what else could contribute to the pursuit of embodied acting. I had a lot of techniques up my sleeve that I could rely on, but consolidating and branching out seemed like a good idea.

The intention behind this book is to offer options for training actors, professional actors and teachers/coaches. The core principles which are integrated into the chapters are:

- You are always working from yourself as the starting point.

- The body can be adaptable and transformative.

- It is beneficial to understand how your body works in order to fully utilise it.

- Creative freedom is enhanced by challenging yourself to embrace and flow with change.

- The craft of acting requires continual training.

How the book is organised

The book is structured into two parts: Part 1 contains eight chapters each of which explores a discrete area and draws on factual information and various strands of research. Some of the disciples that are explored are somatic psychology, Traditional Chinese Medicine, bodywork practices, anatomy and physiology, sports science, and the work of established actor trainers, most notably Michael Chekhov. In each chapter the discussion and ideas presented are supported by exercises.

Part 2 focuses on application. It contains 15 shorter chapters on topics that regularly crop up in my work, such as preparing for auditions, making creative choices and being present. It begins with a fundamental approach to applying some of the concepts of Part 1, then provides exercises and working processes for rehearsals and performance.

How to use the book

The book does not have to be read from beginning to end; the reader can dip in and out according to interest. In many ways I touch on topics which could fill entire books in their own right, so see my chapters as starting points to encourage further reading and experimentation.

Part 1

ACTORS AND THEIR INNER LIFE

Chapter 1

YOU
A place to begin the work

Introduction

The starting point for the work of an actor is their own body. It is the primary resource which is used to transition into fictional worlds. Having the facility to be available and as freely expressive as possible is a goal which seems both essential and valuable. The approach encouraged throughout this book is one which emphasises the importance of knowing and understanding your body. We all have a certain amount of awareness, and the aim here is to deepen this, to suggest where to begin or to where we need to return.

There are amazing stories present in your body, all of which reveal the clues and mysteries of who you are and how your past has shaped your present. Understanding yourself opens the gate to accessing and drawing on your own experiences as the fundamental component of creative work. Each one of us is fascinating, with the depth of an ocean. At your disposal is an instrument from which you can both utilise the familiar and shift into the unknown.

With the recognition of the complex layers within the body comes the possibility to sharpen receptivity and broaden your imaginative range. Nothing creatively interesting will occur unless you learn how to play, respond with spontaneity and move from what is familiar into a creative place where anything is possible. Just as your body is your resource, it can also be your obstacle, and to be able to use it like an artist uses clay or a musician a range of notes, there needs to be an investment in working to facilitate the possibilities. The premise is that you are the material from which to build.

In this chapter I look at how the shape of our body has emerged and consider the broader contextual influences. I want to identify what it means to become aware and what to actually notice. This starts with the layers and structures within, your breath, thoughts and vitality, and the idea that by tuning in to changes and transitions you can feel more connected to your own instrument.

Your body shape

Let's look at the whole body as if it is a piece of carved architecture. The shape has not emerged accidentally but rather has been influenced by a response to the joys, pleasures, intellectual tasks, creative pursuits, traumas and shocks. It articulates needs and expresses the relationship to deepest desires, and to a large extent defines identity. Your shape affects how you interface with and are received by others. It is clear to recognise that an open and relaxed body tends to be easier to access and respond to than one which is taut and rigid, as there is less defence. If we look at stereotypical perceptions of body composition, strict and controlling characters, such as dictators or army generals, are usually stiff and inflexible; angels and heroines are soft and slight, and baddies are either huge, twisted or disfigured. Body shape reveals the clues to the traits and qualities of a person.

The outer shape that has evolved through a lifetime has implications for the many shapes inside, as the two work hand in hand. Literally, the organisation of organs, bones and the endless lengths of veins and arteries that form the cardiovascular system, the intricate web of the nervous system which passes messages and stimulates impulses, are all organised into a neatly packed structure. It is like a jigsaw puzzle, with every piece integrated and ideally fitting together to create one complete vibrant landscape through which the rivers of sensation and emotion run. As there are no static moments within a living body, the scene constantly changes and realigns in reaction to the stimulus encountered. During life, layer after layer of experience is laid down and stored, and what is visible to the eye is the surface of a very deep canyon. As Stanley Keleman suggests:

> Life makes shapes. These shapes are part of an organising process that embodies emotions, thoughts and experiences into a structure. (Keleman 1985, p.xi)

There are two aspects to body shape: one that is visible (the gestures and movement patterns which form outer expression); and one that is all that is inside (the inner world, the physiological action which creates feelings, emotions and every impulse which flows). Both aspects are completely intertwined. Figure 1.1 shows how the shape of the spine moulds the external structure.

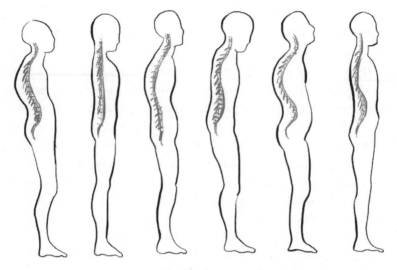

Figure 1.1 Row of bodies (courtesy of Amy Stevens)

Returning to your body as the starting point, there is a lot to consider. Transitions into imaginative worlds affects every molecule, as you continually alter in composition. The given circumstances activate the terrain of the canyon, stirring up changes which instantaneously and truthfully occur. The more the circumstances are believed, the more responsive is the landscape. A significant factor in the freedom to allow for internal change to occur is structure, as it affects the space provided for physiological systems to function. Just like when a pipe is twisted water will not pass, the same applies to the flow of sensation, the range of emotions, the passage of thoughts as well as the quality and amount of energy cultivated to take action.

The acting process involves forming new bodily patterns and the cultivation of fresh vibrations, which may stimulate feelings sometimes beyond what is comfortable or familiar. How often have you read a script and thought that you would never behave in that way (e.g. you would not kill or bully someone or run naked through a street)? The task of the actor is to make the leap and create an authenticity which is believable. As we all have personal patterns and a repertoire of expression, this leap at times may be difficult to achieve. It is natural to have a range of behaviours, but some territory will be new; for example, occasionally you may get angry but never furious; should the scene require fury, you are entering into the unfamiliar. Making a real departure from what is known pushes boundaries, and fury may feel unsafe or unreachable so would require letting go and moving through obstacles that you may not want to experience. This makes physiological adaptability and awareness integral to an actor's craft.

How your shape emerged

Clearly a person evolves through the journey of life, and changes occur according to age and events. There are also some key determinants that define shape, such as genetics and hereditary factors. The chances are that you will inherit some or many of your parents' or grandparents' features, and this may be anything from your height to a frown or the length of your fingers. There are, however, many other considerations which have an effect on your body composition. Let's start by outlining the ways in which shape can impact on your work.

Shape and your work

How you are shaped obviously affects:

- the way you literally move
- the distribution of your weight
- how you use the space around you
- the gestures you make
- the freedom with which you communicate
- how you relate to others.

The shapes within your body affect:

- your range of sensations and feelings
- the emotions with which you express yourself
- your ability to have a sense of your whole body
- the level of energy you have.

Other influences

Sociocultural

The family you are born into plays a significant role in what you will experience and how you perceive yourself. Social class determines the opportunities available regarding a multitude of things, the most fundamental being food and nourishment. On a broader level it influences educational experience, the range and types of pastimes available, the groups of people with whom you interact and the ideologies adopted. What you are exposed to will ultimately inform what you consider to be your norm and will contribute to behavioural patterns.

The codes and rules of any society have a clear effect on how people are able to express themselves. The etiquette of a person living in the United States is clearly different from that of someone in Thailand or Japan. The political systems, the dominant religions and social norms ultimately filter through to body use. This is clearly shown in the film *Babel* as the story follows the lives of characters in four cultures: Japan, Morocco, the United States and Mexico. There is a contrast in the body containment of the Japanese and the Mexican characters, which affects the dynamics of how they use both space and time. Gael Garcia Bernal uses actions which are expansive and move away from his body, as opposed to Rinko Kikuchi, the Japanese actress, who contains and holds. This could be attributed to many factors, including the dos and don'ts of each culture and the dominant social and political systems of the country which contribute to the social conditioning. Geographical considerations also present some insights into your body shape.

Geographical

Where you are from is intrinsic to your outlook and the sets of values adopted. The simple fact of living in a city or rural setting is considerable, the level of ease in the bodies travelling on a packed train or walking along a street in the financial district of any country will be a total contrast to those working the fields in rural areas. The environment triggers the internal pace and provides the type and range of stimuli to which you are exposed, which affects the choices made.

Lifestyle

Lifestyle choices range from occupation to how the body is treated, exercise and nutrition. What a person does for a living is pivotal to the structure and habitual bodily patterns adopted. It also affects how you use your body. For example, teachers often develop the ability to think quickly and strategically plan ahead, whereas mechanics or carpenters will automatically use their hands to make or fix things. The subtle details of how action is executed usually derives from what a person spends most of their time doing. It is noticeable when an actor dedicates the time to really explore the physicality of their character's life, as there is an authenticity to the action, as seen in the performances of Daniel Day-Lewis in *There Will Be Blood* and *The Crucible*. During the process of preparation, Day-Lewis immersed himself into the active world of the story. For *The Crucible* he helped to build the house in which his character lived. Therefore, the embodiment came as a result of experiencing the physiological effects of what it would be like to live the lives of John Proctor in the late seventeenth century and Daniel Planview at the turn of the nineteenth century. The period in which a story is set establishes an interesting dilemma for physical experience, as it is hard for the current generation to imagine what life was like prior to mobile phones, let alone the Internet. What is fashionable or in trend is particularly influential on somatic use.

Trends

In the twenty-first century the crude influence of consumerism bombards most of our lives, driven by physical images which can be considered to be the norm. To be thin and gaunt or over-muscular may establish the tribe to which a person belongs. The codes and conventions of each group also distinguishes the behavioural tone, the gestures, and to some extent the morals. If you reflect for a while, it is easy to see the influences that affect what you do and how you do it, be this going with or rejecting dominant trends.

These examples are glimpses at some of the factors which affect not only body shape but how you function and respond internally to the environment. Through understanding the process of how you have evolved, and what has shaped your structure, driven your actions and determined your expressions, you can come close to developing roles which have the same fascinating layers of complexity that you possess.

Figure 1.2 shows the various factors that are instrumental in contributing to how you are shaped.

Character work requires investigation, a detailed survey of the context that makes up the facets of the situation. Looking at you as a character is a way of seeing how small details may provide answers. It will also help with identifying the differences between you and the character, a necessary discovery for what Lakoff and Johnson (2003) call 'empathic projection', which is when you use the life, values and experiences of the other to influence your choices.

Individual
Hereditary, gender genetics, sexuality, family composition

Sociocultural
Class, ethnicity, education, geographical location, social organisations, dominant rules/codes, peers/friendship groups, religion, time/period the story is set in

Experience
Events Encounters, incidents Happenings

Which informs
Values Morals Belief systems

Figure 1.2 Factors and shape (courtesy of Daniel Hughes)

EXERCISE: YOU AS CHARACTER

The purpose of this exercise is to reflect on what defines you and consider the various factors that may have contributed.

1. Use the terms in Figure 1.2 as a starting point, jot down anything that comes to mind. An example could be:

   Hereditary – one of my parents is from Ireland and the other Lancashire. I was exposed to a number to belief systems: one parent was Catholic and the other Anglican (Church of England). One parent came from a family where there was real financial struggle, which instigated a survival instinct to fight and affected the attitude to authority. Being brought up by someone who needed to stand their ground instilled a strong sense of justice in my own attitude.

2. Once you have made a few notes, turn them into a diagram. This can take any shape, for example, a spidergram, a circle with circles within or the shape of a body (e.g. see Figure 1.3). This will help to make connections and form the links between the facts.

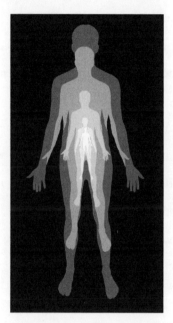

Figure 1.3 Bodies within body (courtesy of Daniel Hughes)

Awareness

Let's continue with the self-character study but take our attention to *how*, and the way in which you do what you do. It is not necessarily usual to really analyse movement and thought. How you move and speak and whatever you feel is right for whatever your situation. So making observations such as 'I am lopsided when I walk' or 'My voice is really high pitched' or 'I can't feel the emotion I am meant to feel in this situation' is likely to be alien. Self-observation is an integral part of acting, a reflection which notices rather than criticises. The value in observing routines and default patterns, which personality traits are dominant and which are more hidden, is that it brings growth. As Peter Levine suggests:

Awareness means experiencing what is present without trying to change or interpret it. (Levine 1997, p.81)

The level of awareness which is really valuable is one that concerns biological and physiological processes, as this will provide the answers to the questions that, in my experience, regularly crop up for actors, such as:

- Why am I thinking too much?

- Why do I get nervous before a performance?

- How can I find a deeper emotional engagement with the scene?

- Why does my body feel so tight?

- What can I do to channel my concentration?

- How can I connect to the text with more believability?

- Why do I find it difficult to remember my text?

- Why do I repeat the same vocal patterns?

- How can I find the right emotional balance to my performance?

The following exercises are designed to encourage you to make some general observations about yourself.

EXERCISE: LOOKING AT YOURSELF

It is sometimes difficult to obtain an objective perspective on your own body and identify how balanced, locked or tight it is. This exercise in pairs is a very simple way of receiving feedback on your overall body shape:

1. In pairs, person A is the observer and person B is being observed. Person B should stand in a position that is comfortable and natural for them. Do not attempt to strike a pose; just stand in a way that is easy and usual for you. Whilst being observed, person B should notice the following:

   1) the speed of thoughts

   2) how the joints are responding to being observed

   3) what is happening to your breath and how that is affecting the ribcage, diaphragm and shoulder girdle

   4) any sensations that may arise.

2. Person A becomes the observer. To do this, stand at a slight distance. First look at person B's body to see what draws you. Notice the following:

- where the weight is balanced

- the position of the joints (notice if they are locked)

- the shape of the spine (e.g. curved, flat or protruding in places)

- how person B breathes and how extended their ribcage is on the rise and fall of their lungs

- how engaged the diaphragm is with the breath

- how the head and neck are positioned. Is the head placed to one side? Does the chin jut upwards, causing the neck to bend backwards?

- the position of the jaw (e.g. it may be locked)

- the ease of the expression of the face.

3. Having made these observations, move from either the head to feet or feet to head and say what you see (e.g. your weight is on the balls of your feet, your knees are locked, your pelvis is uneven, when you breathe, your shoulders rise) until you have completed your observations. Do not be judgemental; just say what you see.

4. Persons A and B then discuss their observations, including how person B felt about being observed and what new sensations arrived as a result. The conversation should reflect on any new realisations. Swap so that both partners are taken through the process.

This exercise can also be done solo using a mirror or filming yourself. The points to notice above will help to guide you as to what to observe.

Vitality and energy

During the 'Looking at yourself' exercise it is likely that you noticed various sensations such as tingling or vibrations and perhaps changes in breath or fluctuations in temperature. This could be because you became conscious of being observed, which instigated a response, or the stillness made you more aware of what was happening. If you started to make amendments to how you were positioned, you may have noticed further changes in sensations. Simply unlocking the knees will alter circulation, and shifting the position of the diaphragm will increase or decrease the flow of feelings. As discussed in Chapter 5, we are composed of electrical charges, which are instigated by biological processes, so everything you do involves energy, which can be experienced as sensation. Another element that you may be observing is your vital energy, or vital force. In Traditional Chinese Medicine this would be identified as qi or prana, often referred to as 'energy' in Western cultures, although there is a distinction made (see Chapter 5 for more details). The effects of the constant motion of qi can be changes in heat and sensations like tingling or flutters. What is noticeable is that each person has a distinct quality – a usual level of buoyancy that is their norm, which I call vitality – the quality of which is readable and gives away clues as to how they respond to any situation as well as what they are feeling and thinking; it is a distinguishable dynamism which characterises who they are. In part, this emerges from a combination of factors, essentially internal action (i.e. physiological functioning), such as breathing, heartbeat and circulation, and neurological activity, such as thoughts, feelings and emotions. This fluctuates in response to the immediate environmental factors and the considerations indicated in Figure 1.2. The emergence of this inner activity is not clearly visible as such but can be felt and is further indicated by your movement. It is usually referred to as energy.

EXERCISE: READING THE BODY – ENERGETIC PULL

If you look carefully at someone moving, it is possible to read the body and notice fragments of information. In this exercise the focus is on observing what I call the energetic pull. Energy tends to follow intentions, so it is possible for the body to be moving forwards but for it to appear as if a part of you is hovering behind. You may not want to enter a room as you fear what you may find, and in this instance your hesitancy is active – it pulls back despite your limbs moving forwards. You could be talking to someone but truthfully feel very unsure of what you are saying; again your body will reveal your reality, and you will not fully release all of your power.

The exercise can be done in pairs A and B or in a group where one half observes the other.

1. Person A, or half the group, walks around the room. Being watched will cultivate feelings and sensations which will alter how you move, but try to move as is normal to you. Establish your own rhythm and focus on the action, in this instance simply walking.

2. Person B, or half the group, watches person A walk and is looking specifically at:

   • the distribution of weight through the feet

   • the connection between the pelvis and the legs

- the relationship between the neck and shoulders
- the direction of the torso (trunk and head may be more forwards that the legs; shoulders could be further back than the pelvis).

If you look carefully, you will be able to observe the direction of energy, which may not be forwards as expected. The energy may be backwards, upwards, downwards or contained very close to the body. The direction potentially offers information regarding where the person's attention resides – in the past, present or future – which could be momentary or a regular position. Someone who continually dwells on the past is likely to have a backwards pull, and movement-wise this could originate from any part of the back, but often it is around the pelvis/lumbar region. If concerns about the future dominate thoughts, energy will travel forwards, and it is usually noticeable around the upper regions from the chest up. A body that is very erect and lifted tends to send energy upwards rather than forwards. How the body moves affects how energy is released, and both are inextricably linked to the internal systems.

The layers within

To identify the reasons for your energetic pull, it is interesting to look in more detail at body composition. The next section may seem like a basic biology lesson. I have found that accessing depth is helped by visualising and reminding yourself of the layers within your body.

There are several layers within, each of which has a specific role, but overall keeping you functioning efficiently is a collaborative effort. The skin protects and holds our structure in place. The fascia supports and is a network for neural messages. Muscles and ligaments enable movement. Bones protect and provide form. Organs process, cleanse and circulate, and integral fluids and liquids/gases (e.g. blood, oxygen, qi, water) nourish.

The following exercise will take you on a journey into the layers within yourself.

EXERCISE: FEELING THE LAYERS

The layers for this exercise are as follows:

- your shape
- skin
- fasciae
- muscles/ligaments
- bones

- organs

- liquids/gases.

In this exercise colours are used to explore and differentiate the physiological and anatomical layers. The aim is to tune in to and notice the density of your body and observe the level and range of sensations within.

Standing or lying in a comfortable position, imagine that you are travelling through each of the layers, and as you do so, breathe in and out through the nose, engaging your abdominal muscles. Observe what colours and visual patterns arise in these layers:

- Shape

  Take in the overall form and contours of your body including the harder or softer places.

- Skin

  Observe the details between the fingers and toes, the creases and lines which have formed on your face.

- Fasciae

  The connective tissue beneath the skin which attaches, stabilises and holds organs in place is like a three-dimensional spiderweb. Imagine the web under the skin buzzing with nerves.

- Muscles/ligaments

  Notice the intricacies of the smaller and larger muscles and how the ligaments connect to bone.

- Bones

  Take yourself inside the bones to the marrow and tissue.

- Organs

  Travel through the space and pockets of the dominant organs.

- Liquids/gases

  Feel the movement of your breath, qi and blood within your vessels and channels.

Travelling under the skin can seem like a surreal and strange experience, and it encourages an awareness of the relationship between structure and sensation. I often refer to 'moving through' the body by which I mean feeling all of these layers and avoiding holding at any level. This allows for change and a wealth of sensation.

There are many practices that are valuable for increasing bodily awareness. Frederick M. Alexander (1869–1955) was an Australian actor who early in his career experienced problems with his voice. Through observing his physicality he identified that it was how he used his body that created significant muscular tension. He developed the Alexander Technique as a system to reduce unhelpful habitual patterns. The focus is to encourage the release and letting go of tension through re-education and an increase in familiarity of the patterns of misuse. Alexander identified that discovering the natural way in which the body is designed to function brings both changes to mental and physical health. Another pioneer of somatic practice was Moshé Feldenkrais (1904–1984), a Ukrainian scientist and Judo practitioner who created a method of bodywork which aims to encourage freedom, ease and flexibility through heightening awareness of movement, breath and posture. The integration of both Feldenkrais and Alexander's approaches into actor-training programmes is a recognition of the need for actors to have a technical and physiological approach to freeing up tension and altering unhelpful habits. Both agreed that breathing is an essential component of the level of tension in the body. It is instrumental to all inner processes.

Breath

Breath is obviously fundamental as your supply of oxygen to sustain life. As Hackney (2002, p.41) observes, 'It provides the baseline of flow for shape, change, ever altering, growing and shrinking.' It sustains and feeds all systems and maintains the overall health as well as playing an important role in muscular tension and emotional expression. The natural expansion and contraction of the body is dictated by breath, as is the extent to which we are able to open up and occupy space within and around us. Becoming aware and reminded of the impact of breath is essential if you want to learn to work for a more flexible instrument. The following exercise can be done at any time as a means of noticing your breath.

EXERCISE: THE CYCLE OF BREATH

Find a comfortable position and spend some time feeling your own breath pattern. Taping into the cycle of your breath is a good way to initially observe the natural rhythm of expansion and contraction. There is a four-point phase that occurs:

1. inhalation
2. pause

3. exhalation

4. pause.

Now ask yourself:

- Is the length of your inhalation longer than the exhalation?
- Which parts of the body do you notice move?
- What happens to you in the pause moments?
- Does the body feel tighter, held, or is the pause hardly noticeable?

The pause is not a lifeless held moment. It is more of a time of preparation for what follows, when the cells expand and tone, as fresh air exchanges in the pockets of the lungs. Gymnastic teacher and another pioneer in somatic studies, Elsa Gindler (1855–1961), believed that the synchronisation of breath brings ease to the body and is crucial to overall efficiency. The rhythm of this sequence alters in response to your circumstances and the stimuli to which your body reacts. This visibly changes stature and how you are able to respond.

It will become apparent that you have a natural pattern to your breath. This will fluctuate with the situations you find yourself in, as breath is a barometer for how you genuinely feel. Shallow breathing, when your breath seems to be high up in your chest and you breathe at a quick pace, is likely to bring anxiety and frustration and induce sadness. The opposite is true of abdominal breathing, when you engage your stomach muscles and breathe at a slower, more regulated rate. The diaphragm is the muscle that is important for emotional release as it is positioned close to a plexus point, the solar plexus, which contains a group of important nerves. The tension state of your diaphragm conducts the flow of sensations, feelings and emotions. If you tighten in this area, you will restrict and limit feeling.

What hinders breath?

We are always in a state of tension of some kind; it is necessary in order to be vertical. Unhelpful tension is usually caused when muscle groups are contracted in response to more heightened situations. When you are frightened, it is instinctive to hold and freeze and so restrict the intake of breath. Muscular contraction will play havoc with your voice as literally your vocal cords tighten to affect the sound you produce. This explains the necessity to be able to control and release your breath.

Figure 1.4 presents an illustration of a 'held' body, and Figure 1.5 shows a series of 'held' bodies.

Figure 1.4 A 'held' body (courtesy of Daniel Hughes)

Figure 1.5 A series of 'held' bodies (courtesy of Daniel Hughes)

EXERCISE: USING THE BREATH AS A RELEASE

The relationship of performers to body tension is similar to that of cooks and the discovery of the right flavours. Adjustments and experimentation are always needed. This sequence uses your breath to soften and bring more ease to your muscular and skeletal systems. The steps are as follows:

1. Start with your jaw. Create some space in the joint by making sure your back teeth are not touching. Inhale, and upon exhaling imagine that you are softening the area. Allow your jaw to ease down, freeing your whole face of tightness.

2. Take your attention to your throat area. Begin with observing the tension state of your throat, and breathe in and out feeling the tightness dissolve.

3. Move to your neck and shoulders and repeat the above sequence.

4. Pay attention to the diaphragm area at the bottom of your breastbone. On inhalation feel the diaphragm dropping, and then rising as you sigh out. After a few cycles of breath, extend the exhalation so that it is a few counts longer. You should be able to feel your abdominal muscles rise and fall.

5. In your pelvis area use your breath to open up all the held pockets. Move your pelvis in circles or a figure of eight as you breathe, release and soften.

6. Feel your feet on the ground. Rock on to your toes then back onto your heels. Position your weight just onto the balls of your feet. Make sure your feet are straight, ankles and knee joints soft, and the coccyx tucked at the bottom of the spine. Take a breath in and slightly sink, then rise as you sigh out.

It may be noticeable that as your state of tension changes so does the tempo of your thoughts.

Thoughts

There is a constant chatter going on in the background as we obviously do not verbalise everything that is thought, and words are selected either spontaneously or with some reflection. The thoughts that float into consciousness are all reactions to either past, present or future circumstances. Past events and memories can take over and affect the ability to be present to the current situation or to 'live in the moment' – a phrase familiar to actors which implies that you invest all your attention in what is happening in front of you and sharpen observations to be fully attentive to the person with whom you are communicating. If you can stay with the present, then you are able to really respond truthfully to what is happening and there is no denial of what you are feeling. So you do not pretend to be confident when inside you are terrified; rather, you acknowledge the fear and so your body will shift on and naturally adapt. It is necessary to train your thoughts or become aware of where your attention travels.

Thoughts steer physiology: they trigger a delicate and complex set of reactions which instigates feelings, emotions and ultimately actions. The stakes attached to a thought will determine the depth of what is felt. A simple observation, such as 'It's one o'clock,' could be of no real significance and therefore command no out-of-the-ordinary inner changes; or the time may be the time of an interview or the time you get results from hospital tests, or the time your father passed away in the previous week. When the stakes are high, sensations will rush through the body and trigger impulses to take action. An impulse is a surge of feeling which propels you to do something. At the moment of the impulse there is a choice to either follow it or to squash it. If the decision is made to follow it, movement is likely to be forwards and open; if you choose to crush the sensation, the body will automatically tighten and hold. An example could be that you see someone you want to talk to because they may be able to offer work opportunities, but they are considered high profile so this fills you with fear. There is a desire to move forwards and speak, but this action may be blocked when your fear takes hold.

What to notice about your thoughts

Notice the speed and tempo of your thoughts and how this changes with your situation:

- Do you tend to think in the past, present or future?

- Do you pose questions to yourself?

- What are the stakes of the thoughts that crop up?

- Do you criticise yourself?

- How often do you monitor what you say?

- Do certain thoughts trigger feelings in particular parts of your body?

- Do thoughts have peaks where your feelings and emotions kick in?

- Does your breath change with your thoughts?

EXERCISE: **FOLLOW YOUR THOUGHTS**

Sit quietly and comfortably, and take a moment to observe your thoughts and the sensations they trigger. Close your eyes to reduce potential stimuli. As if you were reading your thoughts off a page, notice what you are thinking. How often do you change to a new topic? Do any thoughts return? Observe what the thoughts do to your breath and any sensations that arise.

EXERCISE: **THE DIMMER SWITCH**

Bring your attention to your thoughts:

- Do you notice a rhythm to your thoughts?
- Do they jump from one topic to another or is there a theme?
- Is there a tempo present?
- Is it easy for you to drift off and follow various thought tracks?

Notice your breath and allow it to drop in and sigh out. Repeat this a few times and then ask yourself:

- Have your thoughts changed at all?
- Is it clearer which thoughts dominate?

Decide where your attention needs to be in this moment. What is your immediate goal? Make a decision to turn down any thoughts which are not related to this goal. Allow them to fade away. Set yourself a target related to your goal and an amount of time to achieve it. Have a particular thought to which you can return to keep you on target.

Dual consciousness

Konstantin Stanislavsky (1863–1938) used the term 'dual consciousness' to explain ability to focus on performing whilst retaining an awareness of what is going on internally for you, the actor. So ideally, when acting, there is only a small percentage which registers that you are in a studio with a crew of 60 people all doing their specific jobs, or that you are in front of a live audience. It is a matter of finding the balance of your attention, which will automatically shift from moment to moment. Physiological processes register the slightest changes in the immediate surroundings, be that temperature, the sound of someone coughing or movement of bodies in your peripheral vision; therefore, the focus of your attention is crucial. The trick is to learn how to direct your attention. The balance of focus is important, as somatic clues are very easily leaked by your body, which cannot lie. The more obvious signs of unease, or drifting off to unrelated thoughts, are general physical awkwardness, locked joints, shallow breath, pushing the neck forwards, a high-pitched voice, sweating, flickering eyes, changes in skin colour and so forth. If you are battling to stay with the story, it is often clear to see, especially on screen when a camera will capture the fine details.

Transitions

It is interesting to notice the journey you go through at key moments, and this can be enhanced by the fact that you are always in a state of flux. There is a liminal state, which lies in the middle of the focus spectrum and is a transitional place that determines the levels of immersion in whatever you are doing. The concept of liminality first emerged in the writings of Arnold Van Gennep (1873–1957) in 1909 and was expanded by anthropologist Victor Turner (1920–1983) in the late 1960s. It has since been embraced by many disciplines, including the theories of learning, which recognise that there is often a period when information, or set skills, are in a transitional phase, as if you go through an unknown phase. For an actor this could be when you are on the threshold of imaginatively shifting into your fictitious world, prior to the commencement of the action; or the moment before 'action' is called on a film set or the waiting in the wings to go on stage. It is a time where potentially inner struggles occur, which could be emotional intervention through nerves or the challenge to feel the depths of what is required to imaginatively commit. This is when the balance of attention is either with you or the story, and your nervous system will reveal your truth. It is also a period to cultivate the appropriate starting state for a scene, when the sensory connections are made with the past events in the story.

The concept of liminality highlights the changes and transitions within the body. It is a reminder that we are always working with complex inner movement such as the beats of your heart, the rise and fall of your breath and the changes of your nervous system. What an actor may travel from and to in relation to their natural physiological patterns in any given moment is often immense. Fictional stories need to be dramatic to interest the audience, so discovering a dead body, being pursued by a monster or destroying the future of the universe are situations any actor may encounter. Such journeys are biological ones.

Developing the sensitivity to automatically tune in to the sensations and feelings that crop up will increase your ability to inhabit the role. Beneath the words is a changing landscape which needs to be tapped into; it is like the bed of a river: it contains the roots for everything to feed off.

EXERCISE: FEELING THE MOMENTS OF TRANSITION

Some moments have a clearer arc than others and stimulate, in most people, dramatic physiological action. Take yourself imaginatively through the following situations and see if you can feel and identify the pre-liminal, liminal and post-liminal stages. Register the feelings and sensations that emerge:

- jumping off a diving board
- falling into deep cold water
- being pushed into a vat of slime
- walking across a tightrope looking down at the Grand Canyon
- going for a job interview
- asking someone for a date.

Conclusion

Potentially there are endless possibilities for our felt senses and physical adaptability. When you are able to tune in to and fully open up to sensation, the depth of your work will naturally extend. Our body is like an archaeological site, and in order to excavate we need to strip away and feel the layers. The embodiment of the stories we decide to tell can permeate as deep as we allow. You can become the architect of a new being, which artistically uses your own body as the bricks and mortar.

In this chapter I have looked at how developing an acute awareness of your body can lead to more adaptability and responsiveness. Now we move on to explore the potential obstacles to this by closely examining the habits we accumulate.

Chapter 2

HABITS

Sharpening awareness of what you do

Introduction

This chapter explores why and how habits emerge, and considers the impact they have on creative freedom. Repeated patterns, routines and rituals are integrated into the fabric of our lives; they serve as memory aids and expressions of what is truly important to us. Each of us has developed many habits, be that a gesture with an eyebrow, a repeated cough or a specific way in which we eat, walk, think, speak and so forth: they are our individual emblems.

The majority of these habits are valuable and in some instances primal, programmed into the body as part of survival instincts like fleeing from danger, sweating when hot, freezing when frightened. For actors there are a few reasons why it is valuable to notice and be able to change your habitual behaviour. The first is to establish an adaptable body which is not hindered by your own programmed responses. The following are also key considerations:

- to reduce unhelpful body use

- to avoid the repetition of actions that signal unease

- to create performances that are not a replica of ones that have gone before.

Unhelpful body use

As an evolving instrument the body changes and adapts; it is a reflection of its past and current circumstances. Like with any design, there is a structure that is more suited to allowing the body to do its job –

to efficiently function and keep you alive – an anatomical position whereby all of the various systems can work in sync, communication is sharp, the senses are alert and sensations flow with ease. Body use is not always ideal, and as observed in Chapter 1, experiences establish shapes and patterns which are deeply integrated into the overall structure. This includes general posture as well as the stress placed on muscles, ligaments and tendons, which affects the efficiency of circulation, communication of the central nervous system, thoughts, feelings and overall functioning. Specific challenges include:

- locking of joints, especially the knees
- holding and tightening of muscles
- restrictions to breath flow
- emotional habits that affect a willingness to experiment.

All of the above will limit the ability to surrender to the story. The unpicking of what is considered unhelpful is a necessary ongoing pursuit of technical consideration.

Signs of unease

It is a useful target to allow yourself to travel to imaginary places without being interrupted by your own signs of unease. Somatic indicators of unease could be a change in temperature, going red in the face, sweating, becoming rigid, shallow breath, a distracted mind and so forth. They arrive when the body is stressed or overwhelmed, and if it believes danger is hovering. Controlling and managing such situations can help you to be present and responsive.

Unique performance

The specifics of personalised behaviour like repeated tics, be that a frown, a fixed stare, a breath pattern or a vocal tone, all affect the facility to create original work. If you are unable to move away from how you enact even the simplest actions, such as walking – which is not that simple when you break down what your body is actually doing – the ability to physically translate the descriptions on a page into the character's behaviour becomes creatively limited. In other words, you will repeat your *own* patterns. Most automatic action is implicit (unconscious), such as most of your movements and breathing, and all psychological functioning; therefore, it could be said that our general level of awareness is limited, and we are only really aware of a small percentage of what we do.

What is a habit?

One interpretation of habits is that they are actions, or a kind of behaviour, which are often repeated and, as such, are physiologically programmed into the body to become a response to a particular circumstance. This perspective would imply that the brain automatically sets up pathways for neurological activity, and when something is repeated, there is a pattern which is instantly recognised and therefore duplicated. Hackney (2002, p.17) explains that when patterns are formed, 'the neuromuscular system has developed a plan or model for executing movement sequences which become a habitual firing of neuromuscular pathways that come to play to fulfil an intention'. It would make sense that the formation and origins of habits occur for many reasons, including the considerations we discussed in Chapter 1 (see Figure 1.2). Another perspective is offered by biologist Rupert Sheldrake: 'Habits develop over time; they depend on what has happened before and how often it has happened' (Sheldrake 2011, p.32). Sheldrake believes that all things in nature have organising systems which draw on a collective memory. He calls this 'morphic resonance', which implies that memory and habituation are not exclusively a result of brain activity. He suggests that we tune in to and resonate with certain behaviour that is organised in morphic fields. In relation to a habit this would imply that a person is connected to other people and the broader environment, and picks up the vibration of frequencies in such fields. So the tendency to put your hands over your face when shocked or bite your fingernails when nervous comes as a result of drawing on vibrations that already exist in a field. The behaviour is not exclusive to you but also enacted by others when the same feelings emerge.

Types of habits

Whichever model is considered, I have observed that habits automatically surface when stress is experienced. On such occasions it could be that, for example, you bite your lip or your breathing becomes shallow, muscles tighten and joints lock up, and all are associated with anxiety.

Other habits become part of automatic behaviour – physical routines such as eating in the same way, saying the same phrases, sleeping on the same side of the bed or always washing your face before you brush your teeth. These are known as habit memories and are made up of patterns which are regularly repeated, and they appear spontaneous but because of repetition have been engrained into the mind and muscles. They are beneath the bed of consciousness, as there is not necessarily a cognitive recognition of the action. They offer security, aid memory and reveal gems of information about a person.

It is understood by Downing (1996) that what is learned in the early stages of life is absorbed into patterns and habits; they then contribute to the shaping of motor and emotional self-organisation. Habitual responses would therefore be a part of the choreography of your brain. Implicit memory, which contains experiences, actions and behaviours of which you are not conscious, significantly contributes to the formation of habitual patterns. Psychologist Halko Weiss explains that learned and repeated responses formulate embodied connections and become embedded into the tissues of the body. 'The conscious, explicit mind has very little power over the implicit' (Weiss 2009, p.23). It is through making the unconscious conscious that change can occur, and this requires the development of the ability to self-observe.

Below are some examples of the different ways in which I have observed that habits can interfere with the work of an actor.

How habits can surface in a performance

Habits can manifest during a performance in:

- gestures, such as twitching your nose or playing with your hair when nervous

- muscular patterns, like tightening in your throat area when you hold back from saying what you want to say

- thought patterns – that is, a repetition of certain thoughts which may be self-criticism when you feel you have not done as well as you could

- the speed and tempo of how you think.

How you express yourself emotionally could also be predictable and form a pattern of behaviour; for example, you may prevent yourself from becoming angry or of feeling pleasure (i.e. there may be some emotions that are unfamiliar to you).

EXERCISE: YOUR HABITS

Make a list of all the habits you are aware of in the following categories:

- Physical

  What tics do you have? When do they occur? Which parts of the body do you use more than others when you communicate?

- Emotional

  Are there some emotions which you express more often? Are you aware that there are particular triggers which stimulate certain emotions?

- Intellectual

  How do you solve problems? Is the process linear or random? Is there a repeated tempo to your thoughts in particular situations?

Can you avoid your own habits?

Within the body there are some patterns which have been with you since conception, when the foetus morphed from one shape to another. The folding and layering of cells is a pattern which constantly occurs during the months in which a baby forms. Even at this early stage, your body is encoding such formations, which have become part of cell memory. There are many movements and sensations that originate at the embryonic stage which may be very familiar to you, such as waves, shimmers, spirals, figures of eight and so forth. We probably all recognise these sequences which accompany particular emotions, like a flutter which comes with fear, but you may not register their origins or how long they have been within you. As an infant in the primary stages sequences are repeated, such as reaching, falling, pulling, pushing and so forth. We learn to judge the effort required for action and the meaning of the gestural shapes we make. Spatial relationships are registered, as these early reflexes are remembered and firmly integrated into your movement vocabulary. The routines and habitual patterns of movement that you find yourself repeating in daily life may stretch back further than you think.

The emergence of unhelpful habits

There are several approaches to addressing how and why patterns emerge. What is known is that just as they took time to emerge, they take time to diminish or disappear. The study of somatic psychology offers some valuable insights which are useful for the craft of acting.

Keleman (1987) identifies that there is a set of *archetypal gestures* which can be universally recognised as responses to patterns of distress or extreme emotional circumstances. These gestures include:

- holding
- tightening
- collapsing
- sinking
- swelling
- becoming rigid.

Holding, for example, may momentarily occur at times when fear or anxiety are experienced, as if there is an attempt to stop the sensation. If this tendency is over-repeated the overall gesture will become engrained into muscular and cellular life. The response will become automatic.

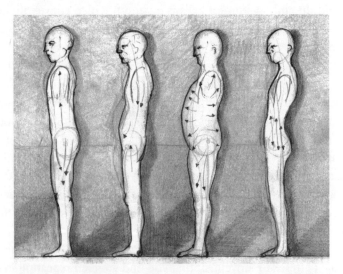

Figure 2.1 Bodies with arrows (courtesy of Valentina Piras)

This will have an overall effect on posture and the general gravitational pull of all the muscles, as seen in Figure 2.1. The arrows indicate the more dominant direction of weight and ultimately energetic flow. The consequences of how you use your body obviously affect internal functioning. Structure either limits or offers space for biological processing, and a collapsed or tight body will alter the circulation of breath, fluids and qi/energetic flow because there is literally no or limited room for a substance to travel freely. Such restrictions inhibit the efficiency of how your body functions and ultimately change and affect the expression of your thoughts, feelings and emotions.

To some extent these gestures are a part of everyday movement vocabulary; sayings such as 'sink into despair', 'swell with pride', 'hold on to a thought' or 'go rigid with fear' are fairly common. With the constant expansion or contraction during a breath cycle it is possible to identify that in brief moments you are always doing one of these gestures, so ultimately such gestures become habitual actions. Examples are when disappointed – the body often sinks – or when in a state of unease – holding seems almost instinctive. If repeated, such habits contribute to your archetypal shape. As seen in Figure 2.1, posture impacts on gravitational pull, the tension in muscles and energetic flow (as indicated by the arrows).

EXERCISE: YOUR ARCHETYPAL SHAPE

Often we may not be aware of the extent to which the body is holding or tightening in the muscles or joints. Holding patterns create form and can be difficult to change.

1. To observe how your body has shaped itself start with your joints, such as the knees, pelvis, shoulders, jaw, elbows, fingers and toes. How would you describe the positions you have adopted? Locked, rigid, held, brittle, soft, flexible?

2. Move to your muscles and notice where you clench. The buttocks, thighs and abdomen are common places. Give the current level of holding a number from 1 to 10, with 10 being the highest. Adjust the level of holding by working with your breath, sigh and release any tightness.

3. Take your attention to your relationship to gravity. Are you pulled in any particular direction? Do you sink, pull back, collapse or lift at the diaphragm area? Are your shoulders held upwards by the muscles, or do they turn inwards as if looking at each other? Pull your shoulders

downwards and imagine your fingers can touch the floor. If you were drawn inwards begin to expand outwards, and vice versa.

4. Imagine that upon inhaling you expand as if the sides of your body touch the walls of the room and your head touches the ceiling. After exhaling you may feel more expanded and feel like you inhabit more space.

To reflect further on the composition of your own body, the following exercise (slightly adapted to suit the needs of the actor) draws on a model from somatic psychology.

EXERCISE: SOMATOGRAM

A somatogram is an image which tells the story of your body. It is used to either assess body composition or to capture how an individual feels about their life story. The depiction can be a realistic, symbolic or imaginative representation with the aim of reflecting on somatic shape. It is a starting place for exploring how your form has evolved and how you emotionally experience your own body.

There are four stages to the exercise, which includes posing questions in relation to how you experience yourself:

1. Using the materials of your choice, draw an image of your body which reflects how you see yourself. Try not to think too much about the task. Follow the first impressions that crop up.

2. Write a brief story to accompany your drawing. (This could be in bullet points.)

3. Look at your image. Pose questions to yourself regarding the shape and how you use your body. Consider the contours, the position of the limbs, weight distribution, the areas that are more emphasised than others and what your shape says about you. Possible questions: Does the position of my shoulders hinder my breath intake? How does the distribution of my weight impact on how I walk? Do I lead with a particular part of my body, such as my chest? Consider the impact your shape has on your performance skills, such as: Do I restrict my voice by placing my chin backwards? When I hold in my abdomen, does it hinder feelings and sensations?

4. If in a group or pair, show your drawing and describe your story.

There are several variations of this exercise, such as drawing your breath or the rhythm of your walk or the arc of an emotional journey.

Body 'splits'

What is surprising is the extent to which repeating certain gestures and prioritising one side of the body can alter overall structure. It is usual for us all to carry bags on one side, distribute weight unevenly and slump in front of the television, but the extent to which this affects the workings of the inner life can be extreme. Let's imagine standing in front of a full-length mirror: what is reflected back is one's whole body, all joined up and connected. If it were possible to look through your skin and see inside, this picture might change. You might notice that particular body use has resulted in twists, squashed organs, protruded bones which do not fit so neatly together and so forth. In some areas there may be less space for efficient psychological functioning, which will affect a number of things. An example is the pelvis: if the joints are held tightly in place, it is difficult for sensation to flow in any direction. There are occasions when we disconnect from what can be identified as natural alignment and cause what Dychwald (1977) calls 'splits'. This is when, in a particular posture, there appears to be a disconnection through locking or holding, which disjoints not only the skeletal system but also the muscular and nervous systems. A common position is at the junction between the head and torso, when the neck is overextended in any direction to prohibit free and fluid movement. The pelvis is another area which can often feel uneven; standing with weight on one side or locking up in the knees are often the reasons. The internal effect of such holding, locking or overextending is to inhibit the work of your central nervous system by restricting the actions of nerves and the general flow of fluids, thoughts, sensations and emotions.

Splits usually occur in the areas of the major joints such as the torso and arms, pelvis and legs, and the midpoint in the body around the diaphragm (Figure 2.2). Long-term effects are felt when a posture is sustained or when the position becomes a part of everyday use. Typical examples are standing with the feet crossed, which will result in a tightened pelvis. Another common habit is the locking of knees which has an enormous impact on the alignment of your pelvis, the solar plexus and the neck/shoulder relationship. This slight action is likely to cause a series of locks in the pelvis, diaphragm, all of the spinal column, shoulder and head/neck. As it restricts functioning, it is as if there is a divide between the head and body. When the skeleton is unaligned, efficient functioning of the anatomical and biological systems is jeopardised.

Figure 2.2 Split bodies (courtesy of Daniel Hughes)

EXERCISE: CHECKLIST OF YOUR SPLITS

We all have disconnecting patterns of which we are not always conscious. Consider the following questions:

- Do you cross your legs, feet or arms on a regular basis? Are you aware of when you do these actions?
- When standing at ease, does your diaphragm area extend or lift?
- Do you lock your knees and pelvis joints?
- Where do you place your weight? Is it more onto one side of the body than the other?
- Is one of your shoulders higher than the other?
- Do you lead with one side of the body?
- Do you jut out your chin?
- Is it usual for your head to be lopsided?

How splits affect your acting

Splits are usual for all of us and triggered in certain circumstances, but they become challenging when they are fixed, as shown in the following case study.

CASE STUDY: A SPLIT BODY

Sam is in his early twenties and had some previous actor training whilst at university, although this did not involve extensive body training. He is not particularly muscular (his body is generally that of a teenager), he has soft features and his presence is quiet and gentle. When I watch him walk, his chest pushes forwards with the chin leading but drooping. He collapses around the diaphragm area. As he moves, his pelvis pushes backwards and is left behind, as if in the past. His body has three dominant splits which have become integrated into how he carries himself: his pelvis, diaphragm and shoulder/neck area. This overall misalignment not only means that it is difficult for Sam to move with any ease or fluency, but also has implications for how he works as an actor. It is challenging for Sam to connect with text, he struggles to express a range of emotion and his tendency is to force and push his neck forwards. As his diaphragm is held, his breath is restricted. His emotional expression is presented rather than felt. It is almost impossible for him to find any modulation in his voice due to the tightness in his throat. His breath is shallow and his abdomen barely expands or contracts during a breath cycle.

The lack of genuine emotion is a result of a structure which has for a long time resisted sensation. Primarily we begin to work on the spine, to allow his nervous system to link up and to enhance the flow of messages to all of his body. We then explore his breath so that he is able to allow his breath to drop in so he can feel the movement of his diaphragm and sigh out with more ease. We imaginatively explore inhaling from the soles of the feet and palms of the hands. Through qigong sequences we work towards moving as one unit, releasing the locked joints, allowing the movement to emerge from the ground. Over time, there is connection between his upper and lower body energy which places Sam in touch with a greater ability to feel and sense. He also becomes more present to the work.

Reducing the splits

There are numerous ways in which you can reduce the possibility of splits occurring. Loosening your joints is a good place to start.

EXERCISE: WORKING WITH THE PELVIS

The pelvis is crucial to feeling a sense of being whole and to fully embodying your experiences. In daily life most people tend to be most aware of the front and upper parts of their body, mainly using the arms and face to communicate. This over-focus often means that some parts of the body are a little more rigid and move with less fluidity.

In this exercise imagery is used as way of inviting change into the body and encouraging self-adjustment. This occurs through the activation of neurophysiological systems which are triggered by the action of your imagination. In Traditional Chinese Medicine the pelvis is considered to be an energetic gateway, as this area houses the lower dantien, also known as the 'sea of qi'. In most forms of martial arts, qigong and tai chi, the dantien is an important concept, as it is considered to be the centre of energy and a place to direct breath. The lower dantien is positioned under the belly button. There are also two plexus points positioned in this area, the sacral and the lumbar plexus, which are like junctions for nerves. Collectively, they send signals down into the legs and up into the torso. It is very easy for this part of your body to become tight and fixed, through poor movement habits such as sitting too much or holding in the surrounding muscles.

Find a comfortable standing or sitting position and follow these steps:

1. Observe how your pelvis feels. Is it tight and held or resistant to movement?

2. See your pelvis as a bowl which is filled to the brim with water, like a small pond.

3. As you inhale imagine that your breath drops into the centre of the pond, and as you exhale a ripple spreads across the surface.

4. Without activating any actual movement, imagine that you are moving your pelvis in a figure of eight whilst trying not to spill any of the water.

5. Alter your breath, inhaling for one half of the figure of eight and exhaling for the other.

6. Do the movement in both directions.

7. After 3–4 minutes, introduce actual movement, allowing your pelvis to create as precise a figure of eight as you can with the aim of not spilling any water.

8. Notice if the sensations have changed in any way once actual movement was introduced.

What could you feel prior to point 7 of the exercise? The stronger the focus and intention, the more active the inner movement will be. The belief that you can alter body composition through mental and somatic practice is a key aspect of several body-centred health practices such as qigong, tai chi, Alexander Technique and reiki.

How to get rid of habits and splits

Trying to change patterns which have been in place for long periods is hard and they take conscious work to undo. It is easy for you or an acting teacher to notice what you repeatedly do, but to unpick and avoid falling into those habits requires making different choices; it is matter of reprogramming. Keleman (1987, p.44) outlines a process he calls the 'How exercise', which is a five-step structure designed to promote somatic awareness of how your use your body and the patterns and sensations that have emerged. At each stage of the process a question is posed to prompt reflection on what you do to sustain the pattern:

1. What is my image of myself in my present situation?

2. How do I muscularly create this image and perpetuate it?

3. How do I end the way I have embodied myself?

4. What happens to me when I end this?

5. What response do I give to this?

The process involves consciously acquainting yourself with the precise details of how an action or posture is retained. The tightening of your jaw does not necessarily begin with the closing of the mandibular joint; the sequence you have developed may start in your throat or further down your body. The pattern is exclusive to you, and to begin to unpick it, the entire train of movement needs to be identified. The How exercise is a means of unravelling the chain of muscular neurological action that is involved in the formation of the habit.

Irmgard Bartenieff (1890–1981) developed a method of re-education which stressed the importance of returning to very early movement structures. Her approach is based on the understanding that the soma stores fundamental movement, which is essential and beneficial for the body prior to the development of unhelpful patterns. Working with basic movements, such as crawling, balancing, reaching, standing and walking, triggers a memory of how it was to operate with ease and freedom. As the body has learned coping strategies to deal with whatever we experience, relearning and unpicking is a little like going back in order to go forwards; it's growth. I tend to begin training with walking and observing weight distribution in an attempt to encourage a reflection on the most fundamental of movements.

How the body is used has a considerable impact on how a person thinks and the attitudes they adopt. In fact, the two are interchangeable. Experimenting with *how* you use your body is fundamental to stimulating sensation and finding new patterns.

EXERCISE: OPENING THE HEART

Opening your body releases the whole of the upper region of your body; it is useful for flexibility and creating space internally. This exercise focuses on your chest and heart centre:

1. Stand in wu chi position (see Figure 4.1).

2. Inhale through your nose and bring your hands upwards with palms facing your body, then raise them up till they are positioned at the top of your head, palms now facing the crown of your head.

3. As you do so, slightly sink allowing the lower dantien to lead.

4. Exhale through your mouth and open out your arms, like angel wings, with palms upwards. Allow your dantien to slightly sink and try to avoid the protrusion of your diaphragm. Stay in this position for a few breaths.

5. On exhalation bring your hands, palms down, along the front of your body and place them in front of your dantien.

Repeat this form a few times. Observe the sensations that arise during and afterwards. When repeated, this exercise will increase your emotional accessibility.

EXERCISE: SPINE AND FEELING

As the axial support of the body, the spine supports the skull and transmits weight down into the legs. It houses the spinal cord and is essential for feeling and sensation. How the spine is used relates directly to sensory and emotional sensation.

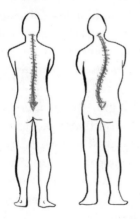 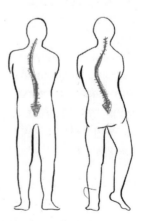

Figure 2.3 Red spines (courtesy of Amy Stevens)

Using Figure 2.3 as a guide, adopt each position, or a similar shape, and retain it for 3–4 minutes. Observe the impact this has on your breath and the sensations that crop up.

EXERCISE: HOLDING THE SPINE

1. Put your hands in front of you to indicate the length of your spine to get a sense of how long you think your spine is.

2. Move your hands to your back and place one index finger on the top of your spine (you should feel an indentation where your cervical spine meets your cranium) and the other hand at the bottom of your spine on your coccyx.

3. Bring your hands in front of you maintaining the positions with your fingers.

4. Walk around the space as if holding your spine. Try to retain the length as you move.

The length of the spine can be surprising. Retaining a clear sense of the length of your spine helps to keep the relationship between your pelvis, neck and shoulders, and allows space between each vertebra.

EXERCISE: SELF-OBSERVATION

Get to know your habits by watching yourself. Use simple scenarios or sections of text, and film yourself in a medium close-up shot. With no judgement, play back the footage and notice if you repeat gestures and mannerisms which are familiar to you.

The practice of qigong

The practice of techniques, such as mindfulness, which increase self-awareness is becoming integrated into a variety of disciplines, including actor training. This form of meditation is a way of training the mind to become more present, to observe and accept feelings, thoughts and sensations. Breath is used to anchor attention, to stay with what is going on in each moment and fully experience sensations and emotional interferences. It is a way of taming wandering minds and tuning in to physiological change.

In a similar way, qigong is a practice that is very effective in bringing awareness to body composition and stimulating changes that bring new sensations and emotional accessibility (see Chapter 7 for more details).

It is an ancient Chinese health care system which integrates still and moving postures with breathing techniques and the channelling of attention. Internal transformation occurs through the promotion of qi flow and opening up tight areas in your body. Integral to the practice is the focus of placing intention behind each movement which unites the body and stimulates internal movement. A posture which is particularly integral to all forms of qigong is wu chi, a position where the body is aligned to create maximum connection (see Figure 4.1). In the stillness of this posture the practitioner just observes what arises and directs attention to where it is useful.

Attitude and structure

The physicality of attitude, whether it is implicit or explicit, is an example of an embodied set of values or opinions which has a positive, negative or uncertain effect on how we behave and communicate. Tiffin and McCormick (1971) define attitude as 'a frame of reference that influences the individual's views or opinions on various topics and situations and influences their behaviour'. According to Stanley Keleman, 'attitude' is not exclusively a mental state, but consists of bodily functions with muscular and emotional components. 'We think of an attitude as a mental set. An attitude is a bodily set. Our attitudes are the framework of our form' (Keleman 1981, p.54). This is partly due to the neurophysiology of emotional behaviour. A question he usually asks of his clients is: 'What layer do you experience that in?' – 'that' being a sensation, emotion or feeling which could be the skin, nerves, muscles, soft organs or bones.

EXERCISE: YOUR ATTITUDE

Reflect on the bodily clues that reveal your attitude. Consider the following:

- how you hold yourself
- how you walk
- any gestures that you do on a regular basis.

What is the central quality you believe you manifest? For example, are you open or closed? Are you soft or sharp in tone? How do you maintain that? How would you describe the dominant force with which you express yourself?

There are many ways in which we reveal our outlook on life. The spine is such a big clue. It has clear associations with particular attitudes, such as overly rigid and straight is considered to indicate an uptight or controlled person. This perspective is mirrored in various portrayals, such as dictators, armed forces personnel or school mistresses. A slumped or concave spine is often read as apathetic or depressed. If the head and chin are jutted upwards, a person is often considered brazen but also defensive. There are examples of characters with a definitive attitude in films and on television. Sigourney Weaver, in the *Alien* films, has a dense, strong and almost armoured stature. She is assertive, dynamic and rarely reveals any softer emotions. She is a warrior, a leader and is unyielding in her fight to survive whatever she encounters. It is not surprising that she reveals no vulnerability as her overall attitude and motto is one of survival of the fittest. Similarly, Jennifer Lawrence in *The Hunger Games* is a perfect example of how body and attitude are integrated and reveal a character's journey. She is brave, she softens when she needs to and moves from being gentle and tender to resilient and assertive. Audrey Tautou, in *The Fabulous Destiny of Amelie Poulain*, portrays a character who is innocent and naive but also very inquisitive with a playful and buoyant imagination. These qualities emerge through a slight, pixie stature, with a childlike curiosity, which is especially shown in her eye gestures. She is sprightly, light and her emotional responses are sensitive.

Conclusion

In this chapter we looked at the need for an adaptable body, one which can be flexible enough to make the transition into imaginary worlds and situations with which you are not familiar. Various strategies and approaches were considered which are useful for *unlearning* and discovering ways of moving that support your work rather than restrict it. Here are some good questions to pose to yourself from time to time:

- Which of my habits interfere with my work?

- What do I do to maintain these habits?

- Is my attitude visible in my work?

- What do I need to do to change this?

In pursuit of this adaptable body, let's move on to look at the notion of receptivity and what that means for the work of an actor.

Chapter 3

RECEPTIVITY
Awakening the body

Introduction

We are always responding to stimuli of some kind, but there is not always a conscious awareness of this; responses just happen automatically. It often takes a heightened situation to fully notice what is being both felt and sensed, such as when an unexpected interaction occurs like being touched by a stranger or having personal space invaded. Being observant of flutters, changes in breath or the increase in your heartbeat is a part somatic sensitivity, a recognition of just how subtle your inner life can be. There are several benefits to noticing and deeply engaging with what is going on in the body. It primarily increases the level of receptivity to yourself, others and ultimately to the needs of the imaginative situation.

To be receptive is to do more than react to a stimulus; it is to fully register and allow yourself to be affected, to surrender to shifts and changes without the interruption or control of mental faculties. It is to be totally receptive. There is a sophistication and intuitive instinct that operates in the body, but how receptive we are to this is greatly affected by the ability to steer mental faculties. Blocks to receptivity may be recognised as an inability to stay present, which often manifests as a difficulty with (a) recalling information, (b) the performance of skills and (c) being in control of feelings and emotions. The roots of the psychological obstacle could be the fear of failure or lack of confidence, and what is often triggered is immense physiological activity, which interferes with clarity and focus, all of which limit the engagement with the material and restrict the facility to completely enter into the given circumstances.

This chapter starts by encouraging a reflection on your level of receptivity to yourself and your environment. We then move on to the central nervous system, examining how it functions and affects the cycle of response to any stimulus. We take a look afterward at the biological process of giving and receiving, and what this means for the actor with a focus on strategies to aid the flow of communication.

How receptive are you?

As we have observed in Chapters 1 and 2, receptivity is affected by the many factors of how we experience and perceive the world, which implies that attitudes and cultural perspectives affect whether possibilities are embraced or denied. There is a direct relationship between what you do as an actor and how receptive you are. Consider these metaphorical questions:

- If you were a door, would you be closed, ajar, wide open or locked?

- Would there be glass through which you could peer, and if so, see-through or coloured glass?

- Of what material would you be made – hard or soft wood, or metal like a jail cell?

- Would you be composed of wool, ribbon, candy floss, ice cream, sponge cake or some other unusual substance?

Your response to the above questions may tell you nothing or something about how you see yourself. There is an obvious difference to being open or closed, hard, soft, pliable or impenetrable. Consider the following questions:

- Are you an observer or do you usually jump straight into action by volunteering and being the centre of attention?

- Of what do you believe you are capable, and do you give yourself permission to act on such possibilities?

- Do you allow your inhibitions to interfere with your creative practice through being hesitant, cautious, controlling or negative?

- Do you have an unconscious mantra which hijacks your actions, such as not being good enough or believing that you do not belong in a particular environment?

- How do you think you are received by others?

- Are you approachable and easy to access?

- Do you show resistance in some instances?

- Do you like to control and give orders?

Checking in with yourself may be low on the priority list. Regardless of how attentive you are, dominant thoughts will instigate comfort or hesitancy, experimentation or safety, defence or an ability to embrace, ease or tension in your body. There is a fickle line between what you determine is possible and whether your reaction is to hold back and block or accept and respond.

Exercises to notice yourself

The exercises in this section are designed to help you become more aware of yourself.

EXERCISE: QUALITIES

If you could select only one quality to describe yourself, what would it be – brittle, steeled, electric, cold, warm, soft, dense, hard, fluid, sharp or something else? What qualities would you like to embrace? In everyday interactions, find ways of experimenting with what is not usual for you.

EXERCISE: YOUR SENSES

How aware are you of your own senses? When you walk into a new space, do you notice smells, sounds, colours and dimensions? Do you tend to be more aware of sounds than smells? Are you someone who touches things and people, and notices textures? Practise placing your attention on the senses with which you are less familiar to broaden your range.

EXERCISE: MIX THINGS UP

Are you aware of doing some tasks identically, such as using the same hand to brush your teeth or sitting in the same chair to watch television? We all become over-reliant on doing everyday activities the same way, almost unconsciously. From time to time, it is beneficial to challenge your nervous system and experiment.

Try putting on your shoes with your eyes closed. With your non-dominant hand, brush your teeth or comb your hair or do your buttons and zips up, place your bag on the opposite shoulder to what is usual and so forth. If you are left-handed, try writing with your right hand, and vice versa.

Felt senses

When we consider the senses, we usually think of sight, touch, smell, hearing and taste. The felt senses are an incorporation of all five and blend to create the background responses of your internal life. Gendlin (1981, p.10) describes them as 'a special kind of internal body awareness...a body sense of meaning'. Although they are always present, we may not be receptive to the subtleties, which are often experienced as a fuzziness. An example of when the felt senses may be more acute is the feelings of unease or anticipation. Levine (1997, p.67) says that 'the felt sense unifies a great deal of data and gives it meaning'. It is one of the ways through which we are able to recognise sensation and decode it. How a response is somatically registered is through sensation rather than thought. A gush of what seems like warm syrup could be recognised as love, a flutter of insects can be understood as unease, and sharp tingles can signal danger or fear. These are examples of the senses working together.

Having awareness of the felt senses helps to:

- ground

- balance

- deepen links to instincts and impulses

- enable the movement of energy.

Subtle and slight changes in sensations are as valuable as bigger, more dominant shifts. Often it is the huge emotional changes that we look for rather than establishing and tuning in to the initial foundation, the felt senses.

EXERCISE: ACQUAINT YOURSELF WITH FEELING

This is a simple routine to do on a regular basis. It is like being with yourself and taking the time to notice what you feel. The more this is repeated, the more observant and receptive you will become to sensation and the felt senses. To do this exercise, sit comfortably and notice:

1. how you feel

2. where the dominant sensations are

3. your breath

4. whether any of your joints are locked

5. the shape you have adopted

6. whether this is a familiar shape.

As you alter anything above, tune in to any sensations. Take the time to observe; it is not necessary to do anything, change will naturally occur. If you feel the need to soften or quieten, direct your breath to the area. If you are someone who overthinks, send your breath to your lower dantien, beneath your navel.

A valuable way of understanding how to become more receptive is to look at the key player in the whole process: the central nervous system (CNS).

The nervous system

There are two main sections of the nervous system: the central nervous system (CNS), which consists of the brain and spine, and the peripheral nervous system (PNS), which is made up of the web of nerves that are connected to, and outside of, the brain and spinal cord (Figure 3.2).

Central nervous system

The CNS controls most functions of the mind and body and consists of the brain and the spinal cord. Together they act as the command centres by interpreting sensory input and issuing instructions, which are based on the memory of past experience and the conditions of the moment. Specifically, it is believed that the brain interprets the external environment and is the origin and control of all body movement, thoughts, memories, planes and coordinates. The spinal cord receives and distributes information from and to muscles, nerves, skin and joints, and runs through the spine (Figure 3.1). It is the bridge to the brain.

Functioning as a signalling device which rapidly sends messages to all the other systems, the spinal cord can calm you down or rev you up, setting the pace of all internal life.

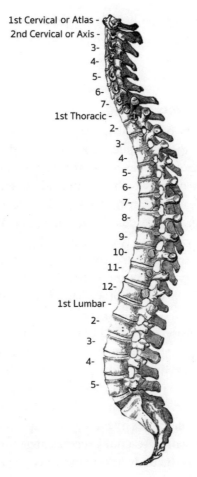

Figure 3.1 The spine (Gray 1918)

Here are the main actions of the CNS:

- It assesses the changes inside and outside the body. It does this through sensory receptors, which respond to any stimuli, and gather information called sensory inputs.

- It combines sensory information in the various parts of the brain in order to make decisions regarding the input. It is a bringing together.

- It activates motor outputs, which initiate the decision to take action.

An example of this process in action could be that you are crossing the road, you hear and then see a car (the stimulus) and you move back to the pavement.

Peripheral nervous system

There are 12 pairs of cranial nerves which emerge from the brain and serve mainly the head and neck area. An additional 31 pairs of spinal nerves pass on information to the whole body. It is a sprawling communication network which is continually sending out signals and instigating voluntary action (i.e. that which we choose to do) and involuntary action, such as your heartbeat and breathing.

The PNS is divided into two divisions, the sensory and the motor. The sensory is responsible for conveying information from internal and external events through the different types of nerves which pass impulses to the CNS via receptors. The motor carries impulses from the CNS to organs and glands to enable physical action to occur.

The motor division has a further branch known as the autonomic nervous system (ANS), which regulates automatic activity such as heartbeat, gland activity, breathing and blood flow. There are two sections to the ANS, the sympathetic nervous system (SNS) and the parasympathetic nervous system (PSNS), which bring about opposite effects. The SNS mobilises the body during extreme situations; it revs up activity creating reactions such as anger and fear. The PSNS unwinds and calms the body as it works to conserve energy.

The SNS and PSNS work together to regulate not only the essential physiological functioning of the body but also the levels of arousal, which determine the strength of feelings and emotions. They control the circulation of blood to a particular area, restricting or releasing the flow which alters sensation and all reactions to the stimuli you encounter in your daily life. These two strands are essential as they connect your whole instrument and enable experiences to be processed.

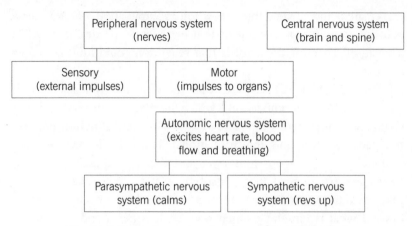

Figure 3.2 Nervous system (courtesy of Daniel Hughes)

The nervous system does not work alone; its main collaborator is the endocrine system, which includes all the glands and hormones that are controlled by the stimulation of the CNS and the chemical receptors in the blood. It helps to maintain homeostasis, the self-regulating process through which efficient and optimal biological functioning can be maintained. This is achieved through adjusting and responding to conditions. Various chemical substances, known as neurotransmitters, all of which have their own purpose, support how the body copes with the potential stressors of a stimuli. An example is that when we need to respond with speed to an emergency, such as running away from an attacker, adrenaline is released to support the functioning of the muscular system.

The nervous system plays a vital part in the kind of actor you are, as it can really dictate your level of receptivity, the extent to which you are able to immerse yourself in your work and your originality. The brain and body connect through neural pathways or networks; it consists of bundles of neurons (nerve cells), which communicate through junctions called synapses. One interpretation of how memory and mental patterns occur is that these networks become integrated into our nervous system. We therefore repeat what is known and what has already been laid down; it is as if data have been formatted. The term 'body schema' is a concept which suggests that the nervous system organises and modifies incoming information at an unconscious level. This activity affects body posture, movement and action. Rhonda Blair suggests that 'Bodily schema are an effect of neural networks, which are created and shaped by the whole accumulation of experience and the cognitive processing of that experience' (Blair 2008, p.57). The significance for the actor is that repetition could limit or reduce spontaneity.

Blair (2008, p.57) suggests that training and rehearsals could be seen as 'brain modification', which implies a conscious effort to change neural patterns. Kemp (2012) makes the distinction between the persona actor and transformational actor, the former working essentially at an unconscious level and therefore drawing on what they have experienced in a consistent way for each character they play. An actor who is more transformative would extend what they do beyond what is familiar to their own body schema and consciously explore various elements of the character traits. This could involve experimenting with different movement patterns – that is, adopting new shapes and bodily rhythms. Considering the biological processes at work, such a process is not instantaneous; rather, it takes time for the brain and body to integrate what is unfamiliar. It requires a type of training which is holistic and prioritises the corporeal – working with how the body functions.

So what does this all mean for the actor? There is one particular part of this process that is really useful to understand: the response cycle. Performers refine their craft such that they are able to recreate exchanges which are realistic and believable, natural conversations. The CNS and its various branches are at the heart of this, and as we have noted, there is quite a complex procedure constantly operating. The senses instigate a chain of events which can easily take you off course, away from where your attention should be.

To summarise, the biological process of receiving and reacting looks like this (this is very quick and much of it is unconscious and automatic):

1. There is a need.

2. This is followed by a surge of sensation.

3. This signals that the information is received and being worked on.

4. A decision is made as to the urgency of this need.

5. The arousal may be downgraded or heightened depending on the urgency.

6. The decision to act in a certain way is made.

7. The receiving stage: your body accepts or resists.

8. The cycle then begins again.

This cycle is constantly happening, thousands of times a day. At the receiving stage, it is possible for the transition from the SNS to the PSNS to be delayed. In this instance there could be a defence to receiving, a shutting down – a result of an overly sustained level of arousal such as anxiety, frustration or a feeling of being unsafe. This is an interesting situation which could be especially relevant for an actor. It is when the embodiment of information could be blocked, and in relation to a creative process this could be when lines are forgotten or when the emotion of the imagined situation is unreachable because the body has remained on high alert and is overwhelmed and stressed. In other words, there are too much data for it to manage. To avoid this, it is necessary to be able to reach a place whereby you can receive and embody your response, as opposed to purely react to it.

So what can be done to encourage your body to avoid halting or delaying the receiving stage of the process? Nerves spread out like the roots of a tree, reaching every inch of your body, so learning how to control your nervous system is a good start.

Figure 3.3 Tree man (Harter 2005)

EXERCISE: CALMING THE NERVES

This exercise works to calm the nervous system and encourages stimulation of the significant nerves in the PSNS. The vagus nerve is one of the largest nerves in the body (see Chapter 8). It moves through every vital organ and has branches along the length of the spinal cord. Its function is to calm, so it is important to get to know it. This is a valuable exercise if you get overanxious and your mind easily becomes distracted. The exercise can be done sitting, standing or lying, as follows:

1. Balance your weight and unlock your joints.

2. Place your hands behind your neck, with your fingers in the slight indentation at the base of the cranium. They should be positioned along the first and second vertebrae of the cervical spine and just above the atlas, C1 (see Figure 3.1). Your elbow should be in line with your shoulders, which should not rise too much.

3. Connect to your breath by regulating the inhalation and exhalation through your nose.

4. Create a mental image of a specific colour moving though the branches of the vagus nerve (see Figure 8.4).

5. Remain in this position for up to 5 minutes or as long as needed.

This does take time to activate, but slowly your body will respond by slowing down.

Having observed the acute sensitivity of your CNS, it is possible to understand how easy it is for your feelings and emotions to get hijacked. It may seem that in some instances you have very little control as to how you respond, such as the times when you turn red from embarrassment, or suddenly start to speak with a squeaky voice when you bump into someone you are attracted to, or when you become nervous at interviews. Here your body is very much being receptive; it is just not consciously controlled, so somehow your internal behaviour is untamed.

Cycle of response when acting

As an actor, initially you have to direct the process and be very aware of the need of the character as the starting point. If you feel strongly about the need, a surge of sensation will occur. Deciding the stakes and how urgent this moment is determines what happens next and the choice as to the course of action. A rupture to this cycle is when the actor stops believing in the circumstances and does not have the need of the character – at the point their own need arises and the body acts on that. This could be any distraction from not wanting to be watched to hearing a sound which is not connected to the scene.

What may prevent the cycle?

The following things may prevent the cycle of response:

- not placing yourself into the imaginative situation

- locking up your body so you are not able to respond to stimuli

- a lack of focus as to where your attention should be in any given moment

- misdirection of your attention

- lack of receptivity to what is genuinely going on in your body

- a lack of rigour in understanding the story of the text

- no clarity about the drives and stakes of the situation.

Interruptions

So what can you do to reduce the possibility of interruptions? Becoming aware of what happens in certain situations is important. An awareness of what you are receptive to is not about controlling what you do, but more to encourage an opening up, to increase your facility to work with your body to embody experience. It is useful to observe what you do in situations when your nervous system interrupts the feeling of being at ease and relaxed. There are classic situations, many of which as an actor you will continually encounter, in which your body will become more alert than in other situations. Consider what happens when you:

- stand in front of a group of people to do a task

- read out loud

- know you are being watched

- have limited time to achieve a task

- are working with a stranger whom you want to impress.

Possible somatic effects

Look at the list below and see if you recognise any of these somatic reactions:

- Your body locks up.

- Your throat tightens.

- Vocal quality changes and loses tonal range.

- Breathing becomes shallow.

- It is difficult to concentrate on the task in hand.

- You hear the words you speak.

- Your temperature changes, often resulting in sweating.

- You cannot feel your body.

- Your thoughts are racing.

- It is difficult to remember what you are meant to be saying.

- You are unable to hear what the other person is saying.

- You do not really notice your environment or acknowledge details.

- Your sensory responses lose sharpness.

What is the problem?

In situations where you become overwhelmed, it is sometimes difficult for the body to maintain normal functioning, and a struggle begins to keep things on course as danger is perceived and how you are able to communicate with both yourself and others is overtaken.

Receptivity to others is affected by how receptive you are to yourself. Recognising the feelings that have emerged in any situation can open up the possibility of choosing how you react rather than resorting to familiar routines or allowing a specific emotion to hinder the outcome of a situation.

Instances that are particularly relevant are when you are unable to fully engage with another person; this could be in a scene, an interview or a performance. In these instances it is useful to be aware of:

- your breath

- your head/neck relationship

- any locking in your body, especially your knees and pelvis

- whether your jaw is closed or locked

- any holding patterns that you have developed (i.e. when you repeatedly hold or tighten particular parts of your body, usually in response to anxiety and worry)

- the diaphragm area and how this affects your breathing.

Making slight adjustments

It is amazing how a slight postural adjustment can bring change to what you feel and think. An example is when you alter the relationship between your neck and head: almost immediately there will be a change in sensations, feelings and your breathing. This may involve tucking your chin or realigning your neck so it does not lean towards one side. At this junction there is a huge number of cranial nerves which transmit messages and send out pulsations throughout your body. If restricted through poor posture or overly taut or rigid muscles, the flow of signals slows and traffic builds up. Another place which is really significant for sensations and feelings is the diaphragm, the muscle that sits at the bottom of the sternum. The nervous system forms a complex web of nerves around the diaphragm. It is located close to the solar plexus, and if even slightly held, tight or out of alignment with the corresponding structures, there will be a significant impact on how in touch you are with your body. This is a crucial position with which to work in order to maximise access to the ability to communicate with yourself and others.

Steps to observing yourself

Take the following steps to observe yourself:

1. Develop a stronger somatic awareness; notice what your body does.

2. If you feel like you are tensing, take action which will bring release.

3. Be affected by what is happening in your surroundings (i.e. alert to your senses).

4. Focus on the feelings in your body, and do not deny what you feel.

5. Register your range of movement. Begin to expand your breathing when you feel uneasy and soften instead of becoming tight.

EXERCISE: JUST BEING

This exercise is a way of allowing sensations and feelings to emerge without monitoring. You can do it anytime and anywhere, as only you know what you are doing. A position that I refer to regularly throughout this book is 'wu chi'. This is a static posture from qigong which requires specific placement and alignment to maximise the movement of qi. It leads to a quietening and calming of all the body's systems.

1. Stand in wu chi position (see Figure 4.1).

2. Inhale through your nose, directing the breath downwards, allowing your abdomen to rise. Exhale through your nose and feel your body slightly elevate.

3. Take your attention to your heart area and see of what sensations you become aware.

4. Imagine that your breath is coming in through the balls of your feet and out through your palms.

5. Observe any changes and sensations that occur.

This sequence is particularly good when you are stressed and feel overwhelmed.

This exercise is also very effective in pairs:

1. Face a partner approximately 3 feet away and retain eye contact. Take each other in.

2. Stand in wu chi position (see Figure 4.1).

3. Follow whatever sensations and feelings arise. This may be to laugh or cry – try not to monitor reactions.

4. Take your attention to your heart and breathe into this area.

5. Change your breathing so it is coming in through the balls of your feet and out through your palms. Note the breathing of the other person.

6. Feel your feet on the floor and just notice what it's like to be with the other person. Observe any changes and sensations that occur.

It is likely that you were able to tune in to the other person with more intensity because you have allowed time to notice and register each other, and allowed feelings to arise. Being with someone means taking time to register the dynamic and how you affect each other.

Flow and receptivity

'Flow' is a word that crops up from time to time in relation to acting. When something does not quite feel right, you may find yourself thinking 'things are not flowing today'. This can be experienced as sensations of tightness, which are often referred to as tension, or an inability to focus on one thing for long. Other examples may be:

- You are thinking too much and find it hard to place your attention on the situation.

- You are unable to remember your text.

- It is difficult to fully engage at an emotional level.

- There is little sensation in a part of your body (your legs, for example).

- Your breathing is shallow and laboured.

- Your body feels awkward and you don't know what to do with your arms or hands.

- There is discomfort, experienced as throbbing or tingling in one part of your body.

- Your body feels robotic and rigid.

Flow is a reflection of the dynamic and pulse of all of your inner life. When thinking about the material that is flowing through the body, you will automatically name thoughts, feelings and emotions, thoughts being possibly the most active – the continual chatter which appears as pictures, words and ideas. They express your opinions and beliefs and articulate what you want in any given moment, some of which is uttered consciously though words, while other thoughts are leaked through bodily and energetic means. What is usual is that mental activity, through the activation of various regions of the brain, is constant. There will never be a moment when you are not thinking.

Behind the scenes, at a deeper level, there is much more flowing, a multitude of substances which are shifting and simmering, all working to keep your body functioning effectively. This range of activity involves atoms, molecules, cells, tissues, fluids and the electrical impulses from your brain to your nerves to a whole network of tissues. At a microscopic level cells are forming and dying, and nerves are reacting to the instructions being given, twitching and vibrating. The activity is immense; it is like a playground, and the possibility for felt experience is bounteous. There is a constant flow of substances which support us and make life possible.

This knowledge and understanding becomes especially valuable when we realise how vital flow is to feeling, emotion, spontaneity and the ability to play. The emergence of tension is one means of identifying obstruction to the flow of your inner life. As we have seen, the natural instinct of the body is to hold, freeze or tighten when anxious, to become overwhelmed and stressed. Tight and overly taut muscles is one way in which flow is interrupted. Other causes of obstruction are:

- poor posture
- injury/bruises
- holding patterns
- restrictive attitudes
- lifestyle choices
- stress and anxiety
- shallow breathing.

These causes of obstruction can lead to any of the following:

- reduced sensation
- overthinking and loss of connection to your whole body
- loss of memory
- loss of alertness
- inability to concentrate
- held and rigid body
- lack of embodied emotion in performance.

Mihaly Csikszentmihalyi explains that there is a connection between a flow state and an embodied experience. He defines it as 'the state in which people are so involved in an activity that nothing else seems to matter' (Csikszentmihalyi 2002, p.4). His theories apply particularly to the achievement of happiness, but he draws a correlation to artists and sports professionals who spend their lives doing what they enjoy, which he believes affects the engagement and control of their inner life. The commitment to an activity is heightened by a goal or target as it channels inner forces. Most of the time we do this naturally; for example, you become less interested in a television show, so the urge and necessary physical energy is generated to turn channels. This is a simple action but actually involves every part of you. For an embodied state to be achieved, there needs to be a high level of integration of the various systems that form your inner life, optimum communication that is working towards one thing. If there is a sense of flow within the body, there is unimpeded movement, which means thoughts, feelings, sensations and emotions travel. This offers the opportunity to be free to play and be more spontaneous.

Achieving a flow state concerns directing the body and becoming really observant about the sensations and feelings present. This is connected to what you are literally doing: you may be locking your knees, pushing your head forwards or tightening your jaw, and any of these actions hinders a flow state. Any structure which is held is hard to move through, and this is the same within your body.

A possible process whereby you register and adjust to increased flow is as follows:

1. Recognise a feeling.

2. Notice your breath.

3. Make an adjustment.

4. Identify what you want in this moment.

5. Recognise the new feeling.

6. Notice your breath.

7. Identify your desires in this moment.

8. Make an adjustment.

This implies that flow requires tuning in and making changes, continually adjusting like a flowing stream.

As discussed in Chapter 1, in Traditional Chinese Medicine (TCM) it is acknowledged that the flow of qi affects not only general health but the day-to-day things you may take for granted, like clear thinking, the ability to concentrate, feelings, sensations and emotional expression. It is present in a number of things, such as blood, food and breathing, and contributes to the movement of oxygen. Transported through the network of meridian channels, which are like energy highways that are mapped throughout the body, qi serves to nourish and detox; therefore, the flow of qi is a means of achieving a healthy and alert body. It too can be obstructed by unhelpful body use, negative thoughts, stress and scar tissue, all of which will affect the direction, tempo and quality of qi flow. Qi can be chaotic, smooth, stagnant, heavy or light, with its overall dynamic affecting energy levels. Working to clear the meridian channels helps to achieve a smoother flow, which enables the levels of communication to sharpen. (See Chapter 7 for a detailed explanation of the meridian channels; also see Figure 7.1.)

EXERCISE: TRACING THE MERIDIANS

Tracing the meridians is a subtle way of keeping energy flowing and balancing how you are coping with the stimulation in the immediate environment. This involves holding the palms of the hands approximately a centimetre above the skin whilst following the path of a specific meridian channel. The intention is to encourage qi flow, so it is not necessary to make contact with the skin to trigger the movement. In TCM it is recommended that you start with your lung channel because of the connection to breath. Other energy-medicine practitioners suggest the conception and governing channels, which follow the front and back lines of your spine respectively. (To identify which meridian channel corresponds to a specific emotion or body function, refer to Figure 7.1.)

This exercises comprises the following:

1. Stand in wu chi position (see Figure 4.1).

2. Place your hand palm down close to but not touching your skin, and retaining this proximity trace the path of the channel moving from the first to the last point.

3. This action needs to be repeated several times for at least 3–4 minutes. Coordinate your breathing ideally so that the inhalation lasts the length of the route along the channel, and exhale as you trace back to the first point.

The hands have a particularly strong electromagnetic energy, essentially because this is the location of laogong, which is point 8 on the pericardium channel. This is an important energy gateway which links three channels: the heart, lung and pericardium.

Breath and receptivity

Breath is a major factor in how receptive we are. Each of us has a breathing rhythm which reflects our lifestyle and somatic awareness. For a few minutes observe how you breathe and the natural pattern of the expansion and contraction. Notice the extent of the movement of your ribcage at the back and front. Place the palm of your hand on your diaphragm and feel the movement of this muscle. How does it feel? Extend the range of movement by taking in more breath and allowing your ribcage to swing outwards.

When breath intake is reduced, this will change both the energetic vibrancy and vocal quality. Though the habits are likely to be unconscious, restricting breath through poor alignment, holding patterns, shallow breathing or the obstruction of any part of the breathing apparatus will affect accessibility to your own sensory life and how you reach others.

EXERCISE: BELLOWS

This sequence draws attention to the natural cycle of the body, which is a rise and fall or expansion and contraction. It can inform you of the ease, or lack of ease, present at any given time, and it can support change to bring calm and self-control. Perform it as follows:

1. Stand in wu chi position (see Figure 4.1).

2. Place your hands about 3 inches in front of your lungs, and try to retain this distance during the exercise.

3. Imagine that your hands are bellows. Place your attention on your palms and direct your breathing to this area.

4. As you breathe in, slightly sink from your centre/lower dantien and rise on the out breath.

5. Focus on allowing your breathing to become smooth and unrestricted. Observe that the whole body is moving in sync as one being.

Becoming more receptive is essential for the transformative actor. It cultivates an instrument which is sharply tuned to allow experience to move through the layers of the body and access sensations at a deeper level. The knowledge that your body is different from that of your character is a significant observation. Accessing their body implies temporarily altering your own somatic patterns – that is, modifying how your brain operates.

Conclusion

Making adjustments to how the body is held is a way of accessing more flow and ease, which will bring a greater range of sensation and feeling. This implies that there are ways of aligning and positioning which are more beneficial to the optimal connection of the internal structures. As we have seen, in order to enhance the ability to be receptive, channelling where attention is placed is vital. This is not exclusively a mental process; it involves the whole of you working as one unit, steering the fluctuations and adapting to what is experienced in each moment. Having introduced the importance of the CNS, we now move on to consider how to order and balance all this activity.

Chapter 4

BALANCE
Controlling inner forces

Introduction

Having suggested that the body is hugely receptive and able to subtly react on a level that is beyond conscious recognition, it is useful to look at what we can effectively manage. As an actor it is necessary to have the ability to steer this complexity and cultivate an inner state that is able to facilitate the embodiment of the story so that you can allow yourself to be moved.

Reaching a position whereby the given circumstances can have transformative effects is fundamental. Transformative in this sense means a shift away from your usual patterns and levels of expression, when you are able to move through any barriers or psychological blocks to experience an altered internal rhythm. To tune and direct all that is flowing offers the capacity for an immense depth of feeling. The pursuit of this can begin with exploring a place from which it is good to start from, and return to, a balanced state.

Anatomical balance is the ability to maintain body weight over its base support, to stay upright and act on sensory input, which makes it possible to control movement, determine direction and speed, make postural amendments and maintain stability. This is led by the vestibular system and is a process that involves signals from the brain to eyes, ears, skin, muscles and joints. I am going to explore a broader definition which involves looking holistically and specifically drawing on some of the traditions and concepts from Traditional Chinese Medicine (TCM). The pursuit of balance is integral to TCM, which sees the body as a dynamic energy system with yin and yang, which are seen as the oppositional forces of nature, being crucial for harmonising. 'Balance is considered to be a complex interplay between body and mind, which is reflected at all levels, ranging from the biochemical components perspective to the energetic control of the physical body' (Wang *et al.* 2005, p.173). This implies that balance concerns the flow and tuning of all activity, physiological and electrical, and as a consequence impacts on feelings, emotions and all behaviour. (See Chapter 7 for more on yin and yang.)

Balance is a word that generally indicates symmetry of some kind, in this instance the body and all its systems. (Chapter 8 gives an explanation of the body's systems in sync.) It is relatively easy for any one of these systems to become inefficient and interfere with optimum functioning. A simple chain of events involving poor posture, such as collapsing around the diaphragm area, will affect your breathing and thereby your vocal quality. Other consequences of the systems not being in tune can be poor concentration, an inability to react with speed, the tendency to be stuck or controlled by an emotion or a lack of energy. At the start of practice, a warm-up, in effect, is working towards being balanced and making biological adjustments. The results of a movement sequence which is designed to energise and focus are usually clear to see, and there is a greater level of receptivity and attentiveness to the felt senses.

With a greater sense of balance comes flexibility, and it is possible to work more effectively from stability than either a heightened emotional state or lethargy. Blocks to creative freedom have been a significant part of the psycho-physical actor training, as seen in the work of Jerzy Grotowski, Jacques Lecoq, Eugenio Barba, Tadashi Suzuki, Phillip Zarrilli, Lorna Marshall and Anne Bogart. The common strands of these various approaches is a recognition of the need to work towards a body which is tuned and receptive. The biologist James Oschman directly relates internal alignment to enhanced communication: 'Performance is enhanced when all of the body's communication channels are open and balanced' (Oschman 2000, p.90). By this Oschman is referring to a body structure that enables ease of movement and the unimpeded flow of messages.

Neutrality

Performers usually go through a process of transition, a move away from distractions towards a focused state. During this stage mental faculties are possibly calming, breath centred and sensations sharpened. This transitional phase is often known as neutral. Jacques Copeau (1879–1949) said that 'Neutrality is a resting state for actors.' He expands by saying, 'It is a state where the actor attains energised stillness. It is a state of readiness' (Snow 2012, p.22). Jackie Snow explains that 'the neutral state is not a passive state but a potent one. It is a place of calm and a place full of vitality. It allows the body to be fully receptive' (p.24). It could be understood anatomically as a point where the skeleton is aligned, the tension on nerves and tendons is minimal and weight is evenly distributed. This position would therefore enhance the flow of all internal activity, because the joints are at ease, creating space for neural stimulation and generally enhanced circulation. Teresa Mitchell acknowledges that it offers the opportunity to calm but also tune energetic forces. 'Neutral is when space, time and weight efforts are resting, but are ready to ignite and intensify' (Mitchell 1998, p.34). If we consider this interpretation, we can assume that the body is settling, realigning its forces so there is more conscious choice as to how it is to be used. Moshé Feldenkrais uses the term 'zero position' which, according to Sullivan (1990, p.46), implies that this is 'an absence of personal movement cliches, idiosyncratic ways of standing or tension in a particular part of the body'. We can see that neutrality can be viewed as an in-between place where there are no committed qualities; tonally it seems to be beige or cream. Other descriptions of this state are 'clean slate', 'blank canvas' and even 'plain'; all suggest that it is a starting place which possesses no real defined ideas – from which anything can be built.

I prefer to use the term 'balance' and see this as a stage when maximum potential or all of the internal network is possible through subtle adjustments. What we experience as balance is in flux: it is not a stuck and rigid position; movement is inherent, as the body registers and is in resonance with its environment. This implies, as Eden (2008) explains, that we move towards balance, momentarily reach it, and then it is disrupted by the interference of a number of sensory possibilities such as a change in light, a memory or thought. This disruption is often seen as a loss of concentration, a diversion of attention or a level of chaos in the felt senses. With this could come many reactions, such as tightening, holding or freezing. The solution is to stabilise and guide the body to where it is fully productive – a balanced state. Becoming aware of a position of physiological ease which is less reactive but responsive is a good place to begin.

Balance and the energy system

To further understand what is being balanced, I am again drawn to the energy system and TCM, whose 2000-year-old practices offer interesting perspectives. In effect, every aspect of your anatomy and physiology is being balanced, circulation is setting a pace which is alert but not overly reactive, breath is flowing freely and there is generally more coherence. With this comes more efficiency and a sharpness, and what you may notice are more vibrations, almost like an electrical pulse. Some bodywork disciplines, such as acupuncture and shiatsu, believe that there are distinct energy systems within the body. 'We are each a constellation of energy systems, just as the body with its immune, endocrine, cardiovascular and other systems is a constellation of physical systems' (Eden 2008, p.109). Eden includes the chakras, meridians, radiant circuits and aura amongst the nine systems she believes are operating. (This is explored in more depth in Chapters 5 and 7. For now we focus on the meridians as the main pathways through which energy/qi flows.)

Working with the meridian channels is the starting point for much of my practice. There are some fundamental postures in qigong which bring efficiency, ease and a stable flow to the body. Wu chi is a standing posture (see Figure 4.1) that offers the potential for connecting up the internal structure, including the meridian channels, and therefore allows all parts to speak to themselves. When the posture is first adopted, it is not uncommon for various twinges, changes in heat and vigorous pulsations to occur. An explanation for such dramatic fluctuations in sensation is that regions of the body are being reunited, having been somehow energetically severed through misuse. Whilst in this posture, new felt relationships are being formed to create an enhanced flow of qi, which will change in tempo, direction and velocity of energy. If wu chi is practised, in time you will be able to tap into internal movement and have a clear feeling of energetic balance. It is then also easy to notice when the body strays off energetic alignment. A common feeling is that one half of the body seems to feel lower than the other inside, which may sound strange, and it is literally as if there is a need to unite the two halves. If an area feels tight and rigid, often known as tension, this is an indication that the energetic system is not as fluent or buoyant as it could be – that is, it is being restricted.

The idea of neutrality is similar to wu chi, as for qigong practitioners this stance encourages a position that is as close to the ideal natural structure of the body as possible, where it can function efficiently. Wu chi is not usually referred to as a neutral stance but provides opportunities similar to the definitions given by Mitchell (1998, p.34) and Sullivan (1990, p.46). It brings a quietening of the mind and an enhanced connection to feeling the whole body. In essence, it's linking up the neurovascular points, and is like turning on a huge lighting grid.

EXERCISE: WU CHI

Wu chi, meaning empty energy, is the starting position adopted for the practice of qigong. It allows for the body's systems to be aligned and increases the potential for qi flow.

1. Place your feet in a parallel position, hip width apart, with the knees facing forwards.

2. Take a small step to either side to slightly widen your step. The sides of your feet need to be straight.

3. If your knees move inwards, place slight pressure on them so they remain over your feet.

4. At the lumbar spine, tuck the coccyx.

5. Moving up the spine, tuck the chin.

6. Allow the shoulder girdle to soften and the scapula to slide down your back.

7. Move your weight predominantly onto the balls of your feet.

8. Place your attention onto the area under your belly button and above your pubic bone. This is your centre, or lower dantien.

9. Inhale and exhale as if through the dantien. Upon inhaling, there is a slight sinking, and rise occurs upon exhaling. This movement comes from the dantien.

10. Have an awareness of the space above your head and the ground beneath your feet.

Figure 4.1 Wu chi position (courtesy of Daniel Hughes)

Centres of energy

The concept of energy flow is further expanded by the idea of centres, which are believed to act as reservoirs and are positioned along the spine. The notion of centres is not new to performance training, as both Stanislavsky and Chekhov developed a series of exercises which explore the notion. Its origins can be traced to Eastern body practice. For the actor there seem to be two main strands to how the idea is used, one being that the centre is the place from where energy radiates, and the other being that the centre changes according to what is being experienced. For example, in one moment you may be thinking and being logical, so the head becomes the centre, and in another moment the hands may take over as they express a feeling of urgency. So the centre is affected by thoughts, drives and wants. Another example would be that if a person wants to be noticed, they would move from the upper body, usually protruding their chest. If it is important to be considered sexy, then the groin area may be the centre. The Eastern perspective takes us a little more into the intricacies of how the body functions energetically.

There are several disciplines that consider that energy centres, known as the hara in Japan or dantiens in China, are essential for fuelling internal communication and the flow of qi. In practices like martial arts, to be centred is to have both a felt connection and control of the whole body, and this is achieved through a strong, balanced relationship to gravity and an alignment which allows energetic forces to function effectively. To be centred is to be in a state of readiness.

In qigong there are three dantiens positioned along the centre of the body like a hanging string of pearls. The alignment of these energy centres is considered to be vital to balance, sensation and the distribution of qi. It is good to imagine that they are like three circles suspended on one line: if one shifts off the place of balance for a sustained period, ultimately bodily connection will be lost.

Dantiens

The three dantiens are as follows (Figure 4.2):

- The lower dantien is positioned in the pelvis. It is the centre of balance and strength, and the storehouse for qi, and it is often referred to as the 'field of bliss' or 'sea of qi', hara or 'field of elixir'. It is a natural balancing point from which energy – or in yoga practice, prana – is stored and distributed outwards.

- The middle dantien is in the chest area and is believed to be the emotional centre. This includes the solar plexus and diaphragm.

- The upper dantien is the spiritual energy centre and includes the head and above. It relates to intuitive awareness and the ability to tap into energetic fields in the boby.

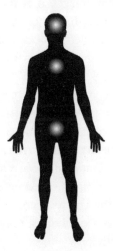

Figure 4.2 The three dantiens (courtesy of Daniel Hughes)

Moving from the lower dantien not only encourages movement as one unit but connects body and mind intentionality. The feeling is one of maximum power and minimum effort.

EXERCISE: CONNECTING TO THE LOWER DANTIEN

Perform this exercise in order to connect to the lower dantien:

1. Whilst standing in wu chi place your hands approximately an inch underneath your belly button with the palms facing inwards.

2. Become aware of your breath and the rise and fall of your abdomen.

3. Remain like this for 3–5 minutes.

There is a general slowing down of thoughts when you are able to operate from this lower centre, not only because you are working in sync with your breath, but because it also activates the parasympathetic nervous system. It is usually in a state of reaction, such as panic or anxiety, that a disconnection from the lower dantien occurs. If you have a stronger link to your upper body, the chest and head region, you will have to work hard to discover this centre. Without a place which encourages a downwards connection from which to orient, it is possible to get drawn into a state of reaction.

When centred, there is ideally physiological harmony, which brings with it physical control, strength and a multitude of sensations such as tingles, heat and shimmers. It is the opportunity to embrace experience, to process through the body, to fully receive; a place to return to when overwhelmed, a bodily and energetic base camp. 'Center is a basic bodily presence, and it is on this presence that other bodily states are built' (Heckler 1984, p.79). This will include breath and the functions of the central nervous system, including thoughts, sensations and emotions.

An individual's primary centre is determined by their physical, mental and intellectual characteristics. There is a position from which each person seems to predominantly operate, for example, the head, chest or groin/pelvis, but in times of extremes this is likely to change. When panic arises, the chest may become the place of heightened sensations and feelings. When anxious, your stomach may be where you notice heightened activity.

The chakra system involves a similar idea: it is believed that there are seven points along the spine, each of which represents corresponding physical and psychological states. An example is that the first chakra represents roots and how secure an individual may feel in the world. The second chakra indicates stability, power and self-esteem. (See Chapter 7 for further discussion about chakras.) It is between these two places that substantial drives are thought to emanate, which is why it is often known as the will centre. Michael Chekhov identified with this and was largely influenced by Rudolf Steiner, who believed that the body could be divided into three parts:

- Head – the place of ideas conscious thinking, reflections, questioning, and the search for solutions.

- Chest – the centre for feeling, the place which mediates between the head and the will centres.

- Legs and feet – associated with a person's will, associated with a person's will, their gut impulses and drives, this centre incorporates the digestive system and creates the force to take action.

This concept makes the distinction between thinkers, feelers or doers, and is a means of recognising which centre a person may naturally prioritise. It may be the head, the heart or the guts where activity seems to be emerging. Classically, a thinker would be an intellectual or someone who is logical and plans rather than acts with any spontaneity. A schemer or controller may be head-bound; Iago is an example. Romeo, who is more impulsive, could be led by his heart. Ideally, as an actor you will have more flexibility if you can fluctuate and move between different centres.

EXERCISE: CHANGING CENTRES

Imagine that you have a ball of energy inside of your body and do the following:

1. Start by placing it in your pelvis. From a sitting position take your attention to this area and experience your weight shifting downwards. Your breath reaches beyond your abdomen and your pelvis expands.

2. Move the ball to your chest around your diaphragm and repeat the breathing pattern. Observe the quality. Do you feel lighter? Has your breathing changed?

3. Place the ball into your head. Notice what you are doing with the rest of your body. Do you have more awareness of your neck and shoulders? Has the rhythm of your breathing changed? Stay with this for a while and see if your thought processes have changed.

4. Take the same exercise in to movement and walk, experiencing what it feels like to operate from each of those places.

5. Have a conversation with someone and experiment with placing your attention at a different centre for each thought.

Michael Chekhov believed the ideal centre to be in the middle of the chest, and he asks that you imagine this to be the place from which energy flows. He believed that impulses stem from this centre and travel through the body. This is likely to be connected to the location of the solar plexus, which contains a cluster of nerves that feed both the upper and lower parts of the body. He also suggested that focusing on the chest as a centre leads to a more united instrument as we can imagine that the legs and arms start from this position. There are various interpretations, and I encourage my students to work from the lower dantien, which has potentially a strong grounding affect and is, according to most Eastern body practices, your centre of energy.

Balance and emotions

Each body has its own sense of balance which has been arrived at over a lifetime. What one person considers balanced will not be the same for another, as each of us becomes accustomed to our own internal state. Also, what you believe to be balanced does not necessarily mean that your internal systems are perfectly in tune or efficient; it is more a question of familiarity and routine. If you are a highly anxious person, you will identify with, and to a certain extent be comfortable in, this condition, as it will be your norm. Similarly, the same is the case if you are laid back and calm.

Balance is, as it suggests, a fine point that exists in a moment as there is a constant interplay between internal systems, what is felt and expressed. When you feel a fluctuation of emotion, the nervous system is put to the test, especially if the stakes of the situation are high and the levels of expression are more extreme than is comfortable. Considering the body's sensitivity, it is useful to be aware of the constant relationship between internal activity and external stimuli.

Every time we walk from one space to another there is a realignment of the senses, as they respond to the conditions of the new environment. This may transport receptors into an alert state, or the transition may be hardly noticed.

Your inner tempo

Biologist Mae Wan Ho compares the activity of internal structures to a jazz band, with each organ having its own beat. Tuning in to one beat will ultimately mean tuning in to others, which merge to form one overall sound. Place your hand on your head and the level of activity emerging from the brain can be felt. Along with your heart, it sets the pulse of the whole body:

> Oscillations of the brain's direct current field, the brain waves, are not confined to the brain. Instead, they propagate through the circulatory system, which is a good conductor, and along with peripheral nerves, following the perineurial system, which reaches into every part of the body that is innervated. (Oschman 2000, p.95)

Often referred to as waves, the currents that control the nervous system stimulate neurons to pulse and vary rhythmically. They help to regulate the sensitivity of the activity of the nervous system, which is susceptible not only to thoughts but other factors such as light, night or day, temperature, the vibration of sound and the quality of air. Have you ever felt the sensation of flutters or waves pass through you when you are nervous or anticipating that something significant may happen? This is the tidal wave of brain activity.

EXERCISE: BODY SCAN

This exercise has two central purposes: first, to encourage you to tune in to your body and observe the flow of activity within, as some areas may be tight and restrict sensation; and second, to teach you to use your breath and the direction of attention to bring ease by softening areas where tissues may be compacted. Perform the exercise as follows:

1. Stand in wu chi position (see Figure 4.1).

2. Upon inhalation, sink from the lower dantien, and as you do this open your arms and move them up the sides of your body to reach above your head. The palms should face each other.

3. Upon exhalation turn your palms down and move your hands along the front of your body until they can go no further. Imagine that your fingers are touching the floor.

4. After four or five repetitions of this sequence, as you bring your hands in front of your body observe any held areas, which will be identified through tension or discomfort.

5. Hold your hands approximately an inch away from where you feel any tension for a few cycles of breath or as long as you need before you become aware that the tightness has loosened, then continue with the sequence. Repeat this a few times until you feel ease throughout your body.

The following exercise also encourages the flow of inner movement with a focus on directing activity through thoughts.

EXERCISE: FIGURE OF EIGHT

This exercise is done in the following way:

1. Stand in wu chi position (see Figure 4.1).

2. Begin by transferring your weight onto the heels of your feet, and move your whole body in the shape of a figure of eight without taking your feet off the ground.

3. After 4–5 minutes, stop the actual movement and imagine that the shape is continuing throughout your body.

4. Restart the actual movement for a minute.

This exercise brings coherence and ease as well as activating your nervous system.

Tips to work with balance and emotions

Try the following tips to help you work with balance and emotions:

• Extend your flexibility by working to loosen your body through activities such as qigong, neigong, yoga or tai chi.

• Explore using different centres. You may notice that each centre stimulates different feelings and emotions.

• Experiment with changing the rhythm of your breath.

- Be bold with your imagination as it is a stimulus for your internal systems and physiological movement. Practise seeing in pictures and creating images.

- Practise wu chi as a way of listening inside and noticing changes and resistance in the stillness.

- Accept what you are feeling and do not try to hide any sensations or emotions.

- Pay attention to your breathing and how this affects the pulsations you can feel.

- Use your full body in what you do, working as one unit.

- Move from a centre, which is ideally your lower dantien.

Conclusion

In this chapter I have considered if there is an ideal anatomical position where physiological balance is possible. Mae Wan Ho uses the term 'quantum coherence' to explain a state which seems similar to my understanding of balance; this is when all biological components are connecting through banks of shared electromagnetic fields. Although this seems complicated, it implies that the body functions better when all parts are communicating, and to do this structure is important. We have looked at several concepts from Eastern perspectives, such as centres of energy and wu chi, and I have introduced the belief that energy systems are important to being balanced. The next chapter interrogates this concept in more detail and relates its importance to the actor.

Chapter 5

ENERGY
Increasing the vibrancy

Introduction

The word 'energy' is a part of our everyday language. Statements such as 'I have no energy,' 'I'm feeling really energetic' and 'I don't have the energy to go out' are common to most of us. In acting, it is sometimes used to reference the quality of the performance: descriptions like magnetic, vibrant, compelling, riveting, mesmerising and captivating all suggest vibrancy, work that is impactful. Equally, when something is not quite right with a performance, the words used to describe the missing ingredients often indicate energetic power. It may appear to be a little flat, lacklustre, on one note, off key, off balance or not have the right dynamic. It is often difficult to define the missing link. I understand this to be energy, which can be quite a confusing and complex topic. It is therefore helpful to look a little further in the search for a clearer grasp and, importantly, to identify how an actor can manipulate and refine how they use their energy.

This chapter considers cross-cultural interpretations and definitions of 'energy' and looks at various perspectives regarding how energy drives and stimulates the inner life.

What actually is energy?

The term 'energy' came into use in the mid-nineteenth century as a substitute for the word 'force' (Mayor and Micozzi 2011, p.325). Generally, energy can be translated as the ability to work, to make things happen (Hamill and Knutzen 2009, p.392). There are many different kinds of energy in the universe, including kinetic, chemical, gravitational potential, electrical, sound, heat, thermal and nuclear. The common factor is movement; it always flows, vibrates and is transformative. To narrow our focus, as the subject is vast and affects virtually every aspect of life, we are mainly concerned with biological and subtle energy.

Biological/chemical energy

Biological or chemical energy concerns the exchange and oscillation of neurotransmitters, the chemicals produced to send messages throughout the body. They pass signals to and from cells through synapses, which are like junctions, and this process connects the whole body. There are different purposes to the various neurotransmitters; some excite, such as epinephrine, and others inhibit, such as serotonin. All fundamental actions, such as breathing, the rhythm of your heartbeat, the speed of thoughts, emotions, moods and any cognitive activity, are affected by this process.

The human body is composed of trillions of different kinds of cells, all of which are designated a specific purpose, such as nerve cells which communicate with the central nervous system (CNS) and muscle cells which contract to enable movement. For a cell to be alive and function it must have three elements: plasma, cytoplasm and a membrane, which allows substances to pass in and out. The movement of electrons and protons across the cell produces a charge which is electrical (Marieb 2009). 'In your body, an electrical current is generated when charges, articles, ions, move across the cell membrane. The nervous system uses electrical currents and nerve impulses to transmit messages from one part of the body to another' (Marieb 2009, p.28). These continual charges can be understood as electrical energy. This is one explanation for the sensations and twitches that can be felt when you tune in and listen to your body and why making adjustments and moving changes feelings, emotions and how you can attend to a task. As Pert (1997, p.276) summarises, 'Energy is produced by various cellular metabolic processes.' We are responsible for our own vitality as chemical energy produces the possibility of potential and kinetic energy.

Potential and kinetic energy

An example of potential energy is the leg before it moves, the jaw prior to chewing food, or any object – a book, boulder, pen or whatever. All objects have the potential for movement, which is produced by their relationship to gravity. If you stand at the top of a staircase, you have more potential energy than at the bottom, because of the gravitational pull of the earth. Kinetic energy is that which comes from motion. Hamill and Knutzen (2009, p.392) define it as 'the ability of a moving object to do work resulting from its motion'. The body needs to develop the appropriate amount of kinetic energy in order to take action of any kind. The production of energy therefore involves the gathering of forces which then instigate a dynamic potential to offer the possibility of movement. There are many books which offer a full and detailed account of how energy is created at a cellular level (see Lipton 2005); this is a brief explanation of what can be a very complex subject to grasp.

Energy is present in everything: your thoughts, feelings, emotions, the actions you take and the inertia cultivated when you decide *not* to take action. What possibly makes it difficult as a topic is that we cannot see it, and some kinds of energy are not necessarily considered measurable. Newman (2011, p.191) explains that 'Energy appears to be an abstract idea only when conceived as an intangible substance or force, although nothing can happen unless energy is involved regardless of whether we can see it.' We may not be able to see it, but we can certainly feel and sense it, even if not at a conscious level. It is not unusual to feel a mood in a room, as if something is hanging in the air, and often we may ascribe a feeling to this atmosphere such as eerie, tense, excitable, flat and uneasy. This atmosphere is created by a number of different kinds of energy, which is affected by elements such as light, space, bodies, colours, objects, heat and so forth.

Subtle energy

Subtle energy is often known as qi or prana. It travels through meridian channels and gathers in particular centres of the body known as the chakras. We have already touched on qi in relation to qigong in Chapter 1 and its importance to Traditional Chinese Medicine (TCM) in Chapters 2 and 3, and here I will expand on identifying its distinction to the other kinds of energy we have discussed. Dating back thousands of years and integrated into various philosophies, such as Buddhism, Taoism and Hinduism, this substance was known to be crucial for health and well-being. There is not an accurate translation of the word 'qi' in English, which makes it difficult to explain. Translated from

Chinese it means 'life force' and is known to flow though and around the body. It provides the vitality to work, which is the translation of 'gong'. Originally referred to as vapour, steam or air, it is associated with breath and provides the vital substance which nourishes and cleanses. Kaptchuk (2000, p.43) explains that 'We might think that qi is somewhere inbetween, a kind of matter on the verge of becoming energy, or energy at the point of materializing.' In TCM it is believed to be 'present in the biological processes of every single one of the millions and millions of cells. It drives all the activities throughout the organism' (Chuen 2005, p.18). Practitioners of several disciplines, such as acupuncture, reiki and shiatsu, manipulate and work with qi, and along with energy practitioners acknowledge that the body has a specific energy system.

Dale (2009, p.xxi) explains that 'the human body is a complex energetic system, composed of hundreds of energetic subsystems'. Some of these systems are more measurable than others, such as cellular activity and emotional expression, which is known as physical energy. Others are difficult to debut and are referred to as subtle. Dale (2009, p.3) suggests that subtle energy cannot be measured because it is 'too high or low in frequency' and understands energy as information that vibrates. Although the presence of subtle energy is debatable for some people, the effect felt once it is cultivated can be significant and experienced as a unifying force in the body.

Scientist William Tiller has been researching subtle energy since the 1970s. His early work centred on the power of mental intention to generate and alter the charges of subtle energy, especially around acupuncture points. In his studies he found that those who were able to direct their mental intention produced higher charges than those whose focus was weak or dissipated (Tiller 1997; Tiller and Cook 1974). Tiller's work has detected that we can direct the flow of energy, powered by thoughts and intention, not just within the body but over a distance (Tiller 1999). Experiments included measuring the voltage of heart and brain activity, with findings revealing that when the subject consciously placed their attention onto the heart and thought of someone they loved, there were profound changes to the electrical activity in the body. This is an interesting observation in relation to acting, where the thoughts and intentions of the character naturally become a focus. Tiller is emphasising that clear and channelled thoughts will generate an active body and a heightened electrical charge.

Pert (1997, p.276) considers that qi is naturally produced through the chemical release of the endocrine system: 'It is my belief that this mysterious energy is actually the free flow of information carried by the biochemicals of emotion, the neuropeptides and their receptors.' Her explanation of the feeling of qi is that when it flows freely sensation increases; if qi is stored or blocked, the body becomes more sluggish. It could be that with the advances in modern science physical and subtle energy will be found to be one and the same thing. As Low (2011, p.136) explains, 'subtle energy may be considered as an aspect of self-organising behaviour arising out of the complexity of the living state', which would imply a combination of ancient and modern scientific thinking.

There remains some scepticism in Western countries around the existence of qi, especially in relation to healing and medicine. What I experience in my practice is that there is a clear difference between movement work which trains the body in terms of expressive range, coordination, flexibility, focus and concentration, and that which involves channelling the flow of qi. This is largely the depth of connection and the capacity of qi flow to bring change, reduce the overthinking and link up all of the body's systems. Disciplined application of qigong moving and static postures brings the ability to delicately notice incredible subtleties and at times an overwhelming level of activity. It also brings a heightened facility to be present to yourself and others.

Connecting into what energy and TCM practitioners call the electrical network or system is a good starting point to enhance the ability to feel and sense (see Chapter 7). The following exercise is a means of beginning to observe and feel the vibrations of energetic motion.

The flow of qi

According to the principles of TCM, qi is fully integrated into the fabric of your body, and therefore there are many factors that affect how it flows. In order for qi to do its job, which is essentially to cleanse, nourish and protect, it needs to move. This enables change and adaptability to occur; it literally supports the overall functioning and vitality of your body. If qi can flow, your body will be alert and vibrant; if qi is stuck or stagnant, the reverse – a feeling of being overwhelmed – will occur.

Direction of qi and emotion

The movement of qi is sensitive and susceptible to change in terms of both its quality and the direction in which it is able to move, and this correlates with your emotional life. The usual directions in which qi moves with each organ are upwards, downwards, inwards and outwards. In the lungs, if there is insufficient downwards movement, you would develop a cough; when stomach qi cannot descend, nausea and sickness will be felt. Everything you think and feel affects the vibrations in your body, which has a cumulative impact on the movement of qi as it follows your thoughts. As Chen (2011, p.6) identifies, particular emotions cause qi to travel in specific directions:

- When one is angry, qi rises.

- When one is happy, qi is relaxed.

- When one is sad, qi dissipates.

- When one is in fear, qi moves down.

This movement will naturally mirror breath control. A clear example is that should you start to panic because you are going to be late, naturally your circulation will change to cope with this perceived problem, as will your qi and breath. It may dissipate or become chaotic, and you may recognise this as distress or anxiety, which causes a disharmony and inefficiency to all biological functioning.

If a significant aspect of your actor training has involved refining and awakening the body, it is likely that you are all too familiar with the sensations of qi. When it is flowing, it brings an alert, sometimes tingling, sensation, as if every cell is active. Once in tune with this state, you will observe that qi travels in distinct patterns and is highly responsive to the situation and environment. Most easily detectable are spirals, figures of eight, and circles. If you are sluggish or non-energised, qi can be either depressed or blocked. This is because it is automatic for the body to adopt a posture which closes inwards in such states, and this impedes flow such that qi becomes trapped. Blockages to qi flow can happen when muscles and joints are tight or rigid as this affects the overall circulation. Emotional distress, and tissue distortion such as scars, bruising and even tattoos, can also cause disturbances. The body signals this by trying to reserve its energy, and you may feel weak, tired, in discomfort and even pain. According to

TCM, if qi is blocked over a sustained period of time, illness could occur. It is therefore essential to retain a flow for health but also for receptivity and embodied connection. Noticing the natural movement of your body, which is to expand and contract as led by your breath, is a useful starting point to cultivate flow and buoyancy.

The fundamental movement: expansion and contraction

Opening and expanding the body is a way of counteracting the possibility of getting stuck in mental and physical habitual patterns, such as tightening up for no apparent reason, or overthinking. Most of us regularly repeat the same tone of expression. Expanding and contracting your body, or just taking in more breath, allows for more energetic exchange at a cellular level and greater qi flow. It also brings the lower and upper regions of your body together and in so doing enhances inner movement and a stronger access to sensation. Expansion is very important to:

- fully experience

- limit habits

- increase breath flow

- provide space within your body

- embrace and receive

- avoid blockages.

EXERCISE: EXPANDING BEYOND

The exercise of expanding beyond is performed in the manner:

1. Feel the rise and fall of your breath for a few cycles. Observe the extent to which your belly and ribcage expand.

2. With the next inhalation, open your body, with your arms reaching outwards as if they can touch the sides of the room. When you exhale, wrap your arms around yourself.

3. Repeat the sequence and take your arms in different directions. One hand may reach to the floor and the other to the ceiling, or both

arms may reach upwards. Your legs will naturally get involved in the movement.

First variation

One variation of *Expanding beyond* goes like this:

1. Get into a child's pose (i.e. kneel on the floor, place your body onto your legs and stretch your arms in front).

2. Breathe into your back and feel it expand sideways upon inhalation and contract upon exhalation.

3. Breathe into your spine and imagine that you are creating space between each vertebra. Direct your movement to different sections of your spine, starting with the cervical, then thoracic, then lumbar and then sacrum.

Second variation

Expanding beyond can also be done like this:

1. Lie on your back on the floor, tune in to the rise and fall of your breath.

2. Upon inhalation open out, stretching your limbs outwards as you exhale fold your body inwards.

3. With each cycle of breath create different shapes and contortions.

The following series of exercises aim to place you in touch with your energy, both physical and subtle.

EXERCISE: ASKING THE RIGHT QUESTIONS

Directing your attention to what you are feeling rather than thinking is a good way to start to increase your awareness away from mental processes to the energetic movement inside the body. Reflect on the following questions:

- What do you feel?
- Where do you feel tight or rigid?
- Where do you have more ease of movement?
- Are there any parts of your body where there is no clear sensation?
- What sensations are you experiencing now?
- What does your breath feel like?
- What happens when you adjust your spine, when you place your weight through your feet or if you lock or unlock your joints?

Notice any of the following as you reflect on possible answers:

- temperature changes
- qualities you feel such as light, heavy or soft
- tingles, pulsations, twitches or waves of sensation.

EXERCISE: QI AND WATER

As movement and flow is vital for qi, the metaphor of water is often used in both meditation and qigong practice. Ergil and Micozzi (2011, p.70) state, 'Flowing water will never turn stale.' This implies that where there is movement there is a level of vibrancy. This simple meditation is good if you feel tired and non-energised.

Find a comfortable position and do as follows:

1. Observe the pattern of your breath and regulate it so you engage your abdominals and feel the expansion of your ribcage.

2. Allow an image of water to emerge. This may be a dripping tap, a stream, a river with a strong current or a stormy sea. The quality of the flow will be dependent on your metal state. Follow this image but begin to encourage the water to have a stable pattern of movement, so the quality becomes calm.

3. After 5 minutes, notice if feelings and sensations have changed.

Water encourages qi flow; as an element it connects with the lower dantien to bring ease and calmness.

An alternative way to use this exercise is to stimulate a mood for a scene. A possible example is a moment from Macbeth, where Lady Macbeth enters the chambers with the daggers to complete the murder her husband failed to do. It would be that she feels any of the following: rage, fury, frustration or fear. Compare the emotion to water; you may imagine a torrent, a hurricane or a thunderous storm. According to the required feeling, you create the image to cultivate the appropriate sensation by selecting the movement quality of the water. Stay with the image for as long as needed; it is as if the moving water is inside your body.

EXERCISE: FEELING YOUR QI

Your palms are like a magnet for qi, as this a crossing point for several meridian pathways; thus, do the following:

1. Rub your hands together for a minute or so.

2. Turn your palms so they face each other. You should feel warmth and a connection between your hands.

3. Move your palms apart, imagining that they are connected through an electric cable. Play around with how far apart you can let your hands

travel before the connection is lost. If you repeat this sequence for up to 10 minutes or more, you will notice that tingling and heat arises.

EXERCISE: HEAVEN AND EARTH

The heaven and earth posture is thousands of years old and part of early qigong practice. If you stand in this position for more than 5 minutes, you will begin to feel a connection downwards to the ground and upwards to the space above. Ideally, there will be a feeling of balance and a sensation of streaming.

Do the exercise as follows:

1. Stand in wu chi position (see Figure 4.1).

2. Position one your arms above your head with the palm facing upwards. Your shoulders should ideally not rise too far. The other arm needs to be in front of your lower dantien with the palm facing down.

3. Regulate your breath by inhaling through your nose and slightly sinking as you do so, and rising as you exhale though your mouth.

Energy and character

As discussed in Chapter 1, there are many factors that make us distinguishable from each other; energetic presence is another. This can be understood as the quality we project which is instigated by how we behave. Behaviour has a force; you may be direct, assertive, controlling, soft or floaty according to the intention in the moment. Often we repeat certain behaviours, so you may be recognised as the person who is hesitant, quiet and shy because you do not speak up or initiate. If we consider that behaviour is energy, as your body produces the level it needs to do the necessary action, just as we display a range of behaviours that are habitual or patterns, we also possess qualities of energy. It is the energetic force by which we can be recognised. What a person spends their time doing may impact on this; for example, a teacher could be seen as direct, forceful and dynamic, as this is what is required to do the job.

Personality types are interesting to consider in relation to dominant energetic qualities. The idea of enneagrams, originally created by Oscar Ichazo in the early 1950s, focuses on personality types and behaviour. The system draws on many ancient traditions including cosmology, metaphysics, spirituality and psychology. There are nine types of enneagrams:

- Peacemaker

- Carer

- Loyalist

- Challenger

- Reformer

- Helper

- Enthusiast

- Achiever

- Individualist.

This concept is very intricately organised and indicates dominant traits and likely behavioural patterns. The suggestion is that every person falls into one of the categories. I find this useful to consider as a starting point, not exclusively because it defines a personality type and a set of behaviours which informs physicality, but also an energetic dynamic or quality emerges. This is the expression of intention and it impacts on all aspects of expression, such as voice, gestures and thought. It is very much related to force, vitality and how the core personality traits are expressed.

How can this concept be used?

If you decide that your character is a Challenger, prior to learning a text or over-analysing behaviour, it is valuable to start to explore the energetic quality of what it is to be a challenger. An example could be someone who always checks the bill in restaurants or disagrees with others for no reason. There will be a specific force attached, a level of expansion and a direction in which the expressed energy travels – in this instance probably forwards and outwards, and likely to be direct. Inviting this into your body prior to making character choices is freeing. It steers you away from the dominance of thinking into feeling and sensing.

EXERCISE: BASELINE QUALITIES

As I have mentioned, we all have a range of behaviour which determines our dominant energetic force or quality. Let's apply this to a scale of 1–10, with 10 being soft and flexible and 1 strong and stiff. Within this range, your expressive range may be predominantly 7–9 and rarely venture below 5 into more vigorous, harsher territory. Whatever you decide can be considered as your baseline. These are the steps:

1. What is the dominant energetic quality present in you? Are you feisty, or soft and pliable?

2. Identify the baseline energy of a character on which you are working. You can do this by looking at what they do in the story. A superhero, like Batman, may behave assertively and participate in aggressive or defensive action, but the behaviour emerges from a strong sense of justice and compassion, so his dominant qualities could be softer than you may at first expect. He may be 6–8 and when required travel to 3 or 2.

3. Consider the less dominant qualities within the character's range, and again recognise this from the action they do.

4. Experiment with either sections of text or moments of improvisation where you play with the baseline energy, taking it up or down.

It is important to realise that we each have the potential for a broad expression of energetic range.

Energetic exchange

The cycle of exchange, which occurs in all situations, is energetic. Consciously or unconsciously you send out messages, and this can be with or without spoken words, which have been cultivated by vibrations from within the body. This is received and triggers the effect and response from the other person or people; therefore, a frequency can be picked up very easily by reading energy. It is for this reason that when you begin to work with someone it is beneficial to acknowledge the energy that exists between you before you start. This serves as a clearing or a move towards joint neutrality prior to the emergence of the energy of the situation.

EXERCISE: CONNECTING TO A PARTNER

At the start of scene work, it is valuable for there to be a brief period of focusing on and connecting with your partner, to allow for the emergence of an energetic exchange. This gives time to acknowledge with whom you are working, to enter into the dynamic of their energy and then to settle into the frequency of the dramatic circumstances.

Do this exercise in the following manner:

1. Stand opposite your partner, or in a position that enables you both to take each other in from a sensory perspective.

2. Observe your breathing and how it is flowing. Allow it to settle and regulate.

3. What do you notice about your partner? Can you identify a quality which emanates from their body? Observe what it feels like to be with that person.

4. Make eye contact with them and hold a gaze for a few minutes.

5. Once you have registered their presence, let the circumstances of the scene drop into your awareness. Who they are to you, what you feel about being with them, why you are with them and what you want to do to them can now be realised.

6. Notice how that alters the energetic dynamic of the meeting.

Words emerge from intentions, which also have a quality related to the need and its urgency. This exists before anything is spoken. It is easy to miss this layer of communication, sometimes known as subtext, and speak the words as a priority. Energy exists before spoken text; it is identified as feelings and emotions. A dynamic exists between people, and it is useful to practise reading this dynamic and experimenting with how to cultivate it. Working with impulses is one way.

The electrical nature of impulses

Impulse is a familiar term to actors. It is usually connected with finding genuine impetus for action. Impulses happen as a result of an electrical charge which has been generated by the activity of your nervous system. At a cellular level there are impulses occurring continually to keep you functioning. When directed by the mind (i.e. the will), the potency and charge to cultivate action and stimulate senses, feeling and emotions is created; therefore, to do anything there needs to be a generation of desire or drive. It is highly possible that you may not be conscious of what your body wants to do, but gestures which automatically occur, such as folding your arms when you hear what you consider to be criticism, may give it away. When the body wants to respond to any stimulus, the electrical charges will increase, the choices that follow may be to go with the impulse, halt it or divert it, each of which results in a different quality and direction of energy. When the impulse is halted or blocked, energy travels inwards, often manifested in a holding or tense posture and held breath. A diversion is a place of indecision when there is not total commitment to rejecting or accepting the impulse. Energetically this is slightly chaotic; it is neither released nor held. Going with an impulse is when there is free expression and a release – that is, there is a flow and exchange. The choices you make will always emit some vibrational information, and the strength is determined by the power of intention and whether you follow this. This leads us to consider energy fields.

EXERCISE: FOLLOWING YOUR ELECTRICAL IMPULSES

The ability to tune in to electrical impulses is possible by practising what appears to be doing very little. Impulses can be experienced as unpremeditated feelings, often felt as a surge which is prompting action. (See Chapter 7 for more on impulses.)

To tune in to your electrical impulses, do the following:

1. Stand in wu chi position (see Figure 4.1) or lie down.

2. Close your eyes and observe the flow of your breath.

3. What are the sensations which crop up?

4. Try following an impulse as if it is a travelling spark. This could be a thought, a sensation, a twitch, a pulsating beat or an urge to get up and move because you are restless. If you stay with observing inner actions for a while you may observe that before you move, there has been a sequence of impulses which have given you the energy to take action. This is such a quiet and simple activity which is really about listening to yourself, being with yourself.

We are filled with electrical charges; this becomes especially noticeable in high-stakes situations when the body is on alert, and may manifest in sensations such as butterflies in the stomach or a fluttering in the chest. This is a fight-or-flight response, which has triggered an increase in blood pressure, heartbeat and rate of breathing. (See Chapter 7 for further details on fight-or-flight responses.) Here the CNS activates the adrenals to release adrenaline and cortisol which causes sweating and heat changes. Such effects are controllable by the manipulation of your energy and qi flow. Let's look at the latter to see how this can work.

Energy field of the body

'The subtle energy fields are bands of energy that do not stop at the skin' (Dale 2009, p.9). There is a direct relationship between the strength of your intention and how much you affect other people. When you release your energy it is able to travel and reach outwards; in other words, it can disseminate. The ability to send out your thoughts and intentions is affected by how you hold yourself: the tighter and more held your muscular and skeletal systems, the harder it is to freely release. In some traditions and complementary health practices, such as reiki, chakra healing and qigong, the existence of a human energy field is important to how your body releases information. Like a layer surrounding the body (Figure 5.1), sometimes known as one's aura, your energy field can be described as the extension of heat or vibratory activity which has been cultivated by internal life. The strength of this field is dependent on a number of factors. If the transmission of subtle and physical energies is hindered, what you are able to send out energetically is reduced, as is the power of your field. An example is if you want to successfully communicate to a large group of people and affect them with your thoughts, from necessity your body needs to open. A held or hunched physicality will hinder how far your energy can travel. Energy is more powerful when the whole body is connected like a huge network, as seen in Figure 5.1.

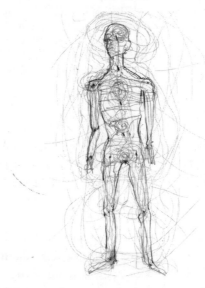

Figure 5.1 'Nerve man' as energy body (courtesy of Valentina Pirus)

Various research studies have demonstrated the importance of intention and the transmission of energy from the heart. It has been shown that the inner emotional state affects the coherence of the electromagnetic field (Stronik 1998; Tiller 1997). Schwartz indicated that when two people touch, the electromagnetic field of the heart is activated (Nelson and Schwartz 2005; Schwartz and Simon 2007). Further testing showed that the strength of the radiated energy differs according to the emotion expressed; interestingly, anger and frustration are shown to reduce the rate of the amplitude, and tenderness and appreciation strengthen it.

Tips for cultivating a strong energy field

Observe the following tips for a strong energy field:

- Practise qigong, as it develops the capacity to project strong biomagnetic fields.

- Work to retain an openness by reducing the time you lock or hold your joints.

- Practise breathing exercises, which will fuel your energetic system.

- Tune in to what your body feels like energetically. Notice your vitality.

There has been a curiosity in cross-cultural concepts related to energy since the emergence of early actor-training methods. Director Leopold Sulzerzhitsky (1872–1916) introduced the practice of yoga and the exploration of prana to the Moscow Arts Theatre from 1905. The experimentation provoked Stanislavsky to develop a series of exercises that focused on communicating through invisible forces. In *An Actor Prepares* he explains an exercise where students are asked to communicate their character's objective through the use of energy rays. This involved sending and receiving rays from their partner, which is described as the 'unbroken line of communication' (Stanislavsky 1980, p.252). The sensation of currents, which Stanislavsky explained appeared like 'hot air', is an accurate description of the movement of qi. It is clear that he understood the importance of energetic activity and transference in communication. 'It is like an unbroken river, which flows continuously under the surface of both words and silences and forms an invisible bond between subject and object' (Stanislavsky 1980, p.214). He later referred to this as subtext, the unspoken which is cultivated by inner activity.

Michael Chekhov participated in these early experiments as an actor, which had a significant influence on the techniques he developed during his lifetime. His specific work on energy forms one of the key tenets of his practice, the 'intangible means of expression'. The exercises on atmospheres, the elements, qualities, centres and imagination fall into this category. They are designed to increase an actor's ability to sense, feel and create a full and active inner life. He uses the word 'radiation' to describe the process of sending out and communicating with an audience. 'Radiating is the ability to send out the invisible essence of whatever quality, emotion, or thought you wish' (Chekhov 1991, p.12). Like Stanislavsky, he used the term 'rays' to explain the release of this 'invisible essence', which he believed is linked to the strength and control of breath.

Chamberlain (2003, p.67) explains that Chekhov suggests that 'all living things possess an energy body, or a radiant energy field which is interwoven with the physical body'. In many ways Chekhov was ahead of his time, as he explored concepts which were considered to be both immeasurable and a little crazy. In other parts of the world scientists such as Harold Saxton Burr (1889–1973) and Wilhelm Reich (1897–1957) were also undertaking pioneering work on energy. Burr deviated from mainstream medicine to focus his research on energy and its role in the regulation and functioning of the body. Reich was a controversial figure whose work included the study of orgone energy in the 1940s. Such experiments were met with much scepticism as at the time it was not believed that subtle energy could be measured, so his work was considered unimportant. In Russia the notion of the subtle body or prana was disregarded and associated with mysticism and spiritual philosophies such as Rudolf Steiner's anthroposophy, which was suppressed in the Soviet Union from 1922. Chekhov's exile from Russia in 1928 was partly due to his attachment to ideas which embraced the intangible essence of mind, spirit and soul, and rejected the material world. These beliefs were considered to be unsupportive to Stalin's regime.

Mróz (2015) identifies the affinity between Chekhov's practice and qigong, seeing a link to the intention to refine sensitivity and cultivate presence. There are a number of exercises developed by Chekhov which work to stimulate heightened energetic awareness. Engagement with your imagination, and what Chekhov refers to as the 'higher ego', plays a significant role in this work. One of Chekhov's best-known exercises is 'Psychological Gesture', which at first glance may appear to be heightened and over-theatrical. You are required to create a gesture, which involves activating all of your body from head to foot, to expresses your character's overall drive or objective. This gesture is repeated many times, during which you may refine the details of your action, according to the depth of feeling that is being stimulated. A sound can also be added and your breath channelled to discover greater engagement. Once you are satisfied that you have physically captured the extent of the drive, you stop the actual enactment of the gesture but imagine that the action keeps going inside your body, so inner movement continues to be stimulated. You can also use the exercise if you are finding it difficult to engage in an emotion or to embody the meaning of a particular line. With the repetition of the sequence the intention is refined and the level of engagement increases, and it is as if a physiological pattern is formed which later can work as a trigger for activating the sensation. This works in a similar way to internal qigong, where an action, such as a spiral, is actualised for approximately 5 minutes, after which intention is placed on the internal movement to continue. The movement of qi is really strengthened and powered by intention rather than actual movement.

The following exercises are based on Chekhov's work and explore the concept of the human energy field and energetic presence.

EXERCISE: EXPANDING BEYOND THE SELF

This exercise works to both create spaces and enhance flow within your body and to expand your energy field:

1. Stand in wu chi position (see Figure 4.1).

2. Tune in to how your body feels; notice any sensations and how you hold yourself.

3. Inhale, engaging your full breath potential and imagine that your body expands beyond your actual frame, as if you fill a huge space and have grown by several inches in all directions. Pay attention to the space above your head and behind your back. As you exhale, you may feel tingles and more space in your torso.

4. Begin to walk around, feeling that you are making contact with your environment and those around you from a distance – that is, your energetic body is reaching its destination before your physical body.

5. Reflect on how your body feels when it is fully expanded. You should feel alert and vibrant.

EXERCISE: LEAVING A TRACE

Based on a similar premise to *Expanding beyond the self*, this exercise also involves working with the energy field. The idea is that whenever we move, there are energetic traces hovering in the atmosphere. As we all continually engage with the front of our body, it is good to focus on your back, which is where it is often harder to feel.

Perform this exercise in the following way:

1. Repeat the first three stages of *Expanding beyond the self.*

2. Place your attention onto the back of your body, especially your spine. Imagine that your breath touches the wall behind you before you exhale.

3. Start to walk around the space, retaining a strong awareness of sending out energy behind you.

4. After a while, stop and turn and imagine that you have left a trace of your energy.

5. Reflect on the sensations which have cropped up for you and whether you have more of a sense of your back after the exercise.

Conclusion

Interesting acting involves a focused and vibrant exchange – one which is charged with intent – between those with whom you are working. To do this you need to know what it is to feel internally coherent, which is when all your resources are moving towards the same goal and free of restrictions. The manipulation of your energy system brings this freedom, as it will enable subtle change and enhanced sensation, and I believe this is at the heart of psycho-physical performance. When you specifically manipulate and refine energy, you are connecting on a molecular level and it is like swimming at the bottom of the ocean.

Understanding energy can:

• offer a clear way of discovering the unique qualities of a character

- help to stimulate feelings and emotions

- prepare the body for work

- bring more alertness

- increase concentration of all your body's faculties and the ability to channel focus

- clear and open up tight pockets of your body.

In relation to character, understanding energy:

- helps to determine how an action is executed

- brings variety to what you do and how you do it

- translates written descriptions into bodily experience

- provides a way of clearly identifying how to express the difference between your own way of being and your character

- helps expand your ability to be present.

An actor should develop a body through which the energy can flow and circulate, and the subtle and refined can be felt.

Chapter 6

MEMORY
The body as a storehouse

Introduction

The journey of our attention constantly deviates between the past, present and future, settling for possibly only a short period of time. Who you are in the present is largely shaped by what has already been experienced and to some extent what you believe lies ahead, some of which has been planned or fantasised. Antonio Damasio (2012) suggests that we all have 'memories of the future' which could be explained as dreams, wants, ambitions, and that all are very much alive in our 'non-verbal planning'. They exist not only because in each day there are routines and organised events necessary for work, family and personal needs, but also because we set goals and create imagined narratives as to how they are to be achieved. Damasio explains that they are intertwined with our history as 'memory of the future that anticipates the future is there moment by moment and it sort of flanks the lived past'. This implies that we live with anticipation and expectation based on what is known or has been experienced. It is as if we are all sitting on a see-saw, residing between the enormous catalogue of memories and experiences, on one side, and the fantasies of what could lie ahead, on the other. The point of balance is in the middle, the now, where we are able to take from and appreciate both. Navigating the now is of real significance for the actor; it is where the action is, and the more alert you are to it, the more alive, spontaneous and truthful your performance will be.

This chapter explores how to use memory to create layers behind what is spoken to give them significance and meaning. The past is vital to the present moment, as without a knowledge of history there is not real substance on which to draw. We begin with reflecting on your memory, moving on to look at how it functions, presenting the idea that it is more than a mental construct. Incorporating some of the findings from contemporary scientists, the second half of the chapter focuses on acting and memory, the merging of character and actor, as imagination inflation is presented as a strategy for depth.

The extent to which personal history is utilised in acting has been a debatable area for both personal health and the question of distance from the role, which was thought to potentially hinder originality. Whether an actor uses their own stories to stimulate emotion has been at the crux of the debate, with Stella Adler and Michael Chekhov prioritising the imagination over real recollections. It is automatic that to some extent personal experiences, memories and associations are used in creative work. Biologist James Oschman explains, 'It has been well recognised that our individual memories shape our sense of who we are as well as what we do on a moment to moment basis' (Oschman and Oschman 1994a, p.2). We are governed by what we have learned and experienced before, as it affects how we receive, interpret, think, feel and respond to any stimulus. There is no escaping your past: it is located in every facet of your nervous system and every cell of your body. Therefore, because you are using your body as the vessel, it is inevitable that you will draw on your own history. It seems that the extent to which the personal is replicated is the issue. Accepting that your history is a valuable resource and understanding how it can be used and blended with imagination is the strategy which I have found to be successful. The identification of the differences between you and the character comes through understanding your own history and how it has shaped you. What is adopted in performance is the behaviour, morals and beliefs of the character, but somewhere along the line noting your own past experiences helps these distinctions to be identified.

What is memory?

It was believed that the brain functions like a filing system from which memories can be extracted, the implication being that what is recalled remains unchanged, like a static relic from the past. From this perspective, if you recalled a memory of a birthday celebration you had 5 years ago, the actions, what was spoken and your emotional reaction would be identical to those that occurred in the actual situation.

It is now considered that memory is more complex and elusive, that it is not located on one part of the brain but made up of a group of systems each of which has a part in creating, storing and recalling. It is more like a web stretching throughout the brain with various sections triggering, stimulating and working together.

Elizabeth Loftus, Antonio Damasio and Jonathan Foster offer the view that the memory changes over time, known as the reconstructive theory. Loftus has found that a more accurate version of the process of remembering is that we present accounts of what we have experienced; these are based on what has gone on since the original event, and how you may feel at the time the memory is recalled. There are shades of the original memory present, but this is mixed with other elements that reflect what we feel now about the actual event: some memories are therefore constructed rather than copied.

Charles Fernyhough believes that autobiographical memories, those that are from your lifetime, 'are mental constructions, created in the present moment, according to the demands of the present' (Fernyhough 2012, p.5). This view suggests that autobiographical memories are reconstructed, determined by the present and affected by additional information, such as altered opinions, belief systems and environmental conditions. So the retelling of, or drawing on, memories is as much about the present as the past. It could be that when you fill in the backstory of a character, you initially shade it with the type of events that you may have recently encountered or perspectives that you have in the current story. You work from what you know and perceive, and notice what your own experience tells you is relevant.

Many experiments have examined this theory, seeing memories as flexible narratives that suit the conditions of the moment (Mazzoni, Scoboria and Harvey 2010; Suddendorf and Corballis 2007). To test their hypothesis, Mazzoni *et al.* (2010) asked subjects to recall a series of four events: three were true and one was invented. Findings revealed that 25 per cent of the participants believed that they had a clear memory of the event – which had never actually occurred. This indicates that it is not uncommon to inflate and imaginatively expand; it is a natural activity. Scientists use the term 'imagination inflation' to describe this phenomenon. Studies show that when a person recalls an event and adds information that is not true or accurate, listeners are more likely to believe them (Manning 2000; Thomas and Loftus 2002). The fragments of past events, therefore, act as the foundation upon which fabricated layers are added. This implies that, rather than being fixed, the memory system is flexible and 'characterised as a dynamic activity or process rather than a static entity' (Foster 2009, p.8). Conway explains that there are two forces of memory, one that wants to stay consistent with the present and the other that desires to stay true to the past; therefore, it is usual for recollections to be altered to accommodate both intentions (Conway, Justice and Morrison 2014; Conway and Pleydell-Pearce 2000).

The implication of the reconstructive perspective for actors is that when you create a role, as you expand on the given circumstances of a text, you are likely to use your personal experiences and blend them with social or historical facts and imagination. So if you use personal experience, your imagination and memory work together, and what is created is not exactly what was experienced. What is useful is to really identify the distinctions of how the character would behave in particular situations, as opposed to you. It's useful to practise 'imagination inflation'; it is something that most of us probably naturally do, but making it a regular exercise is like an imagination workout and will help you to not select obvious choices.

Your memory

We are starting with you and the subtle nuances of your own memory, and for our discussion there are two main aspects that become of particular interest: how memory can restrict creative freedom, and how it can enhance and enrich it. What and how we remember is specific to every individual. It is irrelevant to compare your own ability to recall facts, images, events or feelings with those of anyone else. We are all unique.

EXERCISE: TESTING YOUR MEMORY

Looking at your own memory will help to recognise how you recall various kinds of information. The benefit is knowing what works for you and the areas that need developing. This exercise tests which senses you prioritise when you remember.

Jot down the first five things that arise from the following memories:

- a time when you have been at the sea
- the first house you ever lived in as a child

- an occasion when you had an argument with someone

- the best meal you ever ate in a restaurant

- the smells of your childhood

- the faces of the people you saw on the first day in a new job

- the last film you saw – what were the names of the actors?

- some historical facts you had to memorise when at school

- the first five lines of a poem you may know

- a song or tune from a concert you have attended

- the details of a painting you like

- the perfume your mother liked

- the taste of a dessert you ate once at Christmas

- the smell of school

- the feeling of silk on your skin

- the sounds of a forest

- the feeling of jumping into cold water

- the heat of the sun against your face

- six lines from a Shakespeare sonnet

- the names of all the countries in South America

- the taste of chocolate.

Reflect on your notes and see if there is a preference for a specific sense. Was it hard to recall smells, sounds or places? Which senses did you primarily engage? Did you find the more factual information easier to recall? According to the results, set yourself a task to improve the most undeveloped senses. If it was difficult to recall sounds, begin to pay more attention to what you hear in your everyday life. If your ability to create images and the visual detail of your memories is limited, spend 5 minutes a day inventing visual pictures. Give yourself a known story that you imagine and indulge in the colours, shapes and textures.

Initially it is easy to consider that memory is a mental faculty through which information is recalled. This is not surprising as most traditional educational systems focus on rote learning, be that times tables, historical dates or the analysis of activities. Generally, the brain is trusted over the body, but there is much more to memory.

How you 'remember'
Body/somatic
Consider the following questions:

- Are you aware of using particular gestures on a regular basis? This could be a facial action such as a frown, a pout, a twitch of an eye or placing your head at an angle.

- What body positions do you regularly adopt? Do you cross your legs? Stand with your weight on your toes or heels?

- Do you notice how you use your voice? Are there vocal inflections that you repeat?

- Are there some emotions which you express more regularly than others?

- Do you often invade other people's personal space?

- Do you withdraw and place your weight on your heels when someone approaches you?

- Do you smile when you are nervous?

- Do you have a particular breathing pattern which you adopt for certain situations?

Mental patterns
Examine your mind and ask yourself:

- Do you repeatedly imagine the same stories?

- Do you use the same phrases?

- Do you follow the same routines on a daily basis?

Emotional and behavioural patterns
Regarding your emotional and behavioural responses:

- Do you notice that you react in the same way to certain situations?

- Are there some emotions that you express more freely than others?

- Do you reflect on what you have done?

Memory and learning

Do you generally prefer to read, watch, experience or listen? When you need to learn a piece of text, is it easier if you:

- read over and over again

- work through the text and create action that may aid your memory

- record yourself and listen to the tape over and over again

- watch a performance or video of the scene

- visualise the scene and imagine other people playing it?

Reflect on your notes to see what they have revealed. Some of what we do is habitual, stored and therefore hard to eradicate. In Chapter 2 we looked at how habits could emerge and be reduced; knowing that memory can be trained and learning how to work with what is specific to you is important to all aspects of your creativity. There has been much research undertaken about learning styles and the processing of information. The VARK questionnaire (Fleming 2001) identified three different learning preferences: visual, auditory and kinaesthetic. This approach is definitely useful for actors who are required to remember a considerable amount of text. Recognising your learning style can contribute to the success of your preparation process; an example is that an auditory learner would respond more to the spoken word, so taping their text would be the most effective aid. A visual learner would benefit from working with images and establishing mind maps. Kinaesthetic approaches are more concerned with movement and spatial considerations.

Breaking the mould

Becoming bound by aspects of your own memory, which has to a certain extent encoded your behaviour, is a regular occurrence at the beginning of a rehearsal process. This is the stage when your own remembered patterns can become the first active response. If you raise your shoulders or open your arms when you greet new people, there is a chance that this will be the first gesture you do when your character meets new people. Responding in an instinctual way is natural, but the impact of this could be that every character you play has actions and qualities similar to yours – that is, they sound and look the same. To break the mould and become more flexible in how you interpret stories begins with working towards a more adaptable body which includes recognising how your body remembers and being alert to your own patterns.

What you can do to widen your approach to work?

If you usually begin by analysing the text, start with exploring how your body *feels* rather than 'thinks'. Investigate the world of the story through different kinds of sensory research – visual, auditory and kinaesthetic – before you commit to precision. This may involve learning to make bread if your character is a baker, or teaching a class if they are a teacher.

Invest in various ways of imagining your character and how the scenes could be played out. Avoid logic and experiment with sounds, atmospheres, objects and images.

Having observed a little about how your own memory works, let's look in more detail at how it functions.

EXERCISE: MEMORY AND IMAGINATION

Do this exercise as follows:

1. Imagine a sunset. It can be against the backdrop of any landscape. Select the colours of your choice. Decide the weather, time of year and what you are doing whilst watching.

2. Recall a memory of when you actually last saw a sunset. Make a comparison between what you imagined and your actual memory.

3. Create another image of a sunset, but add more original features, thereby discarding what has been invented in steps 1 and 2. In your imagination, anything goes. The colours and landscape can be whatever you dream up.

This three-stage process is a good strategy to use when creating images, as it helps you to discard the obvious and discover new pictures.

Structure and stages of the memory system

The duration and capacity of your memory varies from person to person; however, the stages in remembering are identical. We initially engage our senses to recognise information, such as smell, taste, touch, sight or sound.

The process of memory fits into three stages:

1. Stage 1 of the memory system is the engaging of your five senses (touch, smell, sight, sound and taste). As this is initially less than a second in length, some information is lost at the initial stage even before it moves into the short- or long-term memory.

2. Stage 2 is when information moves to your short-term memory, which can be for seconds.

3. Stage 3 is when some information and/or experiences progress to your long-term memory where they can be retained for longer periods (even a lifetime).

When information passes into your long-term memory there are further stages (Figure 6.1). You can be conscious of what is being stored, which is known as *explicit memory*. This is usually the case with the memory of facts, faces, places and significant events. Alternatively, you may be unconscious of what you are retaining, which is known as *implicit memory*. In this instance there are many things that you do which you do not have to recall, as they are automatic, like breathing and motor actions, or actions that, once learned, become instinctive like walking, eating or riding a bike.

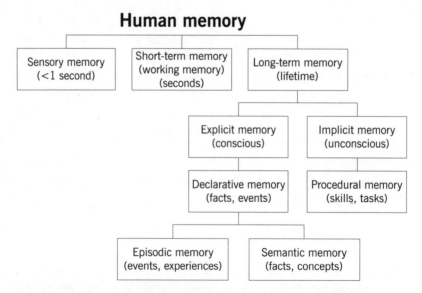

Figure 6.1 Human memory system (courtesy of Daniel Hughes)

At stage 3 there is a distinction made between the type of information that is being remembered, all of which has become long term.

Declarative memory concerns thoughts, facts and information.

Procedural memory concerns a conscious awareness of what you do, including the behavioural acts such as routines, daily functions like brushing your teeth, eating, driving a car or recalling how an action is executed. It includes the storage of general knowledge about the world in which you live.

There is a further division of memory types: *Episodic* is the memory of past experiences and important events, and *semantic memory* is the process whereby objects are recognised and identified.

The process of memorising

In the process of remembering, again there are three stages – encoding, storage and retrieval – which all need to work together for effective functioning.

Encoding

Encoding is the process of changing memories into a useable form such as sound and image. It is when meaning is created and information acquired.

Storage

Storage is the retention of the information – that is, the length of time the memory is retained.

Retrieval

When a memory is brought to consciousness, you may use different strategies to help the accuracy of what is recalled. An example is that when you need to recall the lines of a text, you may use mnemonic strategies which enable words to come to you, such as feeling like a lion or sounding like a trumpet. For example, I was taught a mnemonic for remembering how to spell the word rhythm: **r**hythm **h**as **y**our **t**wo **h**ips **m**oving.

Morphic resonance

The retrieval system is the process that contemporary scientists generally believe to be accurate; however, as discussed in Chapter 2, the work of scientist Rupert Sheldrake presents an alternative view. An opposing perspective to the more traditionalist and mechanical view is the idea of a collective memory, which extends Jung's concept of the collective unconscious. This is based on the theory of morphic resonance – a belief that memory occurs in nature through morphogenic fields, an idea that first emerged in the 1920s. 'What we remember is not inscribed in the brain but depends on morphic resonance. We remember because we resonate with ourselves in the past' (Sheldrake 2011, p.301). The suggestion is that there are fields which surround every living organism. Sheldrake has extended this concept and suggests that there are fields within fields within the body and around cells and molecules. Each field has a memory of what has been experienced, which is retained and remembered; he refers to this as morphic resonance. When you first do an action, a blueprint is established, and the next time you do the action, you draw on the memory of the first occasion. Sheldrake calls this self-resonance and believes that the brain is like a self-tuning device rather than a memory store, and he compares it to a television which searches for the waves in order to clearly transmit. This premise also suggests that there is a broader connection throughout the universe through morphic fields. This occurs when biological structures create patterns and organise themselves into fields which can stretch across space. The act of behaving in a particular way, such as biting your nails when nervous, Sheldrake would argue, began as someone's habit field and was adopted by others who had the same feeling. This perspective places memory in the body integrated into our biological processes and beyond in the universe as a whole.

How we remember: what is actually happening?

The reconstructive theory suggests that remembering an event requires the reactivation of many multisensory domains within the brain. It is quite a complicated process and is largely stimulated by the release of neurotransmitters. Here is a very short and simplistic explanation: The hippocampus is the part of the brain that binds this process together through millions of neurons which send messages across narrow gaps, called synapses. Synapses allow the messages to be sent, and the process of recalling involves the adjustment of the connections between the neurons. When information is only stored in the short-term memory, there is a quick chemical exchange between the synapses. To create long-term memory, neurons need to produce new proteins to allow for the neurotransmitters to move with more speed and consolidate the memory. Memory could be seen as a chemical process.

The senses as triggers for memory

As the senses are the first point of the memory cycle, it is not surprising that they are almost instant triggers for feelings and emotions connected to past events regardless of the length of time passed. An example is that certain smells may be attached to a place (e.g. the overcooked aroma of school dinners can be an instant reminder of childhood). The smell of suntan cream can immediately create the memories of holidays. Sense memory was included in Stanislavsky's early work, and he suggested that it could be used to stimulate both emotion and imagination. More recent studies have verified his early observations. Herz observed that odours stimulate strong memories and create emotional responses more so than visual and auditory cues (Herz *et al.* 2004; Herz and Schooler 2002).

The section of the brain which is known to be responsible for smell is the olfactory bulb, which is part of the limbic system, the area associated with memory and feeling. It is positioned near to the amygdala, whose job is to process emotion, and the hippocampus, which is related to associative learning. When a smell is encountered, a link is forged by the brain and this connection remains as if programmed. Willander and Larsson (2006) identified that smells specifically evoked autobiographical memories with a high percentage of the smell association coming from your formative years, especially under 10 years of age. This could be because as you get older, you rely more on visual and auditory cues. It was found that there is less emotional stimulation with semantic memory when facts, language and statistics are being recalled (Buchanan 2007; Jacobs, Lega and Anderson 2012). It is more likely that odours would affect the semantic memory if the smell was present at the encoding and retrieval stage.

EXERCISE: ENDOWING YOUR WORK WITH SMELLS

Just as objects can be endowed with specific memories, events, other characters or stages in life can have an associated smell which can be integrated into your memory to trigger relevant responses. This selection of smells could be a personal link, so you may use the sensory cues that work for you, or you could make choices based on research and the given circumstances.

Begin to notice smells and do the following:

- Consider what your character does that would have a specific smell attached (e.g. smokes, drinks a lot of alcohol, wears old or vintage clothes, their hygiene routine, works in a kitchen or a sewer).

- Observe the smells of places. There is a distinct odour to some locations such as churches, prisons, schools and bars.

- Select a scent for your character.

- Attach a smell to a memory that is important to the story.

- Use smells as a part of your preparatory process such that when you are creating memories, attach a smell(s).

Music and memory

There has been extensive research into how music facilitates long-term memory and stimulates the retrieval of information. Leung and Fung (2005) observed that background music influences mood. Knight and Rickard (2001) studied the impact that music has on stress levels and found that there was a reduction in heart rate, blood pressure and concentration when calm music was played in the background. It is also believed that tranquil music can enhance learning by altering the levels of focus and concentration. The tempo of the music is significant in stimulating the emotional reaction and the kinds of memories that are recalled. A slower pace was found to induce peace, solemnity and sentimentality, and faster tempo has a more vigorous feel. Webster and Weir (2005) found that fast-paced music had an impact on arousal and performance.

Music remembered from the early years of childhood has been found to evoke autobiographical memories (Krumhansl and Zupnick 2013). The personal and emotional associations of music listened to during the phases of life when there are many first-time experiences and key milestones in the development of ideas and opinions were identified as stimulating stronger emotional responses than music from later life (Schulkind, Rubin and Hennis 1999).

The music from a specific era can act as a commentary of the social and political events of that time, expressing the challenges, cultural patterns, ethics and morals of the period. As we have seen as a curator of our own history, music attaches memories to a specific period and events to stir up a strong emotional response. Each piece of music may have personal associations; for example, a song you remember playing around the time of a break-up could stimulate sadness. There are also cultural associations as reflected in national anthems or pieces of music adopted as patriotic songs such as *Land of Hope and Glory* in the UK or the *Star Spangled Banner* in the US.

EXERCISE: SOUNDSCAPE

Create a soundscape which expresses your character's journey through the narrative. You can select pieces of music which reflect any one of the following: the mood, thoughts, the level of dramatic tension, the character's wants and drives or the feel of the scene.

One soundtrack may suit a whole scene or you may discover that specific moments have a distinct feel which needs exploring. Like the soundtrack of a film, you may feel like there is a specific non-diegetic sound which stimulates your expression of a moment, such as the sound of footsteps for a scary moment.

Sound

In soundscape studies there has been attention placed on how memories are retrieved. Schine (2010) examined the somatic effect of walking through a landscape and how walking whilst actively listening to the sounds improved the act of remembering. She suggests that 'soundwalking' enhances active listening and stimulates an embodied relationship to the environment. Encoding memories and moving through to establish 'soundmarks' is one layer of sensory dialogue that is often missed. She believes that the places a person travels are a part of personal biography, and memories emerge as they wander through different locations.

EXERCISE: SOUNDWALK

There are two variations of this exercise. The first focuses on stimulating your own memories of sound and environment. It is performed as follows:

1. Select a place which has some significance for you; this could be, for example, the street you walked along every day to get to school or the place where you used to go on holiday when you were a child. (You will need to be able to visit the location.)

2. Retrace the steps you have made in this place and pay particular attention to the sounds, which could be voices, objects, weather, traffic, music, wildlife and so forth.

3. Sit and listen to the possible layers of sounds which are specific to this location.

4. Notice what the sounds do to you and if any specific memories emerge.

The second variation, applied to the character and the world of the story, is carried out like this:

1. Select relevant sites in the narrative and create a library of sounds which would be heard in the world of the character. Each period, location and culture has sounds which can be identified as distinct sound cues.

2. Use the cues to potentially cultivate sensations and images.

Why memory is not a mental construction

Tulving (2000, p.13) describes memory as 'the capacity of the nervous system to benefit from experience', the implication being that memories are found in all parts of the nervous system, not solely in the mind. A further development in memory research indicates that every cell in the body, through the cytoskeleton structure, recalls events. Such memories are accessed through the living matrix, a term used by scientists since 1993 to describe the web of connective tissue which connects cells, nerves and fascia. (A detailed explanation is given in Chapter 7.) As Oschman and Oschman (1994b, p.2) observe, 'Remembering involves manipulating coherent wave fronts to "read" information holographically encoded in cell and tissue structures.' It is in the field of body practices and therapy that there have been considerable studies that verify that memories are not a mental construct.

Myofascial bodywork and Rolfing are two methods that focus on release through intense manipulation of the connective tissue. In the 1930s and 1940s biochemist Ida Rolf studied connective tissue and its role in balancing the body. Her observation led to the development of Rolfing, which she identified as working towards structural integration – that is, the realignment of the fascia to reduce tension. Through the manipulation of connective tissue, Rolfers are able to identify and restore segments of fascia where there is misalignment and a hardening of tissue. A typical area may be in the pelvis, where improved vertical and horizontal balance would enable an individual to feel more grounded and in touch with sensation. Practitioners also observe that Rolfing often releases memories in the form of images or strong emotional bursts. The explanation given for this experience is that holding often compensates for and restricts sensations that a person may want to avoid.

When you prepare to work, it is usual to awaken your body through movement; in so doing you are opening up and releasing your potential for personal memories. I often include exercises which involve remaining in the same position for a period of time in my preparatory phase in a class or rehearsal, the purpose being to release deep into the layers of fascia, tissue and muscles. It is common for long-forgotten memories and images to crop up without there having been any conscious recalling – pictures and sensations just flood in. This is especially so when you open up the areas which are tight or bound, such as the lumbar region.

EXERCISE: OPENING UP THE SPINE

Get into a crouch position, if possible with your heels on the floor. If you can, place your head between your knees. This will open up the lumbar region of your spine.

Memory and tension

Memory is affected by how tense your body is. When you are frightened or anxious, it is likely that you will tighten or lock up, as this is a primal response to protect yourself. Let's take a situation such as when you have to stand up and talk in public: the chain of reaction may be that your breathing becomes shallow, your abdomen tightens, limbs lock up and, for a while, you forget what you are meant to say. Your memory has been interrupted by bodily reactions. Once you are able to relax and release your breath, you are more likely to be able to remember and be more alert to the present. There is a direct correlation between tension and memory, the former being a potential obstacle to receptivity.

Here are some tips for releasing tension:

- Work with your breath to open and expand your body.

- Become aware of when your joints lock up.

- Establish a routine of loosening your joints daily.

- Imagine your structure as being flexible and soft like butter.

Memory triggers and actors

A memory trigger is something that summons a memory that is associated with a specific feeling or emotion. It can be used to enable the appropriate emotion for an imaginative circumstance to emerge. Possible triggers include:

- people

- places

- noises

- images

- smells

- dates

- sounds

- body positions

- sensations

- photographs

- objects

- clothing.

There are two main types of triggers, those that arise naturally as they form part of the body's primitive survival instincts, and those that are learned. An example of a survival trigger would be that you would flinch and move out of the way if you perceived something was going to be dangerous to you. Learned triggers are those that we associate with an event that was particularly strong emotionally, such as how a certain piece of music played at a funeral may always trigger sadness, or a smell may remind you of a place or event. An object given to you for your birthday will remind you of the giver of the gift and the surrounding circumstances. You have personal associations with the memory.

Emotional memory works in a similar way: it involves recalling personalised events which stimulate the required emotional response. The idea is attributed to the early work of Stanislavsky, who observed that with the right kind of memory, emotions are stirred, which establishes a place from which an actor can work – the conditions that created the original response being the starting point. If a scene requires happiness, you would select a very specific instance and remember as much detail as you could, such as actions, words, sounds, smells and body sensations. The senses work alongside emotions to trigger bodily responses. Stanislavsky noted that 'emotion memories are not copies of reality – occasionally some are more vivid, but usually they are less so, than the original' (Stanislavsky 1980, p.188). He acknowledges that a direct replica of the depth of emotion is not possible or appropriate.

How actors use memory

Helga and Tony Noice (Noice 1991, 1992; Noice and Noice 1997) have undertaken several projects that focus on how actors utilise memory. Initially the experiments included a study of how lines are memorised, and the findings were then applied to non-actors to assess if her observations had more of a universal basis. They noticed that when the meaning of words is placed in an imaginative context, memory retention is increased. An exercise to apply this could include selecting the keywords of a line and adding a visual image. With the line 'Maybe he is finally reaching out to you,' for the word 'reaching', an image of a person on a ledge with their body stretched out or placed on a mountain with their arms up searching for the next ledge could work as a memory trigger. The research confirmed that applying action is more productive than rote learning and adopted the phrase 'active experiencing' to describe the process, which sounds very similar to Active Analysis, which was developed by Stanislavsky in the latter part of his life.

The intention of Active Analysis is to explore the text through actively doing, exploring possible interpretations through improvisation and arriving at the spoken words organically. The process comprises the following stages:

1. Read the scene and identify the key facts and the main events.

2. Improvise the scene, aiming to cover all the central points of action.

3. Return to the scene and reflect on what was or was not included and decide if there is any information that needs to be incorporated in the next improvisation.

A second improvisation takes place, after which you would reflect on the structure and content with an emphasis on incorporating the significant moments and discovering the character's journey. The improvisations continue with the gradual inclusion of the actual text of the scene.

This approach is very freeing; language is not necessarily prioritised, it acknowledges that feelings and sensations are increased when all of the body is activated. Trying many options also limits the chances of fixing action, as it tricks the brain a little and emphasises that the body is reliable when it comes to memory.

Imaginative embellishment

Imaginative embellishment is a way of working with text to expand the meaning of the words by selecting the key ideas in the lines and layering them with visual images, physical qualities and potential action. Looking beyond the facts and dialogue of the text to discover the subtext and possible surrounding backstory is a combination of imaginative embellishment and a contextualisation of the facts and historical events. The following process is a means of starting to imaginatively explore working beyond the lines:

1. Read the text.

2. Visualise the character in the situation as if you are watching a film.

3. Working one line at a time, identify the key idea or focus of the line.

4. Create a visual picture of each line.

5. Add any sounds to your images. This could be voices or something very particular (e.g. the investigator's shoes).

6. Notice the colours in the space and the clothing the character wears.

7. Imagine the scene being played three or four times. Each time, change what the character does. Focus on parts of the body, such as the feet, hands and facial gestures. Notice what they touch and the textures of the objects.

This process works on several levels, and it will help you to memorise the text, but also through utilising more of your senses, you will stimulate sensation and discover action.

Helga Noice (1991) also revealed that actors who work through rote learning are less successful with remembering text than those who imagine the meaning first through the use of visual imagery. Stanford Meisner suggested that actors rote learn their lines with the intention of not predetermining how to respond when playing a scene. He suggested that actors 'learn the text without meaning, without readings, without interpretation, without anything. Just learn the lines by rote, mechanically' (Meisner and Longwell 1987, p.67). The suggestion is that it is possible to memorise words without any assigned links or interpretation, to clear yourself of any associations, which is a challenge. I find that as soon as we reflect or think about the meaning behind what is said, personal memory is activated. The knowledge and experience we have acquired is deeply integrated into our body, and it is near impossible for it not to be utilised. What the technique does is emphasise the need to be totally responsive to each moment, and to avoid reflection which may take the mental focus into the past or future.

A further observation of Helga Noice (1991) was that clear goals, especially when put into a statement, facilitate the recalling of information. This approach was also integrated into Stanislavsky's practice and further developed by directors such as Mike Alfreds. In his book *Different Every Night* (Alfreds 2007), Alfreds explains how the goals for each line offer actors direction and clarity, and provide a means of stimulating action. By altering the active verb, the execution of a moment can totally transform. There may be a very subtle change in the meaning of the verb, as shown below:

- I want to challenge.

- I want to confront.

- I want to goad.

The actioning of each one will proffer a very different interpretation. Goals engage the body in several ways: cognitively, physiologically and emotionally. If you focus on the level of force which arises from a word like 'challenge', the body will remember the sensation and express this prior to the spoken word. A sense memory is created, and the text will emerge from feeling and sensation.

Choices and imagination

As we have said, when working on a text there will automatically be some assigned associations, such as images of places, people, objects or sounds, which may be based on other performances you may have seen, and/or your knowledge and understanding of the context. If the story takes place at night on an abandoned street, there is a strong chance that you will imagine a street where you have been or seen, one which creates the feelings appropriate for the narrative. Associations form a part of memory retrieval; they are mental operations which are linked to either an idea or stimulus. One interpretation is that links are formed based on what we have experienced, and because they are part of our memory associations, they affect the choices we make.

An example of how association works is demonstrated in the following sequence: You are called for an audition for the role of a police detective. Visual pictures will immediately formulate, including those of other performances of police detectives that you have seen. This may be Claire Danes as Carrie from *Homeland*, Gillian Anderson as Stella Gibson in *The Fall* or Idris Elba in *Luther*, each of which possesses very specific character traits but also some common qualities which match the stereotype. They are highly determined characters – forceful, direct and quick-thinking with a tendency not to conform to authority. There is a combination of archetypal traits with shades of the Heroine/Hero, the Fool and the Warrior which will automatically colour your interpretation. The audition scene reveals a vulnerable side to the character, and you now take another journey into your memories when you have been in a similar situation and begin to identify what you felt. Performances you have seen of similar circumstances will arise. The scene indicates that a particular song is playing in the background, and you recall when you first heard that piece of music and how it affected you. Before long, there is a chain of associations which automatically present themselves to shade the interpretation and possibly hinder originality. The question is then how to use associations rather than be tied to them, and the solution lies in the creative choices you make.

Memory and making choices

We continually make choices, each of which has a consequence – a stake – no matter how small. Deciding which shoes to wear has a consequence. For example, can you walk to the station in them without getting blisters? Do you look trendy, attractive and appropriate for the day that lies ahead? They also reveal a great deal about personality traits, lifestyle and history. How important is it to look good? What statement are the shoes making? Do you care about image? Did you buy the shoes or were they a gift? When did you last wear them? Is the colour significant? If they are red, is this a reflection of you and how you feel? Choices are layered with your own history, associations, perceptions and memories. There is likely to be a predictable element to most of the choices we all make due to our traits and to what is familiar. If this is so for us, it is so for the character being given life. The ripples and layers of personal history have immense vibration, and to create them in a fictional role requires imaginatively delving into given circumstances. Self-scripts are a good starting point.

Filling the moments with self-scripts

Filling your life with fantasy is an activity in which most people engage, as it forms the backdrop to life and usually features stories concerning strong wants and issues of concern. We all have several films continually playing as a commentary on our world. It is interesting to notice key thoughts which take hold and affect behaviour, actions, risks and relationships. An example could be worrying about finances and what can or can't be afforded in order to sustain a lifestyle. The repetition of this concern could influence small actions, such as whether this individual would volunteer to buy a round of drinks or have a generosity regarding buying gifts, which affects how others perceive the person – that is, as generous or mean person – and this influences the atmosphere of a social situation and effectively the layers of the story.

It is also natural to devise scenarios around the actions we do or plan to do. This could be a dialogue around an event that had been experienced where you may think, *I wish I had said...* or *I should have done...* Again, if this is true of you, it would also be true of the character you are inventing. There would be memories, fantasies and thought obsessions that repeat in their inner landscape and consequently affect the choice of actions. To test this hypothesis, it is interesting to reflect on your own patterns:

- Do you often reflect on what you have said or done?

- When you make a decision, do you present options to yourself?

- How often do you think about alternatives to what is happening to you?

- Do you say what you mean, or are there often situations in which you hold back from expressing what you want?

It has been observed, through a series of practical tests on imagination and memory, that subjects tended to repeat imagined scenarios which were often linked to specific goals that they wanted to achieve (Andrews-Hanna *et al.* 2010; Spreng and Levine 2013; Spreng *et al.* 2010). The details and outcome of the fantasies were not part of their actual reality, although fragments of the narrative may have been true. An individual who enjoys singing, and may quietly have an ambition to be a singer, could repeatedly imagine a scenario where they are on a stage singing in front of thousands, or receiving an award for their talents, or getting mobbed by fans. The theme of their daydreaming is singing success and may intermittently occupy varying amounts of thought space.

EXERCISE: DAYDREAMING BACKDROP

This exercise is about establishing a backdrop of daydreaming for your character:

1. Identify the main goal of your character for the whole story: the main objective. This goal may not be realistic, but it must be something your character dreams of achieving (e.g. Lady Macbeth may want to take over the world). It will surface throughout the narrative and will be present in the drive of action in every scene.

2. Imagine a sequence which involves you achieving this goal. (This does not have to be in the text; it is the character's fantasy.)

3. Repeat the sequence and add a few changes as to how you achieve the goal.

4. Allow yourself to travel away from obvious tactics, as anything is possible in the imagination.

5. Use the events in the story as the basis for your character's daydreaming (e.g. Lady Macbeth may see herself wearing a crown standing in front of her subjects).

6. Spend some time each day daydreaming in character.

EXERCISE: CARTOON SKETCH

You have read the script, so you know what happens and have a clear memory of how the events affected your thoughts, feelings and emotions. This exercise is to imagine that it is as if you have no memory of your character's destiny through presenting choices which could shape decisions and action:

1. Select a scene.

2. Identify the turning points of action, including the starting moment.

3. For each of the turning points, in cartoon style, draw three versions of the possible sequence of action which they imagine could happen, one of which must be what does happen in the script. (Each version may involve a few sketches, and the outcome of each may be different due to the choice they make.)

4. Applying this to a scene when you come to a point when a choice needs to be made, consider a few options before you opt for the one taken in the text. Each time you play the scene, think of different options.

Inner monologue and visual image

Inner monologue is internal chatter, the full range of what is being thought, an expression of what is truthfully felt. Consisting of language or visual representations, images, pictures, sounds, feelings and sensations, it is the real story of the moment. It is an expression of:

- what we want to say but find difficult

- goals and intentions which reside in the body

- questions one may want to pose

- the preparation for what is about to be spoken

- memories, fantasy and dreams of the future

- the truth about what is being felt

- secrets and private thoughts.

Internalised conversation that happens prior to an intended action is referred to as proactivity. Honeycutt, Zagacki and Edwards (1989) found that imagined interaction (i.e. what you want to say) is more common prior to interaction. At this stage thoughts, images, questions, reflections and imagined sequences are potentially extensive and play out what we may want to happen. Creating a depth of activity prior to a start of a scene is just mirroring what we all naturally do. Before an outcome anything is possible, as the energy is active and expansive and goals are possible. Obstacles arise when interaction occurs; this is when thoughts are often very active as strategies to achieving goals are considered.

Internalised dialogue and imagined interaction that occur after an event is known as retroactivity. According to Edwards, Honeycutt and Zagacki (1988) this is less common, but I have observed that this tends to be more analytical and involves questioning the outcome, reflecting on the opportune moments that went unfulfilled. For example, you attend an audition and you feel it does not go well, so you chastise yourself for not responding in another way or asking what you now perceive to be the right questions.

Visual image is enhanced by connected associations, which could be objects, sensory stimulation or ideas about the specific incident. If you see a photograph of a blue sky, you may then visualise clouds, and this could remind you of travelling, which could then take you to a memory of an experience in another country, which may take you to a face of a person you met. It is like a chain reaction.

How to extend inner monologue

Inner monologue can be extended in the following manner:

1. Dismiss the first choices.

2. Gather a range of visual resources which are appropriate for the context; for example, if the story is set on Mars, research images, paintings, cartoons, clothing, objects and so forth.

3. Have improvised conversations around what is happening.

4. Write about the character's goals in the first person.

5. Create memories of relevant snatches of the past.

Place, space and resonance

Each memory you have will be located in a place, the details of which hold mnemonic reference points. This could be characterised by the dimensions of the space or aesthetic considerations such as colours, textures or objects you observed and with which you interacted whilst an event played out. What happens in a place forms a part of the atmosphere which can be felt; the most obvious examples are churches. The spatial dimensions, which dictate the light and volume of the place, create a distinct relationship between the objects within the space. It is inconceivable that you can be the same person in every landscape you encounter. This could be because each place has associations and triggers memories which stimulate feelings and emotional responses.

EXERCISE: MEMORY AND PLACE – CREATING THE MISE EN SCÈNE

This exercise can be for either the rehearsal stage, when it is unlikely that the location or setting is fully dressed, or when you are working in the landscape in which you will be shooting or performing. Perform the exercise in the following manner:

1. Select the scene on which you are working.

2. Close your eyes and allow yourself to visualise the landscape. Start with marking the fundamental elements that are present, so if it's a room, the shape and dimension, walls, windows, height of ceiling, door, what's on the floor and so forth.

3. Consider the sensory factors such as the light, temperature, colours, smells and sounds.

4. To what are you drawn? Do the colours have any associations for you? Do you smell something cooking which reminds you of another time or place? Is there a photo on the wall which you notice and have a feeling about? Does the aesthetic speak to you in any way? Does it indicate wealth, status or class? What books, newspapers or CDs are around?

5. Consider the associations that the character may have with the space and the objects in it. Is this environment familiar? What has happened in here? Do they feel comfortable here? What memories of specific events do they have about this place? Is there any evidence of such events? This could be seen in the objects or furnishings in the room, such as a broken lampshade, marks on the walls, stains on the carpet and so forth.

6. Imagine that you are standing in the space. Create the story of the specific memories. It could be that the character looked through the window and saw their lover leave every day. Or that they painted the walls when they first moved in. Develop memories of being in the place.

Modes of remembering

There are two main modes of remembering which will affect the experience of recalling memories: *field memory*, which places the person in the memory, as if you are seeing and experiencing the event through your own eyes; and *observer memory*, which is when you place yourself as the watcher, as if a third person. Sigmund Freud (1856–1939) believed the distinction helped to understand the psychodynamic implications of memory. There have been various studies conducted to identify how each position affects the depth of feelings which emerge as a result of recalling.

Nigro and Neisser (1983) identified that it is natural to recall memories from one of these perspectives. They identified that the purpose of remembering and the distance of the memory determines how an individual recalls the event.

Field memories have been found to cultivate strong feelings and emotional responses to the recalled event (Nigro and Neisser 1983; Talavico, LaBar and Rubin 2004). When considering the language, what a person would select is usually more emotional and contains information from an internal perspective. There are fewer references to the environment, such as the location or the objects in it, but more attention to the feelings that emerge (McIsaac and Eich 2004).

When the memory of a significant event was recalled from an observer perspective, McIsaac and Eich (2004) found that there tended to be a decrease in emotion, and even the traumatic events become less emotional in content. They concluded that the more self-aware an individual is, the more likely the memory will be recalled in the third person, and slightly detached. In such instances the descriptions may be dry and factual, and contain descriptive words which paint a concrete picture of the external considerations surrounding the memory. There is a distance from the pain, and the emotions are regulated as if held in a deeper place.

In the retelling of memories it is valuable to begin by noting the mode of remembering. It will help guide as to the distance the character has from what they have experienced and to find the tone of the language. It is not uncommon for a highly traumatic text to be overplayed and to lack the subtle believability which is natural to how we all recount the stories that have deeply moved and shaped us.

Conclusion

This chapter has looked at how memory is believed to function and how it can be used in your creative process. It is natural to want to interpret each character afresh and seek to embody the behaviour which is very specific to the given circumstances. The obstacle to this is usually you: unconsciously your patterns and responses become those of the character, and shades of previous performances surface. A potential solution to this is to learn to blend what you know and remember with your imagination, which will bring new experience into your body.

Chapter 7

CONNECTING
Inhabiting the body

Introduction

The specific focus of this chapter is to examine the ways in which the body can create a maximum level of connection. I use the word 'connection' to mean the organisation of all your faculties which determines how efficient and attuned you may be to yourself, others and the broader environment.

Significantly, the connection you have to yourself affects not only the depth but also the ease with which you communicate. A distracted mind brings a distracted body and makes it difficult to direct attention or immerse fully in an activity. To connect is to bind all your mental and physical forces together so a united instrument is working towards the same goal. As we are in a constant state of flux, connection is not a consistent state, and neither is it necessarily regularly achieved. Akin to a flow, as described in Chapter 3, it implies harmony but also facilitates a condition from which the depth of inner focus is acute and refined. In the world of sport the phrase 'in the zone' is often used to describe the condition an athlete ideally achieves when competing. There are a considerable amount of techniques and research undertaken to enable this optimum position to be achieved with high-level competitors (Caruso 2005; Weinberg and Gould 2011). In a similar way, performers are required to marshal their attention and invest in the imagined circumstances to the extent that aspects of their own reality are temporarily suspended. The goals of the character steer the direction of mental and corporeal conditions. It cannot be assumed that it is automatic for anyone to be able to obtain such a depth of connection with their own body. Like an elite athlete, performers require training to fully harness their attention. The more tuned the body, the more you can cultivate a peak level of concentration and a stronger presence.

Let's start with exploring some of the concepts which are drawn from various fields that may shed light on what biologist Mae Wan Ho calls quantum coherence and, importantly, to what you are actually connecting. The immediate target for an actor is to strive to connect to thought, emotion and feeling. In previous chapters I have touched on what could stop this from being achieved; here I will delve into this topic and what it means to fully function as one unit. I continue to draw on the principles of Traditional Chinese Medicine (TCM) and Eastern philosophies, which provide an interesting means through which connection can be enhanced. This includes a section on the five element theory, fire, water, metal, earth and wood, and how it can be used in training and imaginative work. Having never embraced the concept that there could be a mind–body split, Eastern disciplines fully acknowledge that a somatic unity is a fact. Scientific research and advances in what is known about biological functioning are now positioned to verify this and challenge the belief that the mind is neither split from, nor necessarily rules, the body.

Connecting through the living matrix

In Chapter 5, I suggested that connecting to an audience is related to the organisation of the internal energy systems. James Oschman's concept of the living matrix offers an explanation of how this can be possible (Oschman 2009). The living matrix is the integrated network of nerves and cells which intricately weaves into every corner of the body. It is like the electrical system in your home: it is all wired up to one central box, your brain. Oschman identified that the matrix operates faster than the nervous system. Messages are continually being directed through the vibrations and waves which transmit from the electrical action of cells and nerves. Such activity is highly sensitive to environmental changes: temperature, sound and textures will register and automatically trigger new patterns even before you are *mentally* able to register them. If you have ever felt the sensation of tingles, or goose pimples on your skin, this is the matrix in full flow. It is like an antenna which sets off a series of events to affect how every system in the body functions. This efficiency of the matrix is therefore important to how responsive you are and to the speed and flow of information; however, there are many reasons for a loss of sharpness and responsiveness. If there is an overload or a short circuit in the matrix, it will weaken or partially shut down. We can identify the short circuit as being a blockage or a halt to communication.

If we follow this line of thought, all of your internal activity can very easily be disrupted and optimum connection severed. One of the most obvious situations is when nerves take over and instantaneously trigger holding and tightening. A suspension of breath and tautness of muscles will immediately send messages of unease, which diverts attention, so if you are fighting your nerves whilst attempting to immerse yourself in a love scene, it's unlikely that you will get anywhere close to the passion required; or if you do not fully trust the working relationship, which may result in thoughts of inadequacy or panic, somewhere the flow of vibrations will be unsettled. Disruption affects breath, the release of neurotransmitters, feelings and emotions – all usually on an unconscious level. Oschman talks of the importance of the interconnected body which he describes as 'a body characterised by physical and energetic connectedness' (Oschman 2009, p.8). The waves and vibrations are what establish the connectedness, the strength of which is determined by tensegrity, which is the tension and compression of tendons in relation to bones.

Feeling connected can seem like a strange concept. It may be that you have never considered the idea of being *unconnected*. If you look at the following signs, however, you may change your mind.

Signs of a loss of connection

A loss of connection is occurring when:

- focus and concentration easily fluctuate

- it is a challenge to access the feelings from the text

- when you act the voice and body are doing different things (i.e. voice expresses anger but body shows no sign of this)

- you adopt postures which misalign the spine, creating splits (see Chapter 2)

- breathing is shallow

- the rhythm of breath is out of sync with the natural movement of the diaphragm

- thinking dominates

- the muscles are tight

- there is over-holding in the torso

- you have an unbalanced relationship to the ground, which may mean you largely communicate with your upper body

- you are unable to complete a task due to distraction

- it is a challenge to immerse yourself in the imaginative world

- you have a feeling of not being able to stay in the present

- it is a challenge to block out external stimuli when trying to engage in a task or playing a scene

- if it is difficult to focus your attention.

Any of the above are signs that your body is not functioning with ease, that there are interferences which splinter how you communicate with yourself and others. There are some immediate solutions to enhancing a sense of connection, things you can do to 'tune up':

- Be attentive to what you sense and feel.

- Recognise the value of setting up the environment in which you can work. This will be personal to you and may involve shutting out sound and clutter, playing music, having fresh air in the space and so forth.

- Work with what is going on for you – accept what you feel.

- Visualise the matrix and register where you may feel less linked up.

- Have one point of focus at a time, no matter how short.

- Have a clear target: so decide on the immediate goal.

- Practise selected attention. This requires really attending to one task at a time and fully committing to it. It may be looking at a painting, cooking a meal, writing a poem or painting your nails.

- Notice what is in front of you and be interested in it.

- Invest in the activity you are doing.

- Set chunks of time for each activity.

- Engage with bodywork such as yoga, tai chi, qigong, aikido and so forth.

Spine and trunk

When you feel less in tune with your body or find it hard to engage with an activity, the spine is a good place to mobilise. Developing mobility and retaining a sense of the length of your spine will stimulate the central nervous system (CNS) and increase its facility to feel and communicate. When any section of your spine becomes locked or rigid, which is usually though misuse, there are significant repercussions, such as your nerves get trapped, muscles tighten and the passage of information slows. The spine is one of the main indicators of the level of ease in your body. It automatically straightens, locks, collapses or twists in response to the circumstances in which you find yourself, such as the moment before a take, going onstage or walking into an interview. In these instances the spine will automatically respond by altering in posture, and this will quickly be followed by changes in breathing. The spine needs to be taken care of to retain sharpened sensory responses and a feeling of being connected.

EXERCISE: HOLDING THE SPINE

This exercise is performed as follows:

1. Stand in wu chi position (see Figure 4.1).

2. Regulate your breathing. Check that you slightly sink upon inhaling and rise upon exhaling.

3. Place one hand in front of your body where you perceive the bottom of your spine to be, and the other at the top of your spine.

4. Register the length, and breathe into the whole length slightly, expanding and contracting and rising and falling.

5. Walk slowly, keeping your hands in place in front of your body as if holding your spine, trying not to alter the length.

This exercise is a simple reminder of the shape of your spine and helps to maintain space between the vertebrae and thereby sharpen nerve activity.

EXERCISE: SEAWEED

'Seaweed' is an exercise that immediately activates and mobilises all of the body:

1. Stand in wu chi position (see Figure 4.1).

2. Root your feet to the floor as if they are buried into the bed of the ocean.

3. Imagine that you are a piece of seaweed attached to this bed. Your feet are not able to move but the rest of your body can shift with the current of the water, which may be gentle and quiet or become furious and fierce. The movement should be continual and allow your breath to follow the motion. The ripples that you may feel in your head or arms will have an effect on the structure and mobility of the rest of your body.

This is a really good way of enlivening the CNS and increasing mobility.

EXERCISE: BREATHING INTO THE SPINE

To do this exercise, take the following steps:

1. Adopt a squat position. If possible, keep your heels on the ground; you may need to widen the position of your feet.

2. Allow your attention to travel from your atlas at the top of the cranium down to your coccyx. Notice which sections of your spine you can really feel.

3. Inhale through your nose and, as you do, feel your back expand. Imagine that it is growing beyond your actual body. Upon exhalation try to retain a sense of length and expansion.

4. After a few breathing cycles, as you inhale travel along each vertebra feeling the breath move between the joints. Upon exhalation the spinal fluid will travel through your spinal cord, which you can give a colour.

EXERCISE: GUIDED IMAGES

Guided images are a good way of seeing your body differently. In this instance the aim is to work towards imagining you are connected up like a spiderweb:

1. Find a comfortable position; sitting or lying down is best.

2. Close your eyes. Inhale and exhale through your nose.

3. Imagine that just under your skin there is a spiderweb which spreads to every part of your body. Move from your head all the way down to your toes observing the complexity of the threads.

4. At each juncture of the web visualise small lights which brighten up as your thoughts travel along your limbs and down the length of your fingers. Notice how bright each point is and where there is less vibrancy.

5. Stay with this image and see yourself walking. Visualise how the web stretches and changes shape as you transport your body through space.

6. Experiment with changing your breath as it is powering the currents.

Connecting to feelings and emotions

I often work with actors who struggle to prevent their own emotions from hijacking the imaginative situation. Attention slips in and out of being anxious about speaking in front of others, or it is a challenge to initially engage with the action, usually because it is unfamiliar and distant from personal experience. There are many other potential reasons, such as:

- overthinking

- fear of what may emerge if you engage with feelings

- a tight body, which hinders expression

- not absorbing the detail of the given circumstances

- the range of exploration that you have undertaken

- the approach to preparation, which may not suit the content

- fear of failure

- the environment in which you are working, which may interrupt internal focus

- not having found a process that works for you to channel your attention.

These obstacles can be easily rectified with some understanding of the physiological processes involved. Let's start with emotion. There is a distinction made by neuroscientists between a feeling and emotion.

According to Damasio (Lensen 2005), feelings arise when the brain interrupts emotion:

> The brain is constantly receiving signals from the body, registering what is going on inside of us. It then processes the signals in neural maps, which it then compiles in the so-called somatosensory centres. Feelings occur when the maps are read and it becomes apparent that emotional changes have been recorded – as snapshots of our physical state, so to speak.

This would suggest that feelings are formed by the forthcoming or expressed emotion. Ekman (2010, p.13) defines emotion as follows:

> Emotion is a process, a particular kind of automatic appraisal influenced by our evolutionary and personal past, in which we sense that something important to our welfare is occurring, and a set of physiological changes and emotional behaviours begins to deal with the situation.

The 'something important to our welfare' could be anything from stage fright to fear of forgetting your text or nervousness on a first night. If your body perceives it is in danger, a strong emotional reaction will occur. The fight-or-flight response, which was first described by Walter Cannon in the 1920s, is an explanation of how the body could react to what it perceives as danger. We all have a programmed survival instinct and a need to sustain what is stable for our body, known as homeostasis. When this stability is potentially challenged, your autonomic nervous system will immediately initiate a chain of events. The danger may be a literal physical attack or when you give a presentation, an audition, meeting someone you perceive to be important and so forth. It can be the stakes you place on the event that creates the reaction, but there is not necessarily a logical explanation related to the response; it is primitive and instinctive. The typical physiological process is:

- The body goes on alert.

- The adrenal cortex releases stress hormones, adrenaline and cortisol.

- Heartbeat increases to circulate more oxygen.

- Breath speeds up.

- The thyroid gland stimulates your metabolism.

- Larger muscles get a supply of oxygen to be ready to take action.

Other recognisable indicators of unease are flutters in your stomach, sweating, shallow breathing, change in temperature, dry mouth or, in instances of being overwhelmed, you may freeze up. The mobilisation that occurs in the body is about being ready to cope: you either fight and face the situation or run and avoid it. Whatever the choice, the body has been placed out of its comfort zone and is ready for action.

Accepting

The need to be in touch and recognise the constant fluctuations is important to staying connected and to being fully engaged. Recognising and accepting what you feel is a key factor. Through accepting that you are nervous you can potentially move through the experience and respond to changes. According to Ekman (2010) emotions occur over restricted amounts of time. He explains that it is not possible to sustain an emotion for an extended period, and refers to the length of an intense emotion as a 'refractory period'. This is the stage whereby only the information and relevant memories linked to the emotion are considered. In these moments it is automatic for there to be a total focus on what triggered the emotion. This could be a moment of jealousy or when someone bumps into you on a train. There is a surge of sensation which captures and momentarily takes over, and at such times it is impossible to incorporate any other information and possibly think clearly. The response has consumed you.

The refractory period is interesting for an actor to consider, as it is when there is complete absorption in the emotional state. To achieve this, an immersion and conviction of the need is necessary. No emotional outburst arrives out of the mist; it will have been stimulated by either unresolved feelings, goals that are thwarted or unexpressed needs and desires. There is always a chain of events that lead up to the expression. An example could be if your friend has agreed to pick up some food but arrives empty-handed. If this is a pattern you have experienced for the whole duration of your friendship, the outburst when they arrive empty-handed is accumulative. At the speed of light, images of the past occasions will arise prior to your expression of rage. It could be that you do not make your rage known, but the emotion will be present, lingering inside. History is important as it provides a context and impetus to respond.

Fully engaging in an imaginative situation requires that you surrender to your own logic, opinions and perspectives on life. It is a process of letting go and venturing into the flow of what emerges. As has been stressed in previous chapters, there are many potential obstacles to this. What is vital are the prior events, the history leading up to the outburst. This point emphasises the need to support key moments with backstory, reasons for the response. The past events will make sense of the action and increase the chances of genuine emotions emerging. If this is not present, what is often witnessed is a generalisation or an overly sustained expression of emotion which, according to Ekman's (2010) theories, are incorrect.

EXERCISE: CHAIN OF EVENTS

Trace the event back as if it is a family tree. This is to see how one event has a chain linking to your past in some way. The benefit of this exercise is to put history behind the action, as it gives a moment resonance. An instruction in a script might be: *Sara decides not to answer her phone.* The chain of past events could be:

- Sara sees a name flash up on her phone.
- She sees an image of the person; it's a work colleague.
- She recalls a disagreement with her yesterday.
- She considers that she may have to apologise for walking out of a meeting.
- She recalls the conversation and the point of disagreement.
- She remembers when her colleague has irritated her in the past.
- She ignores the call.

This demonstrates that to bring each moment to life, the emotional response is connected with what has gone before, which may be composed of many moments of action connecting you to the past.

When it comes to embodying the emotion of the story, it is simple to say, 'Follow the text and the circumstances will move you,' but this is not always the case. Just as in reality you are moved by some events and less so by others, so it is with fictional circumstances. The direction of attention and focus on the events are crucial, and it is interesting to look at what may get in the way of this.

Getting yourself out of the way

What does 'getting in your own way' actually mean? The phrase is often used when you are not able to find depth or inhabit imaginary events. It is when focus is interrupted by thoughts which interfere with or divert attention. Thinking dominates, with often-repeated phrases which are usually self-critical, and you jump ahead rather than be present. An example may be that you stand up to perform a scene and your thoughts are more about how to act it rather than investing in circumstances. Also, in instances of being under pressure, such as a film set with a lot of people present, it is easy to prioritise in the idea of being judged and getting the performance right.

Being creative ideally means that there is an endless flow of ideas, which move seamlessly forwards so you are able to transcend what is your own reality. The level of immersion is such that you respond with ease and fluidity – that is, it is akin to how you played as a child. A place where there is no wrong or right, just possibilities with limitless boundaries.

The critical voice

The interruption of a critical voice, which may originate from self-doubt, anxieties about whether your work is good enough and/or concern about what others think, is a kind of creative paralysis. Thinking overtakes to such an extent that you are unable to get off the 'thought roundabout', as the repeated phrase or image becomes loud and overbearing. At such times you will find that you may do too much, and the force of your work is such that you may not feel connected to the person with whom you are working or the situation you are playing. The key factor is to stay present.

What can you do to stay present?

You can stay present and connected by doing the following:

- Establish a working environment that is conducive to being freely expressive.

- Recognise what you do, the repeated questions you may pose to yourself and when your critical voice emerges.

- Practise allowing thoughts which are unhelpful to pass.

- Creatively make choices or alter routines. If you usually begin with thinking about a text, start by finding a soundscape or movement sequences.

- Use your breathing to take you into your felt senses.

- Work with images which are associated with the goals of the character.

Meditation

Meditation is a really productive way of training and calming the body. It involves a process of intense concentration and attention to quietening the conscious mind. The intention is to bring about a state of active stillness and a channelled focus where there is awareness but not the temptation to be derailed by overactive thinking or attachment. Breathing is integral to all forms of meditation and is used as a way to bring the body into a cohesive, easy rhythm. There are various strands of this practice which are Eastern in origin and associated with different religious and philosophical traditions such as Buddhism, Taoism and Hinduism. (In Western traditions the practice of prayer is believed to have similar effects.)

Mindfulness has recently become a popular form of meditation, its emphasis being on cultivating the ability to live in the present and be fully attentive to what is experienced. Kabat-Zinn (2003) first proposed this technique. He defines it as 'awareness that arises through paying attention on purpose, in the present moment, and non-judgementally to the unfolding of the experience moment by moment (Kabat-Zinn 2003, pp.144–156). During practice, which was first designed to reduce stress, you sit with an awareness of what is happening around you with no effort to change it or make judgement. This approach works especially well with acting training as a means of encouraging attentiveness to the self, your attention and staying in the present.

Brewer and colleagues (2011) conducted a series of research experiments on the effects meditation has on brain activity. Through the use of functional magnetic resonance imaging (fMRI), a test group were measured whilst meditating. Observations revealed that the posterior cingulate cortex becomes especially active at times of anxiety and deep thought but quietens with a period of meditation.

A technique called fMRI neurofeedback provided a visual representation of brain activity.

Using mental images

There has been much research in the field of sports science on how anxiety affects performance (e.g. Humura 1999). Imagery has been found to benefit sports performance especially in relation to reducing anxiety and self-doubt, improving concentration and helping with preparation for competition (Garza and Feltz 1998; Post and Wrisberg 2012). It is also effectively used in skill attainment and reviewing past performances (Thelwell and Maynard 2002, 2003). A number of strategies and tools for overcoming mental and physical obstacles, including self-doubt and low self-esteem, have been tried and tested. Self-talk is one of the recognised methods that is successful with sports men and women. This approach links thoughts with performance through the process of repeated scripted phrases which are spoken during training and competition. The statements trigger a technical or mental response (e.g. to adjust a golfer's elbow to a certain angle, the mantra might be 'elbow up' as a reminder). The words are often joined with a visual image which is associated with the desired goal, so the athlete is encouraged to step into the feeling of what it is like to achieve their objective. Such approaches are familiar to the processes used by actors, notably in techniques where the imagination and mental imagery is crucial to the process.

There are systematic stages to how self-talk is utilised in sport, which involves the inclusion of sensory cues, such as the feelings within the body of the sportsperson when they hear the sound of the crowd. Attention is paid to the tone of the inner voice to assure that the pitch stimulates and encourages the desired effect. Thoughts are edited, with the script providing the guide track, and this avoids the mind from wandering into unproductive thoughts. During training the recording, what actors would recognise as an inner monologue, is encouraged. This limits and trains the critical voice which, in times of stress, can run wild (Hatzigeorgiadis 2009; Todd *et al.* 2009).

Manipulating your CNS is a direct way of quietening the mind and reducing overactivity. This can be done though working with particular points on the spine and controlling your breathing.

EXERCISE: HOLDING THE POINTS

The parasympathetic nervous system (PSNS) is partly responsible for slowing down activity; one of its jobs is to save energy and allow the process of digestion to occur. We can manipulate the PSNS to bring a calmer state by holding two places on the spine. These connecting points are at the bottom of the spine in the sacral region and at the medulla at the base of the cranium.

To achieve this calmer state, do as follows:

1. Place your palms on each point of the spine; your touch should be light.

2. Close your eyes and regulate your breathing so that it reaches the abdominal area.

3. Observe the rise and fall of the body.

4. Hold this position for 3–4 minutes.

Yin–yang theory

Some of the principles of TCM can offer interesting insights into internal organisation. In TCM there is a belief that there are two polar opposites which coexist within all things. These opposites are like the extremes of a continuum such as hot and cold, black and white, hard and soft, calm and anxious, good and evil, pull and push, forwards and backwards, night and day. The yin and yang theory, which dates back as far as 700 BCE to the *I Ching* (also known as *Book of Changes*), is an element of the classical framework of TCM. The belief is that there is yin and yang in everything, they are not separable, but each has specific characteristics which also makes them opposites. Yin is considered to be interior, located in the lower and the front of the body, below the waist, and has a downwards energetic direction. Yang is linked to the upper regions and to the back of the body, and its energetic direction is upwards and outwards.

This principle is integrated into every aspect of the body; for example, vital organs are attached to either category:

- yin – heart, kidneys, spleen, liver, lungs, pericardium

- yang – stomach, gall bladder, bladder, small intestine, large intestine, triple burner (a TCM concept).

In TCM it is considered that there are seven central emotions: anger, joy, worry, pensiveness, grief, fear and fright. Associated with each organ is a mood, an emotion, and an overall quality. Yin is generally considered to be heavy and yang is lighter. You may recognise that whenever you feel sad or disappointed, there is a downwards pull as if you are collapsing inwards. Joy is the opposite: you are lifted and more expansive.

The ideal is to find a balance, whereby yin and yang equally coexist and can nourish each other. What this brings, as explained in Chapter 4, is sharpened senses and a feeling of flow where all internal processes are working together as if being moved down the river by a current. Likened to being 'in the zone' in the case of athletes, this state brings heightened concentration and the ability to let events move through you.

A slightly different angle is wu wei, which derives from Taoist philosophy and is a state of being whereby there is an alignment with the changes in the natural world, an ebb and flow with nature and a position of ease rather than reaction. Wu wei is a state where you watch and allow rather than react – hence, it is defined as non-action or non-doing. The qigong static position of wu chi is a means of practising wu wei.

The alignment of yin and yang has a fragility and is affected by the fluctuation of internal and external factors, such as the environment as well as one's mental and emotional states. It is easy to shift to reactive behaviour, which results in disengagement and a loss of focus. Reactive responses could be distress at receiving feedback which may not be what you want to hear, or a rejection of positive comments due to a lack of belief in oneself. In all instances there is a choice which results in a distinct change in the balance of yin and yang. If a person is drawn into conflict, an instinct either to rise and connect to more yang energy and so become anxious, angry or volatile, or sink and link into a heavier, more sustained yin quality is possible. In this instance behaviour would be calmer or more stoic, possibly immovable. Too much yang will overwhelm and bring anxiety, frustration and possibly anger or fear, and too much yin can result in sadness and depression.

You and yin–yang

Factors related to how you use the body and your lifestyle, as well as mental and somatic patterns, are key influences in the equilibrium of yin and yang. As previously discussed, we all fall into habits, and it is useful to reflect on what they may be and realise that we have the capacity to significantly alter how we feel and react.

Both energies exist within us, but you may observe that you have more yang than yin (or vice versa), or that you rarely fully express particular emotions associated with one state. Consider the following questions:

- Do you move inward or outward in social situations?

- Do you use more of the upper or lower part of your body in general communication?

- Do you express particular emotions more than others?

- Are there certain emotional states that are hard for you to reach?

- Does your concentration flit in and out?

- Is your breath centred or primarily high up in your chest?

The ideal state is to be able to access both yin and yang energy and work for a balance. This will support the ability to obtain an expressive range and remain in control. Maintaining balance is difficult as the environments in which many actors work are not necessarily conducive to it. On a film set there are often time pressures, such as that the shots need to be achieved before the light goes or within the set period that the location is available. Technical setups can take time, and the number of people involved means there is an orchestration of different needs and expectations.

Starting from balance and knowing how to bring your body back to this state is a core skill. The forces of yin and yang are a reminder that we are constantly in transition, and within this state there are oppositions. We are never exclusively one thing or one dimension, but discovering a place where you can feel fully connected and in touch with possibilities is a good starting place.

Yin and yang and character

Working with the opposites of yin and yang is a valuable tool and a way of expanding expression and creatively interpreting behaviour. Someone who is violent can also be tender, just as the calm and collected person who manages pressured situations can rage. It is easy to play what is dominant and fail to identify qualities which potentially reside in a character.

Considering a character like Lady Macbeth, yang seems to govern her personality. She can rage, command, worry, and become frustrated and anxious, which are all yang qualities. She also has a strong connection to her drives and how she can achieve them; this is yin. She can be both cold and warm. These observations inform how she potentially uses her body: she is connected downwards to her strong yin will but also has an upwards pull when she is drawn to fire and she becomes enraged about her husband's failings. It is evident that she has an affinity to her back, which is yang. This is associated with her awareness of the environments she is in, her social and public image.

When I coached actor Fiona Graham on her role as Lady Macbeth in *Shakespeare Must Die* in 2010, our initial approach to working was to apply the yin–yang theory. We explored the interior quality of yin, from which ambition and strength emerges, and we decided that it resided in the character's pelvis, legs and connection to the earth. The downwards direction signals her ability to be steady, reliable and resourceful, and she is able to adapt to situations and find solutions when required, such as when Macbeth fails to go through with the murder and she takes the dagger and finishes the job. Working with the back of the body, Fiona and I explored the more yang aspects, which reflect moments of unease, such as when Macbeth walks out of the dinner displaying his confused state. We were attempting to convey how aware Lady Macbeth is of her surroundings, how she is literally watching her back and protecting intentions. We created the idea that her back expresses her doubts and suspicions about people's loyalty. In this area she could also hold a combination of fury and anxiety which has to be contained and not revealed. Working with the concept of yin and yang offered a broader range of expression, such as the opportunity to draw out oppositional forces and the various dimensions of the character. All too often it is easy to focus on dominant traits and miss the subtle changes.

There are the more obvious oppositions which present an immediate guide to both physicality and inner expression:

- up/down

- open/closed

- sustained/unsustained

- strong/light

- slow/quick.

Other traits which can be considered to be behaviourally driven by thoughts are:

- introverted/extroverted

- aimless/ambitious

- aloof/friendly

- inhibited/spontaneous

- bold/timid

- honest/deceitful

- passive/active

- controlled/chaotic

- boundaried/non-boundaried.

Examples of emotional opposites are:

- cheerful/gloomy

- calm/excitable

- happy/sad

- calm/nervous.

The yin/yang principle also relates to another area of TCM, the Five Element theory, which is woven into Chinese culture. The theory further explains the dynamic of opposite forces and the process of change in the inner landscape of the body.

The Five Elements

The hypothesis is that there are many associations and fundamental qualities that could influence health, expression, vitality, communication, internal rhythm and your general outlook on life. It is clear that every individual possesses some dominant temperamental qualities which are expressed through their actions and how they interact. The categorisation of types is familiar to most cultures, especially in relation to medicine. In early Western medicine people and medical conditions were divided into choleric, bilious, melancholy, phlegmatic or sanguine, each of which is partnered with behavioural traits (e.g. melancholy and sadness). Kaptchuk (2000, p.18) explains how the Elements can be manifested:

> The yang fire aspects of a person are the dynamic or transforming, while the yin or water aspects are more yielding and nourishing. One person projects the heat and quickness of summer fire; another person resembles the quiescence and coolness of winter cold; a third replicates heaviness and moisture of dampness; a fourth has the shrivelled appearance of a dry autumn day; and many people display some aspects of the various seasons simultaneously.

Like the other concepts discussed in this chapter, the Elements are a tool for imaginative purposes or to discover how to work in a deeper and more embodied way. The notion is that there are specific qualities which emerge in an individual's behaviour, as expressed by feelings and emotions. Traits are reflective of health and, importantly, environmental factors, which emphasises that all things are universally connected. This also reinforces the need to consider the context and world of the story and its impact on behaviour.

The Elements have formed a part of the pedagogy of many actor-training practitioners, such as Jacques Lecoq, Michael Chekhov and Jerzy Grotowski, who have developed sets of exercises to encourage actors to not only work imaginatively but to notice their own dynamic qualities. One aspect of this work is to explore how emotions mirror elemental forces, such as fire, which tends to rise as does its corresponding emotion, joy. Water ebbs and flows, and like its associated emotion, fear, it can be erratic; like a tree, wood is vertical but sends out roots to stabilise, so it has a downwards pull; metal is strong and contained but can also bend and therefore is adaptable.

As with yin and yang, the Elements are interwoven, which means that out of necessity for good health, there are traces of each of the five present in us, but there may be one in particular that is more dominant. A person could have the qualities of fire as a possible dominant force but also have water and earth present in their characteristics. The cycle looks like this: wood feeds fire, fire creates earth, earth bears metal, metal gathers water, water nourishes wood.

It is natural for the body to try to establish a balance whereby one Element does not dominate as this could lead to ailments and the overexpression of the associated feelings and emotions. An example may be that too much water would lead to introspection and a feeling of anxiety and isolation, and too much fire can instigate nervousness and a callous attitude. (This is demonstrated in Table 7.1, which shows the physiological and psychological effects connected with the balance and imbalance of the Elements.)

Table 7.1 Characteristics of the Five Elements

	Water	Fire	Earth	Metal	Wood
Colour	Black	Red	Yellow	White	Green
Emotion	Fear	Elation	Sympathy	Grief	Anger
Organ	Kidney	Heart	Stomach	Lungs	Liver
Sense organ	Ears	Tongue	Lips	Nose	Eyes
Orifice	Ears	Vessels	Mouth	Nose	Tendons
Sound	Groaning	Laughter	Singing	Weeping	Shouting
Animal	Bear	Bird	Dragon	White tiger	Red dragon
Season	Autumn	Summer	Indian summer	Winter	Spring
Weather	Cold	Hot	Damp	Dry	Windy
Taste	Salty	Bitter	Sweet	Pungent	Sour
Virtue	Wisdom	Propriety	Faithfulness	Righteousness	Kindness
Smell	Rotten	Burning	Fragrant	Rank	Goatish
Direction	North	South	Central	West	East
Quality	Yin	Yang	Neutral	Lesser yin	Lesser yang
Development	Death	Growth	Change	Decline	Birth
Planet	Mercury	Mars	Saturn	Venus	Jupiter
Balanced	Courage	Joy/calm	Sympathy	Release of grief	Self-respect
Excess	Fear/panic	Nervousness	Worry	Depression	Anger
Deficiency	Foolhardiness	Depression	Neediness	Inability to grieve	Guilt

How to use the Five Element theory

The Elements can be used in various ways not only to explore expression but also to increase awareness of inner processes. Working with the Elements can offer to an actor:

- stimulation of new sensations

- ideas for physicality

- a means to embody subtle nuances that are present in human behaviour

- a way to extend movement vocabulary

- a channel to extend and become aware of one's energetic range

- assistance with being present

- balance in the body

- execution of action

- emotional expression

- flexibility and range of expression

- techniques to free up habits and routines.

Klocek (2013) has developed a model for communication which explores the idea that the four most recognised Elements in the West indicate a specific type of communication:

- earth – information

- water – discussion

- air – conversation

- fire – dialogue.

In the case of earth, which can be hard and solid, as in conversational mode, this means, according to Klocek, that it tends to be factual; it can stop the flow and there can be silence. An earth moment can lack sensitivity and appear cold and factual. As water flows there is an exchange, a stream of meaning, and there can be opposing forces: when water is turbulent and buoyant the exchange ebbs and flows. Emotional attachment can hinder the flow of exchange, which may bring defensiveness and unwanted ripples. A speaker with air as their dominant quality picks out the potential thoughts that may hinder the conversation; they open up and bring space so a two-way exchange can occur. Personal attachments and dominant opinions are not included in their conversation. Fire brings the highest form of communication, as it is transformative. It can be spontaneous and nothing is excluded from what is spoken. It generates change. It is probable that we use each category at different times, but it is interesting to note if you can identify which is most comfortable for you.

Characteristics of the Elements

This section explains the specific qualities of each Element. As a reminder, yin tends to be interior and downwards and yang upwards and outwards. It is therefore possible for someone to be essentially either yin water or yang water, or yin fire or yang fire and so forth.

Water

Water can flow, trickle, burst, storm, pour, spray, drop. It can be a river, stream, sea, ocean, lake, waterfall, pond, puddle, droplet, flood, tsunami, typhoon.

FACTS

Water is the foundation of life: we are 70–80 per cent water. The impact of water on our body's systems is of major significance to its efficiency: if there is not sufficient water present, the composition and balance of all essential fluids will be affected and communication will break down. Water stimulates levels of arousal and affects your ability to concentrate and channel attention, and the sharpness of how your brain functions in terms of semantic memory.

GENERAL CHARACTERISTICS

Often identified as a calming quality, water can trickle, flow in a steady stream, gush like a buoyant rapid, tempestuously storm and develop into tsunami. Too much or too little water results in unpredictable consequences and, translated into behaviour, this can mean becoming overwhelmed, depressed, overanxious or introspective. If water is balanced, there will be calm and ease.

Yin water can be considered as rain, clouds, mist, rain, frost, ice or a stream. It is changeable and able to camouflage itself and blend into the landscape as it is continually altering its shape and form. Water people like change and, not surprisingly, can be unpredictable, just as light rain can become a storm in no time at all. They can be moody and hard to pin down with a dislike of strict routines. On the outside they may appear soft, but they have a strong interior like the current of a river. As water is hard to see because of its transparency, water people hide and do not easily reveal all aspects of themselves.

In keeping with their changeability, they are usually free thinkers, but as with every Element, their temperament depends on balance. When out of kilter, it is easy for thoughts to be erratic and chaotic with a tendency to go round in circles, worry and become anxious. If balanced, they are highly motivated and inspirational and can think out of the box.

Due to their changeability, they tend not to stay in one place. In relation to work, they are at their best when they surround themselves with people who complement them. They love challenges and can have big ideas but do not always follow them through, or they may take risks and focus on detail rather than the big picture.

Yang water is represented by lakes, oceans and large rivers. They are generally dynamic people who, like water, are both adaptable and can change to suit the needs of the situation and their goals. They are diplomatic and will find a way to achieve what they want, filling in gaps others leave and covering every possible angle in the process. They will either be very buoyant and possess a strength which propels them forwards, or if success does not come their way, will drift and float.

A strong yang water person likes to rise to the top and enjoys being superior; if less developed, they will withdraw and feel hopeless. They can have the depths of an ocean; there is always a lot happening beyond the surface, such as plans, ideas, tactics and so forth. They can solve problems with speed, if balanced, and they do not let emotions cloud judgement. If they are less in control, they become overly analytical. As long as there is movement, they are healthy, and staying still for too long is not helpful, as they stagnate. In relationships they seek balance and prefer honesty and have a dislike of drama. They tend to be hard to get close to because they shift a lot. Some other qualities are:

- sensitive
- playful
- lively

- outgoing
- unpredictable
- uncontrollable.

Fire

Fire can blaze, fume, simmer, burn, singe, smoke, flicker, bake, warm, heat. It can be an inferno, forest fire, barbecue, flame.

Facts

Fire consists of hot gases which release heat and light. Like all the Elements it has extremes, having the power to destroy, endanger and rage, but it can also warm and nourish. Fire is associated with heat and warmth, and within the body it is responsible for the circulation of blood and fluids.

General characteristics

Fire is expressed through a general expansion of joy, laughter and pleasure with the world. In excess, there is an over-abundance of heat and rapture, manifested in over-giving which may be invasive. When deficient, there is no inner mirth or compassion. Relationships may be fraught with anxiety and fear, or rejection and abandonment, and this is accompanied by what may appear as coldness. This is expressed by chills or numbness, as if the thermostat is stuck on one temperature. There may be a sluggish quality to movement, as if there is a lack of nourishment.

Yin fire people are like the flame of candles or the light of a torch. They are soft and gentle, and appear considerate. They are predominately thinkers who like to explore and experience new things. Like the flame of a candle, they can be vulnerable.

Yang fire is associated with the sun and sunlight. Such people tend to be independent and have new ideas and tend not to give up. They can be overly enthusiastic and passionate, not knowing where to stop. They like routine and like the cycle of the day in sunrise and sunset. They can be carefree and relaxed people. When in employment, they like jobs which offer security. They excel in areas of work where they work with others and can give energy and be inspirational, and they are good in teams. As leaders, they are patient and gentle and will help others. They can be fierce if they encounter people who are reluctant to change. They are best not alone but need space to be creative and are good socialisers who easily make friends. They love to take care of others and generate great warmth. Some other qualities are:

- courteous
- artistic
- expressive
- eloquent

- passionate
- intuitive
- dynamic.

Earth

Earth can be solid like rock, gravel, clay, stone, or sloppy like mud. It can dry, crack and quake.

FACTS

Earth is associated with heaviness and weight. Being linked to the earth in many cultures symbolises stability and a strong sense of belonging, having roots and stability. Also earth is associated with growth and fertility as in Greek mythology through the goddesses Aphrodite and Gaea. The earth is believed to be mainly dry in alchemy but takes various forms and qualities: it can be a moist marshland, dry and dusty in a desert, fertile and rich in minerals as farm land, and hard as rocks and mountains.

GENERAL CHARACTERISTICS

The season for earth is late summer, the time of abundance and harvesting. It is associated with nurturing and being cared for, and the emotion is sympathy, which ideally can be given and received. An imbalance manifests as neediness and the desire to seek a connection. An earth person may crave sympathy and love, and when this is not received, either silence or whining is a familiar trait. Alternatively, in excess, over-mothering or a tendency to be manipulative surfaces.

The associated organ is the stomach and small intestine, which has the job of receiving and restoring nutrients. If the processing is not flowing, literally there is a blockage, and psychologically this could be a churning of thoughts and a restlessness which cannot find release.

Yin earth is associated with sand and soil. Such people like to nurture and support growth, thereby producing and expanding. Their purpose is to give and protect. Like Mother Earth, they are resourceful and able to problem solve. They make good teachers, charity workers and coaches, have great adaptability and are like soil that is well used. They are tolerant. They work to find solutions to problems. Some other qualities are:

- supportive
- capable
- productive
- creative
- considerate
- innovative
- intuitive
- patient

- too soft
- possessive
- controlling
- dependent
- idealistic
- hedonistic
- stubborn
- pessimistic.

Yang earth is compared to solid rock or mountains. Such people are steady and dependable. This stable quality means that they can be stubborn and immovable and do not easily take advice or guidance from others. They tend to work hard to build their foundation over time, and this becomes their solid base. To reach their goals they work industriously and gradually; success comes from their foundation, which keeps things together. They weigh everything and access what is right before they act. They are not easily pushed into things but quietly sit in a corner to assess what is needed. Some of their qualities are:

- persistent
- down to earth
- realistic
- wise
- stable
- open-minded
- trustworthy
- stubborn

- indecisive
- perfectionist
- loners
- hot-headed
- moody
- inconsistent
- self-reliant.

Metal

Metal can be considered to be similar to the element of air in Western paradigms, especially in its association with breath. In TCM metal can be both solid and malleable; it bends and moulds. It represents the crystals, gems and minerals of the world.

FACTS

The function of metal is to eliminate what the body does not need, to cleanse and let go of what is not required. The associated organs are the lungs and the large intestine; both are responsible for purifying and releasing. When out of balance, there may be an abundance of grief or sadness. This may also be expressed through depression, stubbornness and a tendency to be negative.

GENERAL CHARACTERISTICS

Metal is associated with self-worth and belief in oneself, so if out of sync, there may be a need to seek affirmation and respect from outside. Behaviour is manifested in attachment to possessions, collections and clutter, and it is a challenge to select and discard what is not needed. This could extend to the letting go of insults and rejection, which are seen as failure and disappointment.

Yin metal is considered to be like precious jewels, fine and refined. The manifestation can be seen in a love for glamour and sparkle and the need to be the centre of attention. Such people shine and consider themselves to have substance and depth. They like to be flattered and admired, often coming across as loud. Image is important to them as is to be good at everything they choose to do. They have strong egos when well developed; the flip side is that when they lose their confidence, they can be impulsive. They can think out of the box and are considered to be highly imaginative. In friendships they are selfless and thoughtful. They are always well prepared and work hard to pursue their passion. They prefer to work in teams where they can lead and delegate. They do not respond well to stress. They are very good in jobs where the public profile is high (e.g. public speaking). Some of their qualities are:

- elegant
- cultured
- eloquent
- meticulous
- multiskilled
- show-off
- vain
- know-it-all

- perfectionist
- oversensitive
- moody
- fickle
- proud
- aloof.

Yang metal is raw and can be as powerful as a sword or an axe. As the image of a sword suggests, such people have strength and can be potentially tough. They can take a great deal of pressure and enjoy extreme challenges through which they grow. They are highly focused and tend to go for their goal. Like a sword slashing though wood or flesh, they are relentless in achieving what they put their mind to achieving. If they are less developed, they become unfocused without goals and tend to lose motivation, with a tendency to want things to come to them. With a lack of clarity, they swing randomly and make mistakes.

When they heat up emotionally, they lose strength, which makes fire dangerous to them. It is important for them to stay cool and avoid heat. Workwise they are industrious and like to run things themselves. They do not like to be challenged by others. Some of their qualities may include:

- hard-working
- proud
- loyal
- stubborn
- responsible
- impulsive
- fair
- inflexible
- realistic
- overly competitive.

Wood

Wood can snap, twist, bend, support, hold. It represents growth and balance like a tree with the roots as yin and branches yang.

Wood is specific to TCM and not included in what Western thought knows as the four Elements. It has the function of creating growth and change; its season is spring. The liver is the primary organ, which governs our driving force through shaping direction, ambition and motivation. The liver removes toxins, cleanses and makes way for fresh energy. The other associated organ, the gall bladder, digests fat and concerns decision-making.

General characteristics

In a desire to shape one's future, wood involves making plans. When a vision is stifled, if in balance, a person can readjust, but if out of balance, the emotional response is usually frustration or anger. If too much wood is present, a person is irritable and difficult, stubborn. Change is a problem if wood is overly dominant; it is characterised by not being able to join in life, and there is a feeling of helplessness. Wood is associated with the muscles and ligaments which often cause a rigidity and lack of flexibility if the system remains out of sync. The sound for wood is shouting, and the vocal quality is often loud and overbearing.

The image for *yin wood* is grass or creeping ivy. Such people are survivors who spring back to life even in times of difficulty. They are very resilient and try all angles to keep going, and due to this, they may lack depth. They can be volatile and become angry quickly. In work situations they can be good at networking and taking ideas from others. They can follow through projects and make good leaders, but alone they can be insecure when making decisions; they are able to make short-term rather than long-term decisions and are quick to react and find solutions. They need friends to keep them grounded and confident. Some characteristics are:

- resourceful
- shrewd

- calm
- attentive to detail.

Yang wood can be seen as a huge tree with long roots. They are people with strength and do not move easily. Traits which are most common are that they can be single-minded, pushy and stubborn, and are very straightforward. They make quick decisions and do not dwell on things once they have made up their minds. As the image of a strong tree trunk suggests, they can have a tough exterior though inside this is not always the case, and their confidence can be fragile. Their branches will move in the wind. From this low self-confidence can come a tendency to become angry.

In their careers they spread their roots wide and can take over if allowed. They can also be cut down and may be removed from the positions they have created due to inflexibility and dislike of change. Once they select a career, they tend to stay there. They are not good at starting a business from scratch but can take over once the groundwork has been laid by others. They do not have the patience for slow growth and can take risks to speed things up. They like to gamble. They need space and territory.

How to use the Elements as a part of a process

The Elements provide useful ideas to apply during the rehearsal process, especially while ideas are forming. They are an inspirational and imaginative resource for character interpretation, especially ideas for movement.

EXERCISE: CHARACTER AND ELEMENT

The Elements can be applied to the tempo, behavioural traits, emotional expression and overall energy of a character. Here are a series of steps to follow to begin to formulate ideas:

1. List what your character does in the story. This will provide you with a profile of their behaviour.

2. From the descriptions under each of the Elements (see above), see if you can recognise the traits and select an Element which suits the situation.

3. Create a visual image for the whole body which relates to the Element. If you were yang wood, you could imagine a tree with roots, and decide the shape, structure and expanse to suit the traits. If yin wood, you may be grass which is 8 feet high or creeping ivy which tightens on everything with which it comes into contact. Does this image stir up any feelings or ideas for movement?

4. Working from this image, explore the idea of centre and alter your weight and structure to experiment. Visualise your character moving from this centre. If you decide to explore more yin, have a downwards pull; or yang, the tendency to move upwards.

5. Taking a short piece of text, experiment with imbuing your actions with the quality of the Element. If you selected water, explore fluidity, linking the tempo and force to the emotion. Feelings could trickle, rush like a fountain or surge like a tornado.

6. Place the quality of the Element into your breathing. How does this affect your speech? Experiment with the speed and tone of the text. Use Klocek's work to identify the kind conversations your character partakes in.

7. Select sections of the text where there is a clear emotional arc and translate this into movement using the Element as the stimulation. Fire

may simmer, burn, spark and then spit. Once you have played abstract movement, take this into natural action, considering breathing, space, proximity and the planes of movement.

Internal movement

Internal movement consists of thoughts, feelings, sensations, emotions, mental images and all biological activity. The imagined situation, combined with the given circumstances, affects the tempo, rhythm and fluctuations of all action. Embracing the idea of the Elements and their association with inner expression is a way of cultivating the feel of a scene. This can be done by imagining the quality of an Element and allowing this to stimulate your inner tempo. It is particularly useful for establishing a starting state and considering how it affects the following:

- mood
- feelings
- interaction
- reaction.

Sensations may gush through you at speed like water moving over a waterfall, creating an erratic and uneasy mood. This would affect the speed of discussion, and there might be a buoyant exchange with others. Keeping the image inside, allow your breath to follow automatically your vocal quality, and movement will be inspired.

EXERCISE: OBSERVATION

Do some observation studies of the Elements to build up references for ideas, to stimulate movement and the expression of character traits. This can involve watching nature films or heightening your awareness of the weather and how it affects your senses:

- water – liquids, rivers, streams, droplets, rain, waterfalls
- earth – terrain, mountain ranges
- air – wind, breeze, tornado, stillness
- metal – iron, steel, gold, silver
- fire – smoke, steam, sizzle, burn, blaze.

As an experiment, select a piece of text and just consider what images of the Elements arise. See what happens in transition moments when a character is changing or experiencing a strong emotion. Use the image to imagine what may happen to the body. It could be that water becomes more solid like ice or that you take on earth-like qualities – a moment of indecision which could be fluid and soft, and then becomes firm and definite like a rock. This is when the character makes a choice.

In TCM the Elements are connected to every aspect of life, including nature. Table 7.1 provides a guide to the various categories.

As with all aspects of TCM, with the Elements emphasis is placed on establishing stability, where there is a balance of expression. Too much fire will overexcite, and too little will cause a detached and cold attitude. Table 7.2 shows the effects that are likely for either consequence.

Table 7.2 Balance and the Elements

Element	Balanced	Imbalanced
Water	Easy Articulate Deep in thought Calm Integrity Reflective	Tight Rigid in beliefs Isolated Introspective Despondent Detached
Fire	Laughter Joy	Anxious, fraught Chills, cold Sluggish Lacks compassion Numbness
Earth	Nourishes Cares Openly loves Sympathetic Transforms	Overly mothering Manipulates Rapid thoughts
Metal	Flows Sinks Contracts	Sad Holds on to thoughts Negative
Wood	Clear thinking Direction Goals Digests Rises	Chaotic Overthinks Over-plans Rigid Inflexible

Elemental qigong

In Elemental qigong there are a series of moving and static postures which aim to bring balance and efficiency to the body. This may require diminishing the presence of a particular Element or allowing another to emerge. This type of work is valuable for improving concentration, cultivating a more vibrant and energetic state, and changing moods. The postures are particularly helpful when preparing to work and can reduce overactive thinking and put you in touch with your felt senses. It is also a means of achieving balance in how your body functions, the consequences of which affect all modes of expression. One way to notice which Element is more prominent is to observe your feelings and emotions. If your tendency is to become anxious or overwhelmed, there will be a strong presence of fire, and a means of reducing or balancing this would be to work with water to calm and earth to ground. If you overthink and lack flexibility, this is a sign of too much wood, and it is useful to work with metal. A tendency to hold on to negativity and sadness would dissipate with more fire.

The static postures also have the potential to stimulate feelings and emotions, especially the ones that are associated with the particular Element. An example is that working with metal can create feelings of sadness and grief. In this instance the central organ stimulated is the lung. If a person's usual stance is one of collapse in the chest area or a tightening almost to shield and prevent feelings, the impact of the static or moving metal posture would be to open and create space for new feelings to emerge. The practice of qigong is thousands of years old, but the work of somatic psychologists, such as Stanley Keleman and neuroscientist Susanna Bloch, has explored how postures and body patterns stimulate emotions. Bloch has developed a process which is based on accessing emotion through adopting body postures.

The process of unravelling complex body structures, which may have taken a lifetime to develop, presents the opportunity to discover new ways of moving and sensing, but it also can overwhelm. There are highly subtle effects felt with qigong practice, as it slowly gives access to the deepest structures of the body. With this in mind it is always advisable to adopt the earth-static posture at the end of a session. This is similar to wu chi, but your palms are facing downwards. It is important to keep your breath strong and feel the rise and fall of the abdomen. This helps to balance and calm, and brings stability to your CNS.

EXERCISE: BALANCING HANDS

This exercise works to balance out the Elements and bring more calm to your body. Practise it as follows:

1. Stand in wu chi position (see Figure 4.1).

2. Place your hands in front of the lower dantien.

3. One palm faces upwards and the other towards the earth.

4. Allow the lower dantien to sink, and as you do so, the palm-up hand rises to the chest and the palm-down hand moves down to the level of the pelvis.

5. The hands then reverse and move in the opposite direction along the front of your body.

6. Regulate your breathing by inhaling through the nose evenly, in as you sink and out as you rise.

These postures are structured to work with one particular Element. They work most effectively when the position is held for a substantial period of time. It is useful to start with 5 minutes and then build up the number of minutes each time you practise. (See Sumner 2009 for further information on postures.)

Meridian channels

As explained in Chapters 2 and 3, the meridian channels are believed to be a transportation system which weaves in and out of the body like a gigantic spiderweb (Figure 7.1). Invisible to the eye, the 12 central channels travel though specific organs, then branch off extensively like tentacles and reach every part of the body. In Chinese medicine they transport qi and subtle energies, and are vital to the overall health and energetic systems.

The significance of the meridian channels is that they are a means through which we can access every part of the body and energetically align. 'When I envisage the Meridians as a particular form of coherence domain within the connective tissue, I see them as a sort of watery sheath encasing molecular chains' (Stefanini 2011, p.217). If we follow this thought, lining up the pathways will put your body in touch with all physiological activity. Using the analogy of a hose pipe, when there is a kink, the water does not gush through; in fact, it ceases until unblocked. The meridian channels work in a similar way: circulation of energy and qi is hindered through many ways, most commonly when we become overwhelmed in instances of heightened anxiety when we are likely to freeze up, or our muscles become held or tightened. Rigidity inhibits flow and movement, which ultimately puts emotions on hold.

Aligning the meridians is a way of tuning and activating your body. When the channels position themselves to maximise the movement of energy/qi, it is as if the last piece of the jigsaw puzzle has been added. The systems of the body are joined and you are more able to feel a sense of wholeness, an embodied state, where you are moving and sensing as one unit. Like a radio frequency, unless the precise point of connection is achieved, there will not be clarity or sharp tones. When the meridian channels are lined up, the capacity for optimum synchronisation is immense. It is like being 'in the zone'. However, a toned athletic body does not necessarily mean that the individual has access to their felt senses or is even able to blend energetic forces to fully unite the body. An example is with classically trained dancers in whom it is usual for the upper body to be slightly lifted, around the solar plexus point. In ballet this position may be one of perfect alignment, and hours of practice are spent trying to achieve it. In terms of the meridian alignment, this position disconnects the upper and lower sections which, in time, affects accessibility to senses, feelings and emotional expression.

Actors need to have bodies that are malleable, that are able to move with absolute ease, not only with the muscular system but with the deepest physiological layers. The meridian channels are a means of achieving an intense bond with yourself, where the capacity to feel is extraordinary and at times overwhelming. There are many instances when whilst practising qigong I have witnessed a person suddenly really feel a gush of sensation, like the flood gates on a dam have been opened, and unfamiliar sensations and emotions have arisen. Holding and tightening is usually a more familiar sensation for most people than flow and ease. Holding restricts the meridian channels and will disrupt what is natural and desirable for the body, the smooth glide of our physiology.

Tuning the meridian channels can be done through various ways. If you are following the approach of most styles of qigong, you would start with working on mastering the wu chi stance (see Figure 4.1).

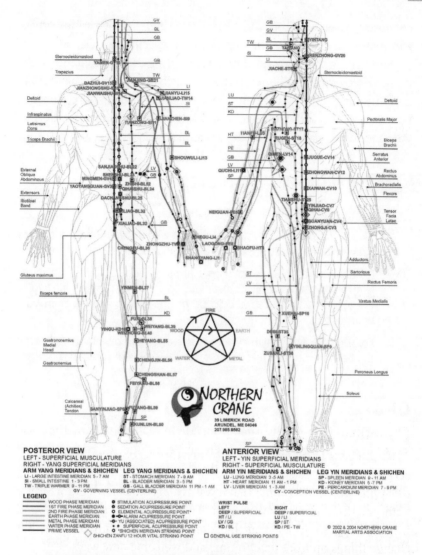

Figure 7.1 Meridian channels (courtesy of Sensei Phil Perez)

Any qigong postures and sequences aim to connect the meridian channels and maximise the efficiency of qi flow. In movement and acting classes, alignment and posture are consistent features, used as a reminder that posture is directly related to sensations, feelings and emotions. Discovering what is often called a 'neutral position' takes on a new meaning when the meridian channels are considered. In TCM the direct relationship between emotion, posture and vital organs is very much a key aspect. If an individual has a habit of sinking and collapsing, over time this will hinder the efficiency of various organs and potentially stimulate the expression of specific moods.

Stimulating the meridian channels can bring energetic vitality to the body. Discovering an aligned position which supports internal fluidity over the long term will expand your capacity to feel and connect to your body. The following exercises will encourage an activation of your meridian channels and encourage qi flow.

EXERCISE: BREATHING INTO THE HEART

1. Stand in wu chi position (see Figure 4.1).
2. Moving from the lower dantien, slightly sink as you inhale and allow your arms, palms down, to rise above your head.
3. Exhale and rise as you open your arms to the side, palms upwards. Drop your head slightly backwards. Stay in this position for two or three full breath cycles and focus on the breath coming from your heart area.
4. For a further two breath cycles, imagine you are breathing in through the balls of your feel and out through the palms of your hand.

Chakras

The chakras work on the same principle in relation to how the body stores and distributes energy. There are a number of traditions and cultures which are associated with the chakras, including the Mexicans, Sufis and Peruvian Incas. The most accepted belief is that the system began in India approximately 4000 years ago and is linked to the Vedanta philosophy. Essentially the chakras are believed to be stations which store energy located along the central column of the body and are therefore linked to the CNS (Figure 7.2). Most cultures consider that there are seven places in which these pools of energy are cultivated and transmitted. Each chakra is thought to influence the body in a specific way and is associated with a particular organ, gland, and emotional and mental expression (see Table 7.3). Dale (2009, p.239) explains that 'chakras interact with the flow of subtle energies though specific energy channels to affect the body at the cellular level, as reflected by hormonal and physiological levels in the physical body'. In TCM the channels are the meridians, and in Hindu culture they are the nadis. The strength and buoyancy of the vibrations emitted from the chakras is dependent on a number of factors and can be depleted due to misuse and physical disharmony.

The exercises on centres, developed by various practitioners including Michael Chekhov, draw on the same principles as the chakras and offer a way of enhancing connection to your senses and balancing your body. Where I believe the concept is most useful is as a starting point for translating the given circumstances into physical language – that is, for sketching out ideas for how the described behaviour can potentially be experienced physically. Through the use of the symbolic representations of each chakra point, a map of how the body could potentially move, the dominant direction of energy, weight, balance and how a person may see themselves in the world can be created.

Starting from your own familiar modes of expression, it is likely that you may notice that when it is difficult to say what you feel, your throat – your fifth chakra – tightens. At times when you are doubting yourself or you are anxious about whether you can succeed, be that in an exam, a proposal of marriage or something else, it is in the stomach, or third chakra, that you will notice the most activity. If you find it difficult to express love and compassion, there is a strong chance that there is rigidity in your chest area. At times when you may be unstable, you may automatically rise and not connect to your second chakra, the place of security and stability.

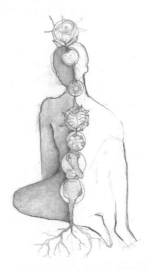

Figure 7.2 Chakras (courtesy of Valentina Piras)

How the chakras can aid your work

Working with the chakras can help with the following:

- receptivity

- your ability to connect the whole body

- getting ideas for physicality

- restoration and maintenance of balance

- the cultivation of presence

- achieving an openness to express freely

- the ability to tune in to shifts and changes in your body

- empowering you to adapt and make changes.

Table 7.3 Chakra-point meanings

Chakra	Developmental theme
Root (first point)	Survival and sexuality; connection to your roots, home, belonging
Sacral (second point)	Creativity; money, security and stability in the world
Solar plexus (third point)	Identity and power; how you see yourself; confidence in your abilities
Heart (fourth point)	Love and compassion for yourself and others
Throat (fifth point)	Communication and expression; speaking the truth and what you are feeling
Third eye (sixth point)	Perception and understanding
Crown (seventh point)	Transcendence of the self; deep connection to the whole body; a feeling of unity

For character development, working with chakras helps the following processes:

- physicality

- mapping out developed or underdeveloped aspects of a character's personality

- noticing somatic behaviour such as from where a character may lead

- understanding the dominant feelings and emotional expression.

The following exercises will help you to tune in to your chakra points.

EXERCISE: BREATHING INTO THE CHAKRAS

Either sit in a cross-legged position or lie flat on the floor. Breathe in and send your breath to the first chakra point, and stay here for four breath cycles. Add the following:

1. second breath, imagine a colour

2. third breath, imagine a circular space which expands as you inhale

3. fourth breath, imagine a sound.

Repeat the above process for each of the seven chakra points. Observe the feelings and sensations that arise and places which feel more comfortable for you to rest.

EXERCISE: MEDITATION

The purpose of this 5-minute mediation is to tune in and calm the thinking part of the body:

1. Sit cross-legged.

2. Observe your breath and regulate it so you are aware of the expansion and contraction of your body.

3. Imagine a piece of string which travels the full length of your spine, on which there are the seven chakra points which can light up. Upon inhalation the lights become brighter, which is maintained as you exhale.

4. Go through each chakra point and as you exhale imagine lighting your whole nervous system, with the light spreading along each nerve. Try to go through each chakra point and stay there for a few breaths.

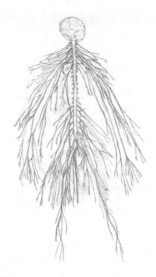

Figure 7.3 Brain and nerves (courtesy of Valentina Piras)

Conclusion

In this chapter we have looked at how to connect to the body from various perspectives, drawing on several cultural interpretations and philosophies, and scientific research. Understanding the complexity of your internal life has a valuable place in your work as an actor. At first glance interrogating neurophysiology and the advances in biology may seem unrelated to acting; however, as creative artists our body is our only source of inspiration, and learning how to fine-tune and embrace the potential for personal change seems to me to be an essential ongoing pursuit.

Chapter 8

INNER LIFE
Finding the depth

Introduction

This chapter explores the term 'inner life', extending the interpretation beyond thought, feeling and emotion to include the biological and deepest layers of your physiology. Taking a journey inside your body will introduce you to the amazingly intricate and interwoven systems which function as one unit and support the discovery of ease and efficiency. As an actor, you are working, of course, with *yourself*.

It seems that by using the word 'inner' there could be a distinction being made between internal events and movement or action which is visible, often termed 'outer action'. This could imply that the physical actions we do are somehow severed from the body's internal processes. This is, of course, not the case, as there is a complete interchange between inside and outside, and all physical actions are a result of an internal response to outside stimuli, to what is in the immediate environment.

There are many approaches to acting, some of which have become identified or labelled as starting with the outside in (Michael Chekhov's approach) or the inside out (Lee Strasberg's approach). In fact, inner and outer are the same; as Zarrilli (2008, p.20) says, 'Inner feeling and outer (physical) form are two sides of the same coin.' It is the key tenet of psycho-physical acting that 'inner feeling and outer expression happens at the same time' (Merlin 2001, p.27). I have found that there is a need to cultivate a sensitivity towards inner movement and extend somatic intelligence. Having some understanding of the intricacies of how the body functions is really important and will help to move through the unconscious barriers which at times arise to inhibit and sabotage immersion.

This chapter touches on anatomy and physiology and some of the processes of the body which drive the inner life. There are a few terms which are used to describe inner activity; for example, Marshall (2001, p.29) talks of the 'inner landscape' when referring to conscious activity: 'Your inner landscape includes thoughts and feelings, but it also encompasses images, sensations, memories, dreams and indescribable impulses.' I consider 'inner life' and 'inner landscape' to be interchangeable and imply the same thing. Although the words do perhaps signify different elements: landscape seems to particularly embrace the imagination, fantasies and memories of the past and future, whereas 'life' references a force, a tone of vibrancy which triggers impulses. For the sake of simplicity I will use the term 'inner life'.

Anatomy of acting

It is interesting to consider that imaginative journeys instigate huge shifts: every time an image is created or a story invented, immense vibrational surges occur. Allowing and registering such changes is important to fully experiencing, inhabiting and owning an action. Listening and being fully attentive to sensations and impulses is therefore crucial. 'The body that you listen to must be alive. A body that isn't alive can't tell you what it wants. It doesn't know what it wants. It is a "dead" body' (Oida and Marshall 1997, p.35). Being alive concerns how alert and attentive an actor may be. Oida and Marshall imply that being able to access the most subtle physical changes will alter your inner state and therefore enrich the depth and resonances for you and the audience. If *you* connect, the audience will too.

As discussed in Chapter 5, lived experiences leave a trace, like a pathway, so if the body remembers what we have felt, the physiological paths have been laid down. Peter Levine's work focuses on the somatic effects of trauma. He has identified that the impact of events that overwhelm, stress and emotionally disturb the body leave 'the frozen residue of energy that has not been resolved or discharged: this residue remains trapped in the nervous system where it can wreak havoc on our bodies and spirits' (Levine 1997, p.19). It is not exclusively in instances of trauma that the body retains an energetic memory. What has already been experienced would therefore have some familiarity; for example, if you walk down a road you have been down before, it is probable that some landmarks will be recognisable. By tapping into what you know but also making new routes, you are able to take your body on journeys which will bring surprise. It is your job to utilise what is at your disposal and expand imaginatively to be able to embrace narratives not experienced.

Developing somatic awareness and anatomical knowledge provides an insight into how the body actually functions and responds. It is easy to focus on what the character is thinking or what they psychologically want at any given moment and to ignore your own behaviour – the locked joints, shallow breath and protruded chin, all of which will prohibit sensation. The elements which make up each beat of action involve immense inner movement which alters depending on how we grade the action. Consider the image of a shoal of fish which constantly darts in sync: the quality of movement changes according to the stakes of each moment, and with the emergence of a large predator the shoal will instantly alter pace and rhythm. So it is within our body, as we are composed of many shoals of electrically charged fish.

Body systems in sync

This section provides an elementary and brief account of how the body functions. There are many books on anatomy and physiology which you can draw on for a more in-depth study, for example, *Hole's Human Anatomy and Physiology* (Shier, Butler and Lewis 2015) and *Anatomy and Physiology: The Unity of Form and Function* (Kenneth Saladin 2014). Marieb (2009) explains that the body is organised into systems, each of which has its own job to enable a smooth, efficient and healthy organism to function. The systems totally coexist and cannot be engaged independently of each other (Figure 8.1).

To bring all these systems into harmony, your body is always seeking homeostasis, and in order for this to occur, there is a continual adaptation to achieve the right temperature, oxygen levels and acidity for cells to survive. Marieb (2009, p.12) describes this as a 'dynamic state of equilibrium'. The nervous and endocrine systems in particular are the main players in sending out and coordinating the necessary information. As discussed in Chapter 5, messages are passed through electrical charges from the CNS and are then transferred through hormones and nerves. The three elements to the control mechanisms of homeostasis are:

- The receptors, which are specialist cells that detect changes in the environment, known as stimuli.

- Control centres, largely the brain, which analyse the information and make decisions as to the action which will be taken.

- The effectors, which provides the way in which the choices will be actioned by muscles. This response has acted upon the stimulus and will alter the functioning of the body by either a negative or positive reaction. This will affect the strength of the electrical charge. If the response to the stimulus is negative, the effect will be to attempt to shut off or reduce the intensity; if positive, the tempo will usually accelerate. This process affects the excretion of chemicals into the body.

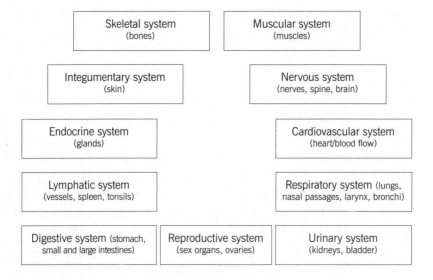

Figure 8.1 Body systems in sync (courtesy of Daniel Hughes)

There is an automatic response cycle, as discussed in Chapter 3, and it is in operation throughout every minute of our lives through the mechanisms of the heart, breathing, temperature regulation and the levels of minerals circulating in the body. This natural cycle of giving and receiving of information, at the deepest physiological level, fully engages all the body systems in sync and is the basis for the activity of our inner life. As you sit in a studio participating in an acting exercise, trying to relate to a scene partner, this natural cycle is occurring – and you, to a large extent, are in charge of how this process operates, as you can downgrade or upgrade the response and literally trigger more or less chemicals into your system, which will affect how you feel.

The endocrine system is responsible for the secretion of hormones, or chemicals, of which there are many kinds. Each substance has target cells or organs which are aroused as a result of the chemical emission. The function of this system is to alert and stimulate activity, which may be the digestion of food or the stimulation of glands. The action instigated cultivates instantaneous change at a cellular level by firing up the nervous system, which then sends out a cascade of electrical impulses. An example of this response is in an instance of high stress when the sympathetic nervous system produces epinephrine and nephrine in an attempt to cope with the immediate crisis. It is easy to see how the endocrine system is of massive significance to how we feel, think and cope with every event we face. In situations of stress the endocrine system leaps into action and over- or under-produces chemicals. The ability to focus and concentrate on a task, retain stability and possess the balance required to cope with life is the responsibility of the endocrine system. In the next sections we will look more closely at the other main players: the heart and the brain.

Heart

There is a constant conversation between the heart and the body whereby the rhythm of the beat directs signals to every nook and cranny. At times, prior to consciously recognising the significance of a stimulus, the heart provides the clues by the strength of its beat. The most obvious signal is the response to what is perceived as danger, and without negotiation, the autonomic nervous system will activate, sending neurotransmitters and an increased blood supply into your circulatory system. This brings the state of alert which your body believes is required for the action.

According to Mae Wan Ho there is no doubt that feelings are directly connected to the heart. She describes it as the most 'powerful generator of rhythmic information patterns in the body', acting as the 'global conductor in the body's symphony to bind and synchronise the entire system' (Ho 2008, p.172). There is a synthesis which functions with almost instantaneous activity to such an extent that it is difficult to identify who is the conductor – the head or the heart. References to the heart are integrated into language and mythology; it is associated with a range of emotions and expressions which validate its status in the body. When sad, it is heavy, shattered, broken or bleeding. When met with love and affection, it is referred to as open, throbbing, or it 'skips a beat'.

It is our heartbeat which provides the clues about our emotional state and is a very clear sign of the truth concerning what we are feeling and thinking. To control the heartbeat, it is necessary to manage responses to the stimuli you encounter, as the heart is at the centre of physiology. If we consider its electrical power, this is no easy feat. The electrical voltage of the heart is about 60 times greater than the electrical activity produced in the brain and penetrates every cell in our body. 'The magnetic compartment of the heart's field is about 5000 times stronger than the magnetic field produced by the brain and it can be measured several feet away from the body' (Ho 2008, p.177). The heart of an actor takes on a military-style assault course whilst working on a role. It is required to respond to dramatic situations, and usually at some point in the narrative, the heart is plunged into the depths of extreme emotion. This demands agility and potentially endangers health and well-being. Who would choose to relive a story daily in which you are asked to believe that your father has been murdered by your uncle, who then marries your mother and takes the throne which is rightfully yours? Or get hunted by a gang of assassins because you innocently witnessed a murder on the street? When filming scenes you will be asked to repeat the action until the director believes they have the performance they want. This is physiologically very challenging. Placing yourself into situations which demand high states of alert will flood your system with chemicals and alter the tone of the CNS. It is beneficial for performers to develop strategies to monitor and manage internal rhythms, which primarily implies coping with the triggers that stimulate strong emotional reactions. The heart is a way of tuning in to the rhythm of the body and achieving a harmonious state or nimbly shifting feelings and emotions.

There is bidirectional interaction between the heart, internal activity and external environments. This instantaneous response collaborates with your brain to monitor homeostatic regularity, perceptual awareness and emotional processes. Scientific research since the mid-1990s indicates that heart rate variability (HRV) is crucial to how an individual manages and copes with their life. It is the measure of your cardiovascular flexibility that indicates your overall ability to cope with physiological stress (Childre and Martin 2000). Heightened levels of stress hijack creative expression and the ability to be present.

The relationship between the heart, brain and the ability to think clearly, and carry out our work efficiently, cannot be underestimated. When under pressure, the heart rate increases which creates a chaotic pattern in the brain, especially in the frontal lobes, which are largely responsible for managing emotions, judgement, problem-solving, short-term memory and some parts of speech. Stress can cause the frontal lobes to cease optimal functioning, through freezing activity. Instances of memory loss in pressured situations, forgetting lines, not being able to remember factual information in exams and so forth are a result of the brain struggling to cope with overload. When plunged into situations that threaten and demand too much, your physiology will enter into confusion, resulting in a loss of control.

We can generate a different HRV which allows us to adapt to the situations in which we find ourselves. The electrical input to the brain from the heart can be controlled in a more stable way through cardiac coherence. This is a means by which the heart rate retains flexibility but has a more stable pattern and is not likely to launch the body into physiological distress. Watkins (2011, p.317) explains that this coherence enhances brain function and activates the frontal lobes. Control of breathing is the most effective way of altering the tone and rhythm of all of the body's systems. When you inhale, your heart rate increases, and on exhalation it slows. Developing the capacity to regulate your breathing will immediately influence your capacity to communicate with yourself and others. Importantly, it will also help to create a feeling of ease and unity where one system does not dominate. (See the breathing exercises in Chapters 1 and 3.)

Brain

In Western society the brain is often prioritised, and this is evidenced in educational systems where achievement is measured by passing examinations, often through rote learning. On the whole, somatic education is absent. Rarely would there be a curriculum which explores the importance of breathing on mental and physical well-being or of emotional expression as a means of creative exploration. Generally perceived to be the centre of operations, referred to as the storehouse or hard drive of the body, we are programmed to believe that the brain dominates all of our activity (Pinker 1997). Since the work of Albert Szent-Gyorgyi, as early as 1940, there has been an increasing amount of research available which confirms that the body is a huge network, its branches stretching to every crevice of our organism (Dharani 2014; Oschman 2000). A slight shudder or reorganisation of one cluster of cells, be they neurons in the brain or T cells which fight infection, triggers waves of information in a similar way to how the Morse code functions. It is known that the brain has many parts, each of which takes responsibility for specific functions, be that movement, motor skills, speech, memory, the release hormones, processing information, swallowing, breathing or controlling emotions (Dharani 2014, pp.9–17). What is also understood is that these parts do not work in isolation; there is a collaboration operating at all times.

In his studies from the 1960s, Sperry (1977) suggested that there are divisions within the central cortex, with the right hemisphere being responsible for more creative expression and the left prioritising logic and factual processing. This perspective has since been largely discarded by much of the scientific community. The division would suppose that there is little analysis in artistic pursuits, which is clearly not the case. Musicians use the left side of their brain to analyse when processing and creating music. This is confirmed by the work of Beckett, who states that playing music involves the whole brain (Beckett 1997; Zatorre and Beckett 1989; Zatorre *et al.* 1998). Using magnetic resonance imaging (MRI), she monitored the activity of the brains of musicians whilst they were improvising, and her findings confirmed that even when recalling a melody through mental imagery, both hemispheres of the brain are engaged. In a series of studies Nielson *et al.* (2013) examined the neural connection between the hemispheres whilst undertaking specific tasks that required logic and reasoning, and found that all regions worked together. Neuroscientists use the term 'lateralisation', which is when one hemisphere is used more than the other. Neilson *et al.* (2013) found that for one individual it could be that there is greater lateralisation in the left or right networks, but that this is not a global phenomenon. They generally identified that the left side of the brain is associated with language and the perception of internal stimuli, and that the right side is more active with regard to external stimuli, especially spatial and visual action. When applied to acting, it is the left side which is responsible for language, words, definitions and the right side for time, tempo, volume and inflection, which implies that for an understanding of what is being spoken, both hemispheres are equally active. (A detailed explanation is offered by Blair 2008, pp.18–24.)

Speech and movement

When working on a text, the language does not originate from you: they are not your own thoughts, which clearly affects how the words emerge. The process is not as natural as when you speak your own thoughts, so it is not surprising that there is usually a gap between speaking a text and its embodiment. A physical clumsiness, such as awkward gestures with the hands, often occurs before the language can be owned. Research confirms that thoughts generate both language and movement, and that there are neural links which connect gesture and speech during its formation (McNeill 1998, 2005). Despite this, Kemp (2012, p.63) believes that 'The difference between how the brain processes written and spoken language is at the heart of the challenge that actors face in bringing a script to life.' This is because language and gesture operate in different ways despite being part of the same system. Kemp explains that actors who have not been able to make the leap from language to gestural imagery will find it hard to fully engage their body. Kemp refers to the work of cognitive linguist David McNeill who has demonstrated that when we speak, there are two aspects to the communication: one is language and the other is visual in the form of images and physical action. He believes that gestures are natural to speech, and with this comes the engagement of all of the body. A movement of the shoulders involves moving the whole instrument; the same with the hands, head and face. Actors who solely repeat the words on the page without engaging with gesture 'have not made the mental leap from the linear nature of written language into the gestural imagery of spoken language' (Kemp 2012, p.66). One of the challenges of screen acting is that working in a tight frame can limit movement, so in this instance the trick is to work with inner gestures, to draw on mental pictures to stimulate inner action.

Gestures are also known to influence neural activity in areas of the brain that are responsible for semantic information. This offers an interesting consideration when it comes to memorising, and techniques such as Michael Chekhov's 'Psychological Gesture', not necessarily used as a mnemonic, could also aid in the recalling of information.

Thoughts

The process of how thoughts emerge is complex and remains under scrutiny by neuroscientists. A good reference book is *The Biology of Thought* (Dharani 2014) which examines in detail what a thought is and how thoughts are produced. A simple explanation is that thoughts are caused by brain function and are generated by immense activity occurring largely at an unconscious level in response to sensory information. The process involves patterns of electricity created by the billions of neurons which produce approximately a thousand signals per second as they move across networks. The signals pass through the peripheral nervous system (PNS) and CNS, providing information to all the body systems in sync, which results in action.

Thoughts can be facts, ideas, memories, reflections, observations, beliefs, notions, mental pictures, images or opinions. They occur over a period of time which is dependent on the type of thoughts they are. It could be that you are unravelling an idea, giving an instruction, pondering a concern, doubting an action, posing a question and so forth. Thoughts can appear as idle thinking, recollections, daydreams, reflections, factual recollections, musings, brooding, speculations and so forth. They have a quality which is dependent on what the thought is and its stakes. Thoughts can float, dart, sift, penetrate and/or be broody, shallow, deep, light or heavy.

Thoughts can be short-lived and appear as constant murmurings which are repeatedly in the background of your world such as worries about money, obsession with someone you love, fears, regrets, hopes, ambitions and so forth. Every thought has a time frame and is either in the past, present or future. This is very important to the energy and the action that emerges, which could be conscious or unconscious. If an action is unconscious, you will not be aware of doing it. An example could be that consciously you want to be at an event with a particular person but your body action is to withdraw and reject, which is instigated by past experiences of such situations in which you have felt uncomfortable.

One way in which a character is understood is through what is said, the dialogue that expresses thought, but what is spoken is clearly just the tip of the iceberg. As the brain mediates between the conscious and unconscious, with the former representing a small percentage of brain activity, it is easy to see that to truthfully portray a person in any situation, it is necessary to look beyond the spoken word.

Unspoken thoughts

Spoken thoughts tell us something about how we want to present ourselves; they are one of the means through which we communicate. What is not spoken is usually more interesting and forms the undercurrents of the inner life. Although not necessarily visible, thoughts are detectable through somatic behaviour, by gesture, movement, breath, and temperature changes affecting skin colour and perspiration.

Not on thought

We never not own our own thoughts; they emerge from us as an expression of our wants, needs, perceptions, opinions, cultural and social heritage. However, it is possible to not own the thoughts of a fictional text, to speak without a real internal connection that stimulates genuine feelings and emotions. An indication of not being 'on thought' is when the linking thoughts are missing, the journey from one line of text to the next is absent – a result of not enough attention being placed on inner conversation, the development of the thought. Without this, there is a gap in emotional growth, as if a few notes are missing in a piece of music.

In moments of dual attention, when personal thoughts emerge to side-track those of the text, the body is usually the giveaway, as seen by tightening, holding and/or a change in breath pattern. The solution is to keep your thoughts active, as if they arrive just as you speak. *Active* thoughts are fresh, alive and roll off the tongue.

Finding a balance between reality and fiction

All forms of creative expression require a surrendering of logic and an ability to get lost in the activity. Making art does not necessarily make sense, as the process draws on the wealth of the experiences which an individual may have encountered and the unknown, in the form of fantasy and imagination. Having the ability to shift from reality into make-believe is a matter of balance, and being locked too firmly in either territory does not necessarily ground the work being made. It seems that there could be three stages to this process:

1. recognising your own reality

2. identifying the fictional reality

3. fusing the two, so you use what you know and explore what you don't know in the attempt to understand and apply the perspectives, morals and opinions of the character.

We have talked a lot about balance and how to achieve it. To refresh the point and add further to the definition, we can say that a balanced body is when you are able to vacillate between bodily systems equally – to move from thinking to feeling simultaneously – and direct your attention so as to avoid mental dominance. The benefit is that you will be more present and therefore free to respond. It is as if everything internally is working towards one goal.

Controlling the mind

The mind is potentially wayward and unruly, as it has at its disposal the possibility to travel to the unknown through the imagination. To stay present to any situation, it is necessary to control the monkey mind. Here are some tips to avoid overthinking:

- Loosen your body by practising a daily routine to free up tightness.

- Work with your breath to open up the spaces inside your body.

- Practise going with your instinct and impulses rather than holding.

- Tune in to how you feel and where you feel most.

- Work to release the lower part of your body, especially your feet and pelvis, through movement sequences.

How is mind control achieved?

There are a number of ways to train your mind and develop an ability to tune in to your whole organism. The activity of your mind has a tempo which is reflected in thoughts and pictures, like your own independent movie which is constantly running. There is also a density and a quality to mental activity, which is sifted according to priority and investment, in so much as we decide whether to dwell on a matter. This is evident by common terms and expressions such as:

- I have things on my mind.

- My mind is buzzing.

- My mind is in a spin.

- Stop playing mind games.

- My thoughts are running away with me.

- I have heavy thoughts.

- My mind is playing tricks on me.

- I can't stop thinking.

- I feel like my head will explode.

The mind is like a sea which weathers both storms and calmer waters, and we have the authority to direct the passage.

Techniques for calming the mind

Meditation and other practices to achieve mindfulness are great for calming the mind. Tuning in to the quality and tempo of your thoughts is a good place to start. This can be achieved though the visualisation of a mind map which may have many sections or layers. Observe the pulse and vibratory sequences which are being created as if you are watching a screen of an MRI scan. There may be a dominant movement pattern evident, such as a whirling, spinning or floating sensation. Use the breath to work like the wind to direct the movement of thoughts, sending them to the lower parts of the body or slowing them down.

EXERCISE: MOVING THE WHOLE BODY

It sounds simple, but by moving the whole body the composition of your inner life will change: what was dense will dissipate, and your centre of energy will shift. If you are overthinking, move and engage the whole body.

EXERCISE: CONTINUOUS MOVEMENT

Do 5 minutes of continuous movement, which may be either the repetition of a sequence or a combination of stretching and movements that open and close the body.

EXERCISE: SHAKING

In qigong there is an exercise which involves shaking the body; it aims to stimulate the nervous system and encourage qi flow. The way into the exercise will differ according to the form of qigong you practise, but it is beneficial to start from the wu chi position (see Figure 4.1), which aligns the meridian channels and centres the breath. Working from a lower centre, the lower dantien, move down from the coccyx and begin to generate a shake involving the whole body. The shake can vary in force and is generated by the centre rather than the shoulders.

EXERCISE: CALMING THE MONKEY MIND

1. Stand or lie and observe the activity within.

2. Place your hand on the top of your head and feel the pulse and beats of your heart and any other inner movement. Breathe to the rhythm of the pulse.

3. Slide your hands to the back of your neck so they rest on the indentation between the cranium and your cervical spine. Hold this area with a light touch.

4. Run your hands down the neck so your fingers are spread out and breathe deeply as you do.

5. Place your attention on this area.

6. Build up your breath so you extend the length of the exhale to more beats than the inhale.

An alternative way of doing this exercise is to stand or lie and listen to the activity within you like it is a radio programme. Hear the chattering but do not follow it or invest in it. Notice the volume of the thoughts: do they become busier and more raucous, developing into an anxious frenzy? If they do, increase the intensity of your breath and upon exhaling imagine that your thoughts are dissolving or fading as if they are passing mist.

EXERCISE: SENDING YOUR THOUGHTS

Tune in to your inner activity through your breath and notice if you recognise any thought patterns. Are the phrases familiar to you? Imagine that as you breathe you swallow up the thoughts and move them from your head to another part of your body (e.g. your big toe or your knee). Spend a few minutes visualising the chattering in the new place.

Skeletal and muscular systems

Looking at rows of bodies at the start of a class is an interesting experience. It is like viewing a landscape with various architectural designs, some of which are tough and hardened by their environment, others shrinking in an attempt not to be seen, and others standing firmly connected to the earth, able to shift and adapt to what is coming. It is usually detectable who will be able to embrace creative work in the spirit of exploration and be prepared to make changes, be that in outlook, attitude or habits, and those who will resist and struggle with new concepts. There are several clues, but the skeletal and muscular structures are immediate giveaways.

The structural alignment of the skeletal system is paramount for many reasons. How you stand and move will contribute and reflect how you feel and reveals the truth about inner experience and self-perception. It is symbiotic with mental processes. The skeleton is the framework upon which other systems are built; its structure is therefore crucial for internal alignment and the flow of activity. A collapsed spine will impede the speed of messages from the CNS. Locked joints will affect overall circulation and restrict the space for muscles and soft tissue to function. If you explore the placement of weight through your bones, it is easy to feel huge changes to fundamental bodily functions. Place your weight onto your heels and see if you can identify how your breathing alters. As this action affects the position of the ribcage and how the diaphragm is positioned, it is likely that your breathing will become lighter. The body automatically alters in alignment according to the circumstances in which it finds itself. When frightened, the bones may lock; when relaxed and happy, they soften and open.

Wu chi is a structure which is particularly useful for internal alignment as the joints are unlocked and structured to allow for the muscular, cardiovascular and nervous systems to function with ease. Attention is paid to weight distribution and the ideal energy centre with breathing controlled to follow the natural rhythm of the vital organs. (See Chapter 4 for a description of wu chi.)

EXERCISE: CONNECTING TO THE SPINE

The spine is the core of the body, and when you are in touch with it, there is more of a feeling of being whole. Imagine that you are at least 1 foot taller than you are, so your spine extends beyond your head and drops down like a tail. Inhale, sending your breath down the length of your long spine, and as the breath travels, lights flash on. At first you may only reach half way down, but your aim is to reach all the way down to switch on the last light at the top of the coccyx. Upon exhaling the lights glow.

A variation of this exercise is to take it slower and stop and breathe into particular places which are harder to feel, such as the thoracic spine in the middle of the back or the lumbar region.

Another variation is to imagine that the spinal fluid has a colour as you inhale; like a thermometer the liquid moves down the centre of the spinal cord as you inhale, and upon exhaling it rises. The aim is to reach all the way down to the coccyx upon inhaling and up to the atlas upon exhaling.

EXERCISE: LEADING WITH THE WRIST

Working towards both unpicking unhelpful postures and habits and finding more ease in movement can be achieved through visualising how the skeleton moves. This exercise, performed in a pair, explores the effect of the transference of weight through the skeleton and encourages an appreciation of the connection:

1. Establish a structure in which you have a low centre with joints unlocked.

2. Become aware of the distribution of weight through your skeleton.

3. Connect to your breath and notice the movement of your diaphragm.

4. Place the outside of your wrist against the outside of your partner's opposing wrist.

5. Begin to gently move with one person leading. All movement is initiated through the wrist. The movements may be very subtle. There is always a leader, but this can change without verbal negotiation.

6. Work towards fluidity as if you two are one.

What you may observe is that very slight movements significantly affect the structure of all of the body.

If you tune in to the feeling, the impact of lifting a wrist very slightly can be felt through the chest, diaphragm and all the way to your feet.

Bones and joints

The skeletal system is composed of bones, joints, ligaments and cartilage. It is the body's internal framework and is responsible for protecting organs as well as connecting and stabilising muscles to enable movement to occur. Bones come in different shapes and sizes to accommodate the particular function they play. An example is the cranium, composed of eight bones, which are designed to protect the soft tissue of the brain; each bones varies in shape, texture and density. As the hardest material in the body, it is often assumed that bones are rigid, dry and hard in composition, partly because of the weight and force the skeleton bears. Collagen, which is present in all bones, enables them to be flexible. Bone is an active and dynamic tissue which remodels itself according to your calcium intake and the stresses on muscles. The density can increase or decrease mass depending on physical activity. Where muscles are larger and dense in structure, the bones will become thicker to support movement possibilities.

The skeletal framework will change with how it is used and demonstrates perfectly how all the systems work in tandem. How an individual copes with the world around them will be evident in their structure. They may expand to embrace and retain a position of ease whereby they can sustain a flow of activity, or they may freeze or close down. By shutting down, the body often moves inwards and sinks around the diaphragm area, as if shrinking away from the situation of stress. Muscles and ligaments will hold the bones in whatever position they retain and, in so doing, calcify or harden. In the instance of holding, it is often the shoulder region that takes the pressure, and with repeated stress it can appear as if the shoulders are holding up the body.

In qigong practice the joints are considered to be instrumental in enabling qi flow and bringing ease. Locked or stiffened joints hinder the movement of fluids including the circulation of blood and the direction and pattern in which qi may travel. Holding in any of the joints will have an impact on the whole body. Loose and healthy joints are reservoirs for qi. Try locking up your knees and observe the movement of your pelvis and spine – a common habit which causes tension in most areas of the body and fundamentally traps the circulatory flow.

All joints and bones are vital, but I am going to focus on a few which have particular significance. The temporomandibular joint is a hinge joint that connects the mandible, the lower jaw, to the temporal bone of the skull. This bone is positioned in front of each ear at the sides of the head. These joints need to be flexible to allow for chewing, speaking and yawning. The muscles that are attached to the jaw and those that surround it control the position of movement of the jaw. Common causes of a tight jaw are clenching or grinding of the teeth, dislocation of the joint, and stress, which usually leads to a tightening of all of the facial muscles. A held jaw will limit vocal range, tone and flexibility, as it is difficult for words to be clear or legible when the organs of speech become restricted. The ideal position is for teeth not to be pressed together and for lips not to be pursed.

There is a large muscle called the occipitofrontalis that extends from your eyebrows to the back of your skull. When this is tight and tense it causes the shoulders to rise, and like a band it tightens onto the skull, often resulting in headache or migraine. Tension around your head triggers other muscles in your neck and shoulders, which will restrict movement. This also affects both the expanse of breathing and, again, your vocal quality.

EXERCISE: RELEASING THE OCCIPITOFRONTALIS

Place the fingertips of both hands on your forehead. Inhale and slowly exhale as you pull your fingers apart, as if you are stretching the skin. Allow the fingers to slide down the sides of your face to your ears. Repeat this sequence across your head and at the back of your cranium. Breathe in and out through your nose as you do this.

EXERCISE: JUST STANDING

1. Imagine that you can pull your shoulders down to your feet, as if your fingertips are touching the floor.

2. Slide your scapula (shoulder blades) down your back.

3. Move your jaw downwards; keep your lips touching and your teeth should not touch each other.

4. Press your tongue downwards towards your bottom teeth.

5. Tuck your coccyx.

6. Tuck your chin.

7. Allow a little space under your arms.

8. As you inhale through your nose, slightly sink and expand the diaphragm and the ribcage, and as you exhale slightly rise.

9. With your weight slightly forwards, as in wu chi, try to remain in this position for up to 5 minutes.

EXERCISE: OPENING OUT

1. Lie on the floor.

2. Push your body into the floor.

3. Place your arms above your head, with your palms touching and elbows outwards.

4. Bring your legs into a frog position, with your knees bent and your feet touching; hips should be turned out. Try to allow your knees to drop to the floor.

5. Stay in this position for 5–10 minutes. Breathe in and out through your nose, becoming aware of the rhythm, and try to extend the length of the exhalation.

Muscles

The function of muscles is to contract or shorten to enable the movement of the body. There are three types of muscle: skeletal; cardiac; and smooth muscles, which are found in the walls of organs such as the stomach and bladder as well as the respiratory passages. It is the skeletal muscles, those attached to bones, that provide the facility for the body to be mobile. Tense and tight muscles are disruptive to freedom of movement.

A specific area that is likely to create havoc if the muscles are tight is the throat – this condition is known as *muscle tension dysphonia*. Muscle tension dysphonia is when the quality of the voice changes due to extreme tension around the larynx. This can make the voice hoarse, gravelly, raspy, strained, squeezed, tense and generally weak. Such tension will affect all of the organs of speech, and it can take considerable effort to release as the condition has usually accumulated as a result of poor habits and a build-up of stress.

Psoas muscle

We have talked about the importance of grounding and finding a centre that supports balance, freedom and the range of expression. The psoas muscle is a major player when it comes to alignment and the transference of weight throughout the trunk, legs and feet. It forms a muscle bundle around the lumbar spine and the lower transversospinalis muscles. If this muscle is toned, it can sit on top of the pelvis and support movement of the spine, but if it is tight or held, the lumbar spine will be pulled forwards and the upper spine backwards. As a consequence, the diaphragm will lift and divide the trunk resulting in a feeling of disconnection throughout the body. Taking time to stretch and open this muscle will bring an increase in feeling and sensation, particularly more connection to the lower body (see Jarmey 2008).

It is not uncommon for most of us to misuse our muscles; this may be through being over-reliant on the more dominant muscles, holding a bag on the same shoulder or slumping from time to time. The shape of a body may not necessarily support an efficient working state. Energy levels, concentration and sensory capacity are all affected when a body is lopsided or collapsed, because the weight is not evenly distributed. In the 1980s Elizabeth Behnke developed a technique called 'matching', which addresses the stress patterns created when the symmetry of the body is out of alignment (Behnke 1984). A common example may be that one shoulder is higher than the other or the pelvic girdle is lopsided due to the uneven distribution of weight through the feet. Over time, this will cause holding patterns that may lead to stress or the inhibition of the nerves and the flow of fluids.

With this technique there is no manipulation of the body – that is, no attempt to correct the position or to consciously relax; the person is asked to consciously feel the imbalance – for example, that one leg may be shorter than the other. With this they become aware of their own asymmetrical shape. What follows is a realigning, which may mean the higher leg drops to match the shorter one or the other way round. The three stages are:

1. recognition of one's own body shape

2. realigning or matching up

3. allowing the change to occur and embracing the new sensations.

The technique aims to encourage the individual to tune in to how they are using their body and observe the feelings which arise. This effect of the technique is dependent on having the ability to feel the asymmetry in the body, which usually leads to self-adjustment (Behnke 1984). If this technique is applied to uneven shoulders, the person recognises that one shoulder is lifted higher than the other and would then lift the lower one to match the higher side. So although this is not ideal, both shoulders would be at the same height. In theory, the shoulders would drop, possibly because the discomfort would be extreme. This approach is a way of self-adjusting and experimenting with the impact of posture on feeling and sensation.

Seven points for freeing the body

As a starting point for increasing flexibility, I work with seven points in the body that are crucial for alignment and increased sensation. Through loosening the joints and aligning the spine the nervous system communicates with more ease.

Table 8.1 Seven central body points (courtesy of Daniel Hughes)

Point	Function
Feet	The feet are the end or start of several meridian channels and the location of the 'bubbling spring', an important energy point. Place your weight primarily over the balls of your feet.
Knees	The knees are important for the mobility of the legs. Several meridian points pass through the vessels and arteries. The knees are hinge joints – avoid locking them by keeping them slightly open or soft.
Pelvis	The sacroiliac and the iliofemoral (ball-and-socket) joints are important for connecting to the lower half of your body. This area is like the basin of the body as it is a vital energy gate. Tuck your coccyx under to keep your pelvis and spine fully connected.
Diaphragm	The major muscle passing across the ribcage, it is integral for breath control, feelings and emotional expression through key nerves such as the phrenic nerve. There is often a tendency for this area to be lifted or collapsed. Place one hand on your diaphragm at the front of your body and the other on your back at the same height. Assess whether you are lifting or collapsing in the area and, if needed, amend to bring the spine and diaphragm in alignment.
Shoulder girdle	Here five joints allow for a wide range of movement. Several meridian channels pass through this area. There are also two plexus points. It is important to be open across the chest and prevent the shoulders from being raised out of position. Imagine the scapula sliding down your back.
Head and neck	An energy gate which aligns meridian channels and the CNS. Keep your chin tucked to prevent the neck muscles from doing too much work and becoming tight.
Wrists and hands	The end or start of meridian channels. Rotate your wrists and loosen your fingers to retain flexibility in the joints.

By attending to these seven points, you will establish an alignment which supports all of the body's systems including the energetic.

Especially when you feel tense and ill at ease, it is useful to take yourself through these key areas to soften and bring more ease.

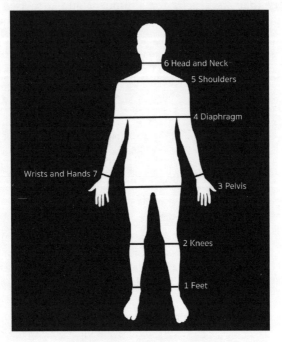

Figure 8.2 The seven points

Parasympathetic nervous system
Plexus points

As discussed in Chapter 3, the PNS is a complex communication system that instigates the felt senses. Getting to know all of this system is important for uniting and maximising sensation. The plexus points, which are the main nerve junctions, are positioned where groups of spinal nerves, known as ventral rami, come together to serve the motor and sensory needs of the limbs. The significance of these plexus points is that, combined with the nerves, they contain a high charge of electrical activity and are imperative to the functioning of the limbs in the following ways:

- The cervical plexus serves the head, neck and shoulders.

- The brachial plexus serves the deltoid muscle and skin of the shoulders as well as the skin and the muscles of the arms, wrists and hands.

- The coeliac/solar plexus serves the diaphragm and the internal organs.

- The auerbach plexus serves the gastrointestinal tract.

- The lumbar plexus serves the lower abdomen, skin, hips and thigh muscles.

- The sacral plexus serves the lower trunk, back of the foot and leg, and gluteus muscle.

- The coccygeal plexus serves the coccyx.

Positioned on the trunk of the body, the plexuses branch off the spinal column and are crucial for obtaining a sense of the whole body.

EXERCISE: JOURNEYING THROUGH THE PLEXUS POINTS

The objective of this exercise is to connect to your trunk and especially your back, which can be a neglected area in terms of sensation.

1. Either lie, stand or sit upright.

2. Tuck your chin and coccyx, and try to achieve a feeling of dropping down at the bottom of your spine and rising up at the top.

3. Imagine that you have a series of network junctions positioned in places where the plexus points reside (Figure 8.3). Allocate a colour which beams out as you inhale and slightly dims when you exhale.

4. Go on a journey travelling through each plexus point. Start with the brachial plexus, by the shoulders, and allow the imagined light to travel all the way down your arms to your fingertips. Move on to the coeliac/solar plexus and feel an expanse and spreading out of the light as your breath expands. At the lumbar point, create a pool of warmth which fills the lumbar region. At the sacral points, visualise and feel the nerves extending all the way down to your toes, sending out pulsations.

If you feel you need to activate your arms or legs due to being under-energised, tap around the areas of the plexus points to stimulate nerve activity.

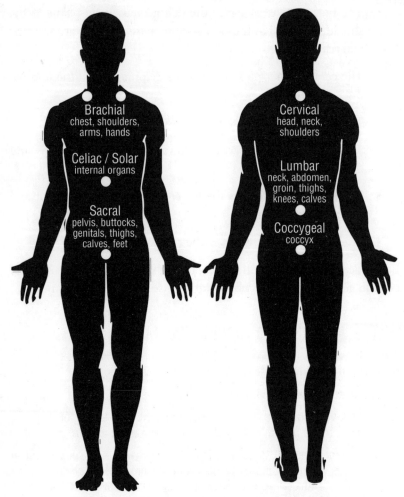

Figure 8.3 Plexus points (courtesy of Daniel Hughes)

Vagus nerve: the calming influence

Just as the plexus points have the capacity to send signals to the outer extremities, there is one particular nerve which is especially crucial to communication and controlling how your feel: the vagus nerve.

The vagus nerve is of particular importance to the PNS, as its main duty is to allow the nervous system to rest and digest. It is positioned on each side of the body, running from the brain stem, the chest and into the abdomen (Figure 8.4). It has many offshoots which take it into every vital organ, including the stomach. This helps to explain why when we feel nervous, our stomach is affected, and this may be felt through sickness or a sensation of butterflies. It also affects the muscles in the vocal chambers and is largely responsible for speech, swallowing and keeping the larynx open, heart rate and the production of chemicals, notably oxytocin, which stimulates positive feelings. It is the tenth cranial nerve and is known as the 'nerve of compassion', as when it is fully activated the sensation of warmth floods the body.

The tone of the vagus nerve will relax the nervous system and monitor levels of arousal. A balance is required for a person to feel at ease and to maximise a range of sensational expression. Breath is important to how it functions, as longer intakes with controlled exhalations provide time for the nerve to be activated. It can be inhibited from functioning efficiently when the intake of breath is quick, which is common in an anxious state, as this does not allow time to calm. A slower breathing rate leads to greater vagus nerve activity, which enables the body to relax and regenerate from potential stress.

There are several ways of affecting the activity of this nerve, including movement sequences from tai chi, qigong and yoga. Exercises such as 'Opening the heart' (see Chapter 2) and working with your head/shoulder relationship will stimulate this nerve.

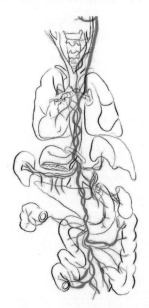

Figure 8.4 Vagus nerve (courtesy of Amy Stevens)

EXERCISE: EXTENDING THE BREATH

If you are feeling anxious and observe that you feel tight in your stomach area, it is beneficial to regulate your breath and activate the vagus nerve. Begin by inhaling and exhaling through your nose for four counts. On each breath extend your exhalation. Observe the point prior to inhalation and create an image of this long nerve reaching into your stomach, bringing calm and stillness. Send your breath to all the branches of the vagus nerve.

The physical sensation we feel as a result of being overloaded is detrimental on many levels, and the immediate effect will be a loss of the ability to focus and respond with clarity. Knowing that you can manipulate your own nervous system to change is valuable.

Conclusion

This specific chapter explores the term 'inner life', extending the interpretation beyond thought, feeling and emotion, to include the biological and deepest layers of your physiology. Taking a journey inside your body will introduce you to the amazingly intricate and interwoven systems that function as one unit and support the discovery of ease and efficiency. As an actor you are working with you.

Part 2

APPLICATION
Exercises to sharpen your craft

Part 2 explores practical application and how these topics relate to various preparation and performance contexts. In some instances I have adapted what may often be group-led exercises so they can be undertaken independently of a rehearsal or class. This is especially valuable for screen work where much of the preparation is often solo.

Each chapter focuses on either a discrete area or a specific detailed process. There is no particular order; it is easy to dip in and out according to interest. In some instances there is a specific structure to follow, such as the whole-script project, which will take you through a potential way of working on a screen role from page to the shoot. Other sections are more of a brief interrogation on a theme or areas that have regularly cropped up for me during my teaching.

Process is key to creative practice. How you decide the order and content of what you do along the way will clearly determine the results. Of course, it is possible to just turn up to an audition or a rehearsal having only learned the lines of a script the night before (or even hours before), as this in itself is a process, and even then the musings of your imagination and accumulation of experience will automatically support you. However, finding what works for you and having a structure to your work is vital. Process is about exploration, play and the immersion into a world other than your own, and it should be enjoyable as well as thorough.

Regardless of how long you have worked as an actor, I believe that adapting and experimenting are crucial, as these processes refresh your inquisitiveness and present challenges. When you feel you know how to do something, it is time to shift and seek other possible ways.

Chapter 9

A SIX-STAGE APPROACH TO TRAINING AND PREPARATION

Laying the foundations

Introduction

This chapter takes you through a systematic method which contains many of the key concepts outlined in Part 1. The six-stage process can serve as a foundation for your performance work, as the contents form the fundamental ingredients of embodied performance. I have found myself returning to these principles, as they provide the solutions to many basic dilemmas which regularly arise for actors.

Six stages to help in training and preparation

The approach below is concerned with developing the facility to be in tune with the body and to work towards maximising an embodied state whilst performing. I have identified six stages between which there is a very fine line as the concepts are all totally integrated. The ideas derive from various sources including bodywork concepts, martial arts and philosophical ideas. These stages are:

1. awareness

2. structure

3. reorganisation

4. integration

5. ease

6. action.

Awareness

Awareness is the first step – it facilitates the possibility of change and creative freedom. When you recognise something, which could be any aspect of your behaviour, you are then in a position to make other choices. Knowing what is useful to notice is the next point to consider.

Observation

Observation is fundamental to noticing and developing an inquisitiveness about your own physicality. The starting point is to begin with observing how you move your body, in particular:

- the transition of your weight

- the quantity of space you take up

- your muscular composition

- how your joints are positioned

- the kind of movements you use

- any sequences which you do in certain circumstances, such as crossing your legs or folding your arms

- the overall physical form which you have created as well as its density and structure

- the rhythm of your breath

- whether you hold and tighten particular parts such as the jaw or abdomen

- whether you lead with a part of the body when you walk

- where you place your weight.

This will change with how you live your life, what you experience, age, environment and the relationship you have with yourself.

Listening

To listen is to pay attention; it implies that you acutely notice all of the internal activity which largely functions automatically – the rhythm and vibration of the multitude of pulsations and beats of your body, which creates a background noise; it is your own tune that is familiar and comfortable to you.

The rise and fall of the breath sets the base for all pulsations. Learning to tune in to the natural expansion and contraction of your breath is fundamental to somatic education. Notice the pause and the length of your exhalation. Is your breathing smooth? Does it shake, rasp or quiver? Is it shallow? Do you fully engage your diaphragm?

Sensing

When you really listen to your body, a range of sensations emerge. The depth of what we are conscious of increases, as does the complexity of the conversations we are capable of having with ourselves. We have a wisdom which is programmed into our physiology, and there are many instinctive codes that are unravelled before we are conscious of them. The fight-or-flight response is an obvious example of this. Fear is sensed and interpreted at lightning speed by the central nervous system (CNS) and the peripheral nervous system. It is not unusual for a sensation to arise before a thought or real recognition of what is happening occurs.

Structure

The objective of this stage is to learn to move through the body, with an emphasis on *through*. A relationship with your whole being is the target, and to allow messages of sensation to become the language to which we automatically pay attention. The three concepts that provide a means of working through the body are: centre, ground and balance.

Centre

In qigong the centre refers to the dantien, usually the lower (see Chapter 4). It is considered to be the natural position of the body's energy and produces stability and a feeling of being fully connected to the whole body. At any time, depending on the environment and circumstances, we may lose this sense of being centred. An example is when overexcited, overwhelmed or stressed and the energetic centre shifts upwards. There is a fine balance between the position and quality of your centre, as it is ideally fluid rather than dense and sharp. Body builders often have a chest centre, as do ballet dancers. Ideally the body should have the capacity to shift the dominant centre from which it operates. At times we all overthink, or feel strong emotions such as grief or passion, but ideally we can shift and have the ability to think, feel and take action. Being fixed and bound by a body which holds the muscles impedes this capacity. An overly defined centre can reduce openness and flexibility as it becomes a stiff point, which would be more like an island rather than being integrated into your whole body. It would limit the embodiment of momentary transitions and reduce receptivity to outside stimuli. The centre is a means of uniting and accessing all parts; it is like a roundabout from which activity circulates.

Ground

To ground is an essential part of being able to feel and obtain a sense of your whole being; it enables sensitive communication with yourself and others. To feel the ground creates a true sense of belonging to the rhythm of the universe. It is a reminder that we are a part of something bigger than ourselves from which we can gain strength and potential inner harmony – a place to return to at any point of unease or overexcitation.

Your physical environment has a significant role in informing your embodied response. The human sensory apparatus, which contributes to how you perceive and orientate yourself, is positioned in the front of the body: ears, nose and eyes. Movement forwards occurs more frequently and naturally than backwards. The same can be said of upwards and downwards movement. The ground can be perceived as blocking physical possibilities and can be tainted with negative connotations related to falling, non-achievement, darkness, heaviness and so forth. Upwards implies more energy, lightness and positive achievement. Possibly due to these associations, it is not unusual for the experience of finding the ground to be new and unfamiliar. A large proportion of the population live without a strong connection to the earth, especially in Western cultures. I certainly find this to be true when working with large groups. The fast-paced occupations which come with stress, and the pressures of the need for material achievement, place emphasis on mental capacity. This contributes to the dislocation of the body and a loss of contact with energy. Functioning primarily from the upper part of the torso will limit communication and a full felt sense of the lower half of your body – the pelvis, legs and feet. When a person operates largely from their waist upwards, it is common to lock up the joints and hold around the diaphragm and abdomen. This response may occur in instances of heightened emotion such as fear, anger or feelings of anxiety. The rigidity will place pressure not only on your skeleton but also on how your CNS functions and on the efficiency of all communication modalities. Holding and locking will make it nearly impossible for anyone to reach their energetic and sensory potential.

Grounding allows for a streaming flow of energy to move downwards. It connects you with reality, because you are able to feel all of your body. If you cannot feel or root your legs, you function from a place of instability – the world is wobbly and has no stability. Spindly or thin legs often indicate a life where the ground is unfamiliar. In these instances the sense of the ground may have been created in another part of the body such as the waist, abdomen or chest. This creates actions and gestures that are generally invented or unreliable. 'By channeling our energetic and bodily experience through our legs and into the earth, we become grounded in the living reality of our situation' (Heckler 1984). A downwards flow of energy is likely to reduce feelings of confusion and anxiety, and will enable you to move from ideas and overthinking into feeling and sensation.

Balance

Balance is the third element that is integral to the overall discovery of integration. To understand balance it is necessary to know what is being balanced, as it is not simply a matter of the alignment of weight through the skeleton; rather, it involves all the systems of the body including your energetic networks. Physiological balance implies access to the whole body and brings with it the possibility of dynamic physical freedom and expressive choice.

Once the concepts of ground and centre have been introduced, finding a balance is an easier idea with which to work. Understanding comes through exploring physical shifts, working with the directions of movement and the transition of weight. Wu chi is a means of achieving a balance. This stance is the basic position which establishes the possibility of physiological connection. The aligning of the internal structures, such as your meridian channels, opens up the energetic pathways deep within the body.

Balance with the ground and the energetic centre will allow for momentary transitions to be felt, but it requires work to achieve and is difficult to sustain. It is easy to be thrown off balance or lose a sense of being centred; for example, anything from receiving news to recalling an incident which created a strong emotional reaction is likely to interfere with balance. Once your body has experienced balance, it will know how to return to it, as it is the place of stability.

Reorganisation

Stage three is when the effects of grounding, centring and balance are felt. The body begins to change in response to the adopted postures, movement patterns start to be noticed and unpicked and new shapes of experience are formed. The changed structure allows previously held connective tissues to expand and new sensations to emerge. This is often recognised as heat, twitches, pins and needles, flutters, shimmers or pulsations. If the person is familiar with a state of balance, they may notice that one side of their body is out of sync with the other. During this stage tune in to your natural expansion and contraction through your breath and begin to expand beyond your familiar breathing pattern.

Integration

Integration is when your body learns to move with the changes and resists returning to habitual patterns and structures. It is the point where there is a choice to return to what is familiar or embrace the new sensations. Shifting away from dominant archetypal patterns, such as holding, tightening or becoming rigid, requires practice. To achieve this, new ways of being need to be explored, and it is through moving with the expansion of breathing that your ability to surrender and let go emerges. This expansion enables a blending to merge with your existing internal dynamic. Shifting away from retaining a held, contained shape will work to create space in the smallest pockets of your body, which may previously have been tight or blocked.

This process of learning to fully go with natural patterns is integral to the ability to give and receive from others. In any form of communication there is ideally an exchange rather than a blocking or clash. In cases of anxiety or fear, an instinctive response would be to hold and block as if to protect from harm. However, moving through this instinct enables a blending to occur which embraces the situation and allows for the body's systems to deal with what is being faced. Moving through the obstacle, which is often a held, tight or taut muscular system, by expanding, an altered state will be created – like when a cork is pulled from a bottle, the substance within will relax and expand.

Pre-planning and action hinders the possibility of a genuine exchange as the process does not consider the energy of the other actor(s). Energy therefore blocks rather than blends with the other dynamic being presented, so a crafted, rather than organic, performance occurs. Through accepting and integrating the other person's energy, there is a spontaneity, a new concoction is brewed. This requires that you work with what is presented to you and avoid resistance.

A means of practising integration is to learn to work through resistance as exercised in many forms of martial arts such as aikido and tai chi. If your natural habit is to hold back, then learning to move towards and embrace, rather than tighten, will greatly benefit you. Movement sequences which encourage your body to feel the sensations of going forwards can instigate a change in habitual patterns.

EXERCISE: MOVING THOUGH

Going with your energetic impulse can be practised in everyday situations. When you are walking along a street or getting into a crowded train, explore what it feels like to flow and swerve to avoid someone rather than stop and freeze, as if the movement is continuous and easy.

A variation on this exercise is that two people walk towards each other on the same horizontal line. It is evident that at some point a clash will occur, but just prior to this action one person steps to the side and continues to walk. A variation is that the person who steps to the side then turns to face the other person who receives the quality of this action and makes another choice to keep the sequence going. The idea is that there is a streaming of energy rather than a stop and start which jolts and disrupts the internal flow.

Ease

Ease is the next stage with which to work; it will allow the body to synthesise the changes and balance the exertion of energy. The ability to move with ease is more than aesthetically pleasing as it offers a way to energise and for bodily unity to be maintained. Ease is unlaboured; it is when movement is economical and smooth. The effort executed is appropriate for the task: it can be heavy or light, as the term does not imply a specific weight, but it does imply flow and simplicity. It is a bodily state which is created by going with allowing the *body* to lead rather than the mind. If the mind leads, it will determine the quality of an action. This could be a walk that is heavy and overly laboured because there are too many burdening thoughts knocking around.

Ease is important for actors for several reasons. Primarily it is a way of being in touch with feelings and emotions. Operating from an open and relaxed body means that there are less obstacles being created by the actor themselves, such as doubt, lack of confidence or the spiral of anxiety which can comes with such states. From the sensation of ease any emotion can come and go, even extreme states which do not need to be imbued with clumsy action or heavy, controlled tones. When animals fight, they do so with grace, and their entire beings are absorbed in the activity. Effort can stifle creativity, as it can be an obstacle to the union with yourself. Letting go of conscious effort whilst performing is this state of ease, when every aspect of your body comes together. Ease will prevent the questions and thoughts from arising which have little to do with the creative moment, such as 'Did I say that right?' or 'I am not feeling anything.' Such questions remove you from the imaginative situation. Whilst performing all that is necessary is to be at ease in what you are actually doing and allow the situation to progress.

EXERCISE: WORKING WITH EASE

A way to experiment and practise ease is to take yourself through what it feels like to be in the opposite state, one of unease. This may sound counterproductive, but the first step towards making changes is to become conscious of the sensation. We all have our own version of what is uneasy. For me, it is to lock up in the joints and hold around my diaphragm.

Adopt a position which feels uncomfortable and hold this for 4 or 5 minutes. Observe what happens to your breath and the level of excitation in your muscles.

Michael Chekhov placed a great deal of emphasis on ease and preferred to use this term rather than 'relax'. He asked his actors to allow the body to let itself down, to open up to expansion and let go of the holding of muscles and tendons. The kind of relaxation that is beneficial to actors is not necessarily a total giving in or collapsing but rather an attentive dynamic, one where thoughts, feelings and sensations possess a readiness. This is the optimal state of the CNS when circulation is free and the communication networks are open.

Action

Action is when all the stages come together and there is a union that creates a deep somatic experience from which any creative options are possible. Through the positive extension of your breath and physical ease, there is a sensitivity to the needs of the situation rather that any imposition arising from your thoughts. A clarity about how far you need to extend in order to receive from the other actors and the timing of the action becomes instinctive. Extending outwards does not need to take you off balance, and imagining your energy reaching beyond you is a reminder to avoid holding or containing. With harmony comes a connection to the impulses that ebb and flow, and an automatic awareness of when it is the right time to do something.

Conclusion

This approach to training and preparation may appear simple and natural, but it is not necessarily instinctive. A good test for how much you feel connected to yourself is to stop and notice where the dominant activity is in your body. Where do you notice the sensations? I would make a fairly safe bet that often it is your head that dominates. Fully connecting to yourself needs daily practice, a time to identify tension and soften those places with your breath. The more frequent you make the journey inside, the more instinctive and automatic it will become to make instant somatic choices.

Chapter 10

WARM-UPS
Shifting the energy

Introduction

To some extent there are always rituals and routines attached to every job, and what you do to prepare is obviously dependent on your occupation. This process may involve thinking, gathering of thoughts or specific actions. A cook may wash their hands, put on whites or an apron, and clean surfaces, or an artisan may gather their tools and organise the area where they are about to work. Regardless of the job, the associated activity involves a combination of internal and external preparation, the balance of which is based on individual need and experience.

For an actor a warm-up is a journey of transition, which can clear the body of excess clutter to create an altered and focused state. It is a structured period when thoughts, or the residue of feelings and emotions from past events, can shift or be channelled to enhance the situation at hand. The process can enable you to move to a place where what happens moves through you, so you are able to receive and be open to receptively experiencing whatever arrives.

Let's consider this process of what scientist Mae Wan Ho would call 'inner organization'. The nervous system is the immediate target, and in particular the sympathetic nervous system which activates the more heightened activity in the body, such as overthinking. As we have observed, it also controls the natural functions, for example, heartbeat, heat and circulation, and physiological conditions which instigate feelings of stress, worry and emotions such as anger and fear. To bring more ease and harmony to the body, the parasympathetic nervous system needs to be prioritised.

There are some given functions of a warm-up such as:

- to heighten your focus on the work

- to bring ease to the body

- to distance yourself from unhelpful thoughts, feelings and emotions

- to balance all of the internal systems of the body.

The selection of what to do as a part of your warm-up depends on the activity on which you are about to embark. If you are going to perform, there will be a specific starting state you will need to shift into, and the journey will involve the transition from you to the needs of the imaginative situation. It requires a gradual narrowing of focus and an imaginative leap.

Key ingredients for a warm-up

The key ingredients for an effective warm-up are as follows:

- All the exercises should be specific and directed towards a goal.

- The order followed should support the body's natural physiological systems.

- It should ideally work to organise the internal energy network (see Chapter 7).

The focus of this warm-up is to connect with and organise your energy systems. (See Chapters 5 and 7 for further explanation.) There are many exercises and sequences that encourage your energy system to become more coherent, and these particular ones involve directing the flow of qi within the body so it moves freely in one direction. The purpose of this work is, overall, to calm the mind and body, sharpen concentration and focus, and enhance the capacity for sensation. Several of the exercises aim to direct the energy, and work to create a state of cohesion. The body can be thought of as a battery: the head is positively charged and the feet are negatively charged. Generally, upwards energy excites, and downwards energy, the natural and preferred direction of the body, calms and balances.

You can pick and choose the combination of exercises and the order in which you place them according to the needs of the scene.

EXERCISE: WU CHI

See Chapter 4 for the exercise steps.

EXERCISE: SETTLING YOUR BREATHING

1. Stand in wu chi position (see Figure 4.1).
2. Observe your breathing pattern.
3. Place your hands on your abdomen and inhale through the nose, and as you do, slightly sink, moving softly though your knees.
4. Exhale though your nose and slightly rise; allow this to be led by your abdomen.

EXERCISE: LOOSENING YOUR HEAD

There is usually a great deal of tightness in the face. To remove some of the constriction, consider the following questions:

1. Can you feel anything in the space between your ears?
2. Can you feel the distance between your eyes?
3. Can you feel the space across the jaw?
4. Touch the roof of your mouth with your tongue and notice the sensations. Slightly open your mouth so your jaw is open and rest your tongue on the bottom of your mouth. Imagine that it can spread right across your teeth.
5. Place the fingers of both hands on your forehead above your eyebrows; they need to be facing each other. Slowly pull your fingers apart.
6. Repeat the above routine on your scalp, working your way across your head.
7. Put your fingers on your temples, add some pressure and take a deep breath through your nose.
8. Run your fingers down along the back of your ears.

EXERCISE: QUIETENING THE MIND

1. Put your attention on your breathing.
2. Notice the length of your inhalation and exhalation.
3. Increase the length of the exhalation, if only for one beat.
4. Create an image for the chatter that may be going on in your head; this may be a throbbing ball of heat, or a pulsating insect, or a thunderstorm cloud.

5. Place this image in your feet.

6. As you inhale and exhale, imagine that the image is dissolving.

EXERCISE: CIRCLES OF ENERGY

1. Centre your breath.

2. Upon inhalation imagine that there are circles of energy moving down the front of your body all the way to your feet.

3. As you exhale the circles travel towards your head. This will help you to extend your breath and connect to the ground.

EXERCISE: FEELING INSIDE

1. Stand in wu chi position (see Figure 4.1) and close your eyes.

2. Place your attention on the area around your heart. Notice any sensations that arise.

3. Move your attention to your pelvis and see if you can detect a pulse around the plexus points (see Figure 8.3). Imagine the flow of fluids in your legs all the way to your toes.

4. Direct your breath to where you feel any tightness, and once you identify any restriction, don't stare at it – just recognise that it is there and use your breathing to dissolve any tightness.

5. Upon inhalation expand, and upon exhalation loosen and dissolve the knots.

EXERCISE: LOOSENING THE JOINTS

Loosening your joints encourages a more efficient chi flow. Changes in temperature are common due to the increase in access through potentially tight regions. To do this exercise, start with your feet and work your way up, moving the joints in a figure of eight in both directions. Include the following:

- ankles
- knees
- pelvis
- ribcage
- shoulders
- elbows
- wrists
- fingers.

Twisting your hands and feet is a good stimulant for the meridian channels (see Figure 7.1). Twisting your hands and tweaking your little finger, for example, will open up the heart channel and you may feel a connection along the arm to the chest, followed by an increase in heat.

EXERCISE: OPENING SPACES

Opening the spaces in your body is a way of releasing tight structures. The back in particular is an area where holding is common. The sequence is as follows:

1. Hug yourself.

2. Direct breath to your spine and allow your ribcage to expand, then twist from left to right.

3. Crouch down so you are in a frog position.

4. Drop your head and place your hands on the floor in front of you.

5. Breathe into your lumbar spine.

6. Sit cross-legged on the floor with your knees dropping down and weight on your sitting bones.

7. Fold your body forwards and place your elbows onto the floor. This will open up the whole of your back.

Conclusion

Warm-ups not only ease the body and, in the case of strenuous work, prevent injury, but are also opportunities to enhance receptivity and channel focus. They provide you with a period to gather and direct the whole self towards the given circumstances and to enable the preparation you have done to shift into action. I often hear actors say that they seemed unable to allow the hours of prep to have an impact and that they did not access the emotional depth which they may have experienced in rehearsals. In such instances it could be that the warm-up or lack of one was not tailored to the needs of the scene. An athlete needs to guide their body and tune it for the important events, and a performance is the same for an actor. When filming, the schedules are usually such that there is no time for a warm-up, but if you have kept your body alive and receptive through snatches of time when you can be alone, or even channelled your mind when in the make-up chair, or on the walk to the set, there will be an impact on what is felt and received.

Chapter 11

BEING PRESENT
Living in the now

Introduction

Where we place our attention continually shifts: in a fraction of a second a sound, smell, visual cue or thought can capture or distance you from the action in hand. Many activities do not require the total focus of all your faculties, and we are all able to undertake most everyday actions, such as driving, walking, washing and eating, without having to fully focus on the task. Although we may be conscious of doing an action, it could be that it does not require the level of focus which is alert, and this creates the impression that we are capable of doing more than one thing at once. We are, in fact, only able to attend to one activity at a time, the length of which could differ from a millisecond to minutes. Often we time-travel, visiting the past and the future with the present seeming fleeting. Being present appears to require a heightened consciousness that is different from the norm. It also needs synchronisation, a command of all of our faculties, which together determine how you are able to concentrate.

For the actor, being present is important on many levels. Primarily it:

- heightens the senses

- brings active responses

- moves the action forwards

- stimulates feelings and emotions

- creates a strong presence.

Becoming more present

To become more present you need to develop an acute ability to be able to tune out what is not relevant and select the information that is. Being able to stay with the present and not cling to the past or race ahead into future possibilities also provides the space to be spontaneous. It proffers natural performances, as in the present you truly do not know what is coming next. Being able to notice and relish what is happening to you in each second is exciting; it's like being on a dangerous fairground ride: the levels of excitement are high and you are fully alert. It is useful to remember that the level of attention you give to any activity is a matter of choice. The more you are able to recognise and stay with internal changes, the more present you will be.

The following exercises are designed to increase bodily awareness and cultivate a state of readiness.

It is useful to begin by noticing how you are in your own environment and what changes when you are in more public or performance situations. Recognising the correlation between presence and energy is also vital, as being present is like being on the starting block: everything is firing and ready to go.

EXERCISE: TUNING IN

Begin this exercise by generally becoming aware of the following:

- the speed of your thoughts
- how you feel
- the quality of the sensations in your body
- which parts of your body you sense the most
- your flow of breath
- how much you move
- the movement of your attention to the past, present or future
- what you look at in your surroundings
- how observant you are of other people
- which senses you prioritise
- how you invest energetically in activities.

The next step involves directing your attention. Diverting and directing your attention is something that you can train yourself to do. The following is a start:

1. Make detailed observations about the person you are talking to, such as their breath, the energy in their eyes, the shifts of their attention, the gestures they use, their overall vibrancy, their patterns of speech, how responsive they are to you and the feelings which emanate from them.

2. Listen to what is being said and register how it affects you.

3. Be inquisitive and curious about the environment, as if you are seeing things for the first time.

4. Tune in to the continual shifts in your body and how they change. Notice the impulses that arise; this could be the need to move away, get closer or change the subject.

5. Observe whether you follow the impulses or stifle them.

EXERCISE: BREATHING CYCLE

Your breathing is crucial to how present and at ease you are. The rhythm of your breathing will reveal how you feel in any situation – that is, it will express comfort or 'dis-ease'. By witnessing your breathing, you may choose to change the flow, potentially extending and deepening.

If you become aware that your breathing is shallow or held, breathe in and out through your nose allowing any tightness to fall away upon exhalation.

EXERCISE: TIME FRAME

It is a myth that we have the ability to concentrate on two or three things at once; hence, the danger of texting whilst driving, as even if it's for a split second, only one of the activities will have your attention. So it is with time: you are always more present to either the past, present or future. More often than not, the past or the future are where we reside, passing through the present as if on the way to somewhere, and in so doing we miss the moment. Reliving what has happened or rehearsing what may happen is usual for most of us, and being present is something that needs attention and, to some extent, training. The action is in the present; it is potentially where we are most alert and responsive.

There are two potential reasons for identifying the time frame:

•   Being more present to the now will enable you to be responsive and spontaneous. By accepting whatever is happening to you in terms of feeling and emotions, you are able to make changes and adapt.

•   The character will always be in either the past, present or future. This observation is crucial to what they do and how they relate to other characters.

Working with yourself

When you are finding it difficult to concentrate, or when you are about to do a presentation or speak in public, notice how you move in and out of time frames. To stay present become observant about your surroundings, work with the cycle of your breath and be specific about where you place your attention. Engage with what is in front of you.

Working with the text

Go through your scene and recognise the time frame through what the character says. Once you have done this, notice what this observation does to your attention and energy. There is a clear distinction between the energy of a memory and that of a present observation.

EXERCISE: LETTING GO

Living in the present usually means letting go of time-travelling, forwards or backwards. Judgements, expectations and concerns can sabotage the potential to fully experience the moment of exchange. Letting go is to surrender to possibilities, to clear away any obstructions and experience what comes. In Chapter 7 we talked about getting out of your own way, and one of the fundamental issues is not releasing personal thoughts that interfere with the ability to be present.

If you find it difficult to surrender to an exercise or a scene, it is valuable to reflect on what is getting in the way, of what you need to let go, such as:

- feeling insecure and unconfident
- planning what will happen in the scene
- worrying about your performance being judged negatively
- wanting success
- wanting to 'get things right'.

Surrendering to the present will allow it to *take care of itself*. If you have prepared your work, letting go will allow the preparation to automatically take over.

EXERCISE: WU CHI

See Chapter 4 for the exercise steps.

EXERCISE: SOFTENING YOUR JOINTS

The softer and more open your joints are, the more energetically connected you will be. Ease brings a more enhanced qi flow. Do this exercise in the following way:

1. Stand with your legs hip width apart. Travel up through your body starting with your ankles and soften your joints by simply placing your attention on the selected area. Imagine that the joints are made of sponge or cotton wool. Notice your knees, pelvis, shoulders, elbows, fingers and jaw.

2. Feel each part of your feet on the floor. Move your weight around the edges, then onto your heels and the balls.

3. Inhale as if you are breathing in from the balls of your feet and breathing out through your palms. As you do this, continue to soften your joints.

EXERCISE: GATHERING CHI

Reaching a coherent-flow state is important to presence. It stabilises the central nervous system, thoughts, feelings and emotions, and will encourage your body to be alert and operate harmoniously. To that end, follow these steps:

1. Stand in wu chi position (see Figure 4.1).

2. Place your hands in front of your lower dantien with your palms facing towards your body.

3. Inhale through your nose, sinking from the dantien as you do so. Turn your palms outwards and push them sideways for as long as you can inhale.

4. As you exhale through your mouth, turn your palms to face each other and return to the front of your dantien, which rises as you do so.

EXERCISE: ENERGETIC BUBBLES

This exercise is based on Stanislavsky's 'circles of concentration'. The aim is to explore the relationship between where you place your energy and being present to your situation. Imagine that there are three bubbles which vary in size that surround your whole body. The expanse of the bubble will determine how far you direct your energy and if it has an inwards or outwards direction, as follows:

- Intimate

  The first bubble is approximately 1 or 2 inches off your body. I call this intimate; the direction of your energy is inwards and does not radiate too far outwards. This is likely to include moments of reflection, memories, times when you need to recall a past event, as well as deep and complex thoughts connected to wants, regrets and ambitions.

- Personal

  The second bubble can include one or two other people. I call this personal, conversations which may be intense or any exchange which requires a focused level of interaction. In fact, most dialogue-based scenes are predominately at this level.

- Social

  The third bubble covers a space which can include anything from a dining table of eight people to a whole room or conference centre. I call this social. Your energy in this instance is wide and expansive. Giving speeches and public addresses, teaching a group, conducting a ceremony and so forth are all examples of when it would be instinctive to communicate in the social energetic circle.

When you communicate under usual circumstances you may not be aware of how you direct your energy – you just do it. This exercise demonstrates that we naturally make energetic shifts, a little like the aperture of a camera. This is sometimes forgotten in an acting context, so it is good to practise. The three places also enable you to have subtle differences in where you place your attention at any moment. Do this exercise as follows:

1. Using a piece of text, experiment with performing all of the scene using the social circle.

2. Repeat the above instruction but change to the personal circle.

3. Repeat the above and adopt the energy of the intimate circle.

4. Reflect on how that felt and which moment seems to suit which circle.

5. Work through the scene finding the appropriate energetic circle.

Conclusion

Staying present needs practice as the lure of memories or future possibilities is a permanent hook. To recognise and accept how you react to the circumstances in which you find yourself is key to being momentarily alert. As in life, when performing, choices are best made instantaneously rather than having been over-planned. It is inevitable that your thoughts and feelings will be different from those you identified when preparing or rehearsing a scene, so instead of trying to capture those identical feelings, work from where you are – the present – and with it will come new choices.

Chapter 12

DISCOVERING ACTION
Working beyond the words

Introduction

If you tune in to your internal life, you will notice how much physiological activity there is: your heartbeat, breathing, heat changes and many thoughts. As we have discussed, a great deal of this is automatic – it just happens – but it is affected by external stimuli such as temperature, light and all that is in the environment. When acting, we are working with conscious thought, as the verbal text is provided, and even the subtext, which in real life could be unconscious, is conscious. There is therefore initially, especially early in the rehearsal process, a high level of control over the action. During the stages of preparation, there is usually a gradual reduction of attentive control, which will only occur once the material has passed into the realm of the automatic. To do this, as with learning a piece of music, there needs to be repetition. The musician is only free to create their interpretation of a piece when they fully know it; then it can emerge spontaneously.

Thoughts depend on what has been done before, what is known and encoded through experience. There is always an enormous amount of material from which to select. If we consider an actor recalling lines, the thoughts need to be precise so the focus is on what the character is thinking.

Thought becomes an action when it requires sorting something out and involves an internal discussion, as opposed to those thoughts which are automatic such as reaching for a glass of water or closing a door. Such movements have not arisen from a complex chain of mental events. They are automatically embedded into a learned behaviour, as are the routines which we have accumulated.

It seems to me there are four potential dilemmas for actors with regard to action:

- There is not enough action.

- There is too much action.

- The action does not belong to the circumstances and is creatively uninspiring.

- The action does not emerge from a driving need and, as a result, is not embodied; it is heightened and performative.

I find that it is common, certainly in training actors, for action not to be attached to or motivated by a central need or intention; or for there to be a confusion concerning the reason for, and the feelings about, the action. What emerges in such instances are empty gestures like arm waving or folding – general clutter. So how can you overcome any of the dilemmas listed above?

Intention becomes the crucial factor in action and instigates a decision. It drives what is often referred to as external action, that which is visibly done to yourself, someone or something.

There seem to be different kinds of action:

- internal action

- personal responses which may be unconscious such as fiddling with hair or playing with a napkin or a pen

- literal action which could be written in the text as a direction (e.g. she reads, she chops and so forth)

- conversing and listening.

As an actor you will be considering all of these categories. The key point to ponder is sticking to what your character would do, which is not necessarily what *you* would do.

Things to do to help with finding a character's action

Here are some tips to help you find a character's action:

- Determine what action is automatic for your character (smoking is an example) and how you can create this.

- Provide your character with knowledge and memories. (To do that, you must know their lives and behaviour.)

- Integrate the practice of what they do into your routine to enable the behaviour to look automatic rather than performed.

Fill your work with depth, which implies that internal actions such as memories, recollections, plans and questions are as vital as action which involves the movement of the whole body. Seeing your character as someone who has many aspects – all the light and dark sides of behaviour – is important. Although the text provides you with the key information, there are additions which you can supply. Having a future ambition alive in the body is a kind of action. My suggestion is to invest beyond what you read. The more facets you interrogate, the more fascinating and distinct the characters you develop will be. You are not one-dimensional; each of us has beautifully intricate ways of being, and your work should also show such complexity.

The following set of exercises are designed to start your process of discovery.

EXERCISE: TRAVELLING INSIDE

Spend some time each day to become acquainted with the activity inside your body, as this will enable you to become familiar with your rhythm and the patterns of your inner action. To this end, try the following exercise:

1. Stand in wu chi position (see Figure 4.1).

2. Take your attention to the expanse of your breathing and observe the rise and fall of your body.

3. Notice any sensations of heat, pulsations or tingles.

4. Observe the speed of your thought processes.

5. Follow your thoughts and see how they change and build. Do images emerge, and if so, do they inspire a need to take action? Are there any strong impulses to speak or act?

EXERCISE: DIRECTIONS OF MOVEMENT

There are six potential planes of movement: up, down, forward, back, left, right. The direction in which you move corresponds to your need in the moment. In one instance you may need to reject, so you move back; in another you may need to embrace an idea, so you move forward. Here is a short process that will help to action a scene and sharpen your objectives:

1. Start by moving in each of the six directions.

2. Speak the first line of the script and feel what you need to do. Is it to assert yourself, in which case you may sink your weight? Or do you need to avoid conflict, in which case you may shift from side to side?

3. Progress through the scene and experiment with moving. Before you speak in response to the text, register the direction of the urge – this may be to move back, move forward or drop down. Feel rather than overthink.

4. To take this a stage further, refrain from moving until you feel the need inwardly. This tends to cultivate your felt senses.

EXERCISE: THREE LISTS

Try the following exercise:

1. Draw up a list with three headings: You, The character, The differences. Write everything that you share in the You and the Character columns. This may include if you both have siblings, can speak a specific language, enjoy a certain type of music, have fallen in love before, feel strongly about freedom of speech, lose your temper quickly, live in a city, own a pet and so forth. Be as specific as you can.

2. In the Differences column write anything your character is or does which you do not share, such as class, education, occupation; reflect on their attitudes, morals, how they communicate with others and so forth.

3. Initially focus on the Differences column and start your interrogation in those areas. If your character was orphaned as a child or has been to prison, or attended public school or worked as a scientist, gather some insight through experience or interviews, and reading, to collate a background profile. If you have identified a set of emotional responses which are new to you, such as happy and optimistic or sad and pessimistic, identify the quality and energetic force attached to this.

4. Using the columns of shared experiences, explore how you may differ in rhythm and qualities from your character; for example, they may explode when they lose their temper, and you may simmer.

EXERCISE: AMBITIONS

Personal ambitions are often unconsciously present in how you behave. They feature in our dreams and fantasies and often creep into the image we create of ourselves. Depending on how absorbed we are with the goal, we invent physical attributes and gestures as well as adopt hobbies and lifestyles which may get us closer to making what we want a reality. In an interview at Royal Central School of Speech and Drama on her work with the director Mike Leigh, Alison Steadman commented on how she has used the ambitions of the character to help to shape ideas for mannerisms, physicality and overall personality traits. She used the example of Beverly in *Abigail's Party*, who she decided wanted to be a model. This one choice brought ideas for how the character walked and gestured, her interests and how she wanted to be perceived. It took her to the make-up counters at high-end department stores, to looking through catalogues, to observing catwalks.

Decide on a driving ambition. Be specific about the character's choices; for example, if they want to be a singer or musician, what type? Who would be their idols? What is the set of behaviours associated with this person?

EXERCISE: OPPOSITES

This exercise explores a way of finding the opposite sides to your character:

1. Using the list of polarities given in Chapter 7, select a dominant attribute (a good one; e.g. your character may be generous, optimistic, kind, soft, loving, caring).

2. Focus on the polar opposite (a bad characteristic) and see when this could influence their behaviour. It may just surface in a thought, before they smile or instigate a series of actions.

3. Select a section of text to explore that reveals various opposite traits, emotions and rhythms.

Conclusion

Action will come from surrendering to the situation, absorbing the given circumstances and really listening. Being active is crucial, not just in thought but to how you feel and what urges are triggered. There is no real distinction between outer and inner action; they are intertwined and stimulate each other. So if someone touches you on the face, this will instigate internal messages and associations which are active. For actors the dilemma emerges when there is not enough investigation into the givens and if the personal (e.g. tightening of muscles, sweats, thoughts which are of no consequence) interferes with the imaginative which results in unrelated action. Finding the right action is therefore a matter of knowing the circumstances as well as being active and receptive to what is in front of you.

Chapter 13

THOUGHT TRACK
Developing an inner monologue

Introduction

This chapter presents several approaches to discovering what is usually known as the inner monologue. The aim of these exercises is to discover subtext, in particular to explore if there are any thoughts other than what is actually spoken. To manifest the full impact of the given circumstances it is beneficial to look beyond the words, to the effect the past has on the present, the memories and events leading to the now which provide the backdrop to what is spoken. I call this work 'thought track' because the thoughts, feelings and emotions have a trail – that is, they are part of a string of events which lead to the origins of what is spoken.

Thoughts can come in various forms such as impressions, concepts, ideas, opinions, images, memories, perceptions, reflections and associations. Conscious thought is when we are aware of what is current and momentarily active, and there is also a wealth of 'unconscious interferences' which feed what comes to mind, some of which becomes part of our awareness. All in all, there is a lot going on surrounding what we commonly call 'thoughts'.

When a thought is tracked, it is as if there is a thread which contains the history and associations. This is especially the case with more complex ideas which have considerable stakes or implications connected to a situation. Thoughts leave deposits which have consequences for emotional and felt senses. The various kinds of thoughts leave different impressions, and although most may be short-lived and related to what we see or encounter, others may hang around and repeatedly crop up like an interference on a radio broadcast.

Thoughts can rise and fall, flash up as if from nowhere, float up and dissolve; they have a rhythm unique to each individual and the circumstances in which one may be. They are composed of knowledge, judgements, facts, fantasies, beliefs, reasoning, imagining – everything that passes though the brain engages the senses and then triggers a response to the rest of the body.

It is an assumption to consider thoughts as being exclusively words and images of what we have experienced which form a large part of the thought process. According to the need and value of what is experienced, you may search, interrogate, investigate, reflect or hunt for additional data.

The words therefore are the tip of the iceberg as the undercurrent consists of constant murmurings which allow us to make sense of the world and interpret our experiences according to needs, attachments, objectives, plans and priorities.

A dramatic script is composed of the verbalisation of characters according to needs, an organised slice of what characters express. It contains the essence of the situation and conflict, and structures the thoughts, but it does not contain *all* of the thoughts. It would be impossible to put into words everything we think and feel at any given time. The text would look like a maze of confusion.

Creating a thought track is similar to devising an inner monologue but with some additions. You are filling in all the mental and physical reactions which are not voiced but registered and relevant to the imaginative situation. You are also noticing the constant murmurs which hang around in the back of the mind and refuse to fade, as well as the short-lived discrete events of passing thoughts.

EXERCISE: A PROCESS OF WORKING BELOW THE SURFACE OF A SCENE

The following exercise can be applied to any text. The words represent the bare bones of the story. This is a process to begin to identify some of the layers behind what is spoken and to put something behind the text:

1. Speaking in the first person, give an account of the character's action in the scene moment by moment. Cover every beat, detail and observation.

2. Engage in a 'thought riff' (a musical term but here you are following your thoughts and just speaking what rolls off the tongue). It's a little like jazz improvisation. You speak the text and anything else that arises.

3. Answer the following questions:

   • What do you think about the other person(s) in the scene?

   • What do you know?

   • What do you believe?

   • What do you fear?

   • For what do you hope?

   • What does it feel like to be in the presence of the other people?

4. Consider what your character is searching to say. Do they have many thoughts, questions or statements which are on the tip of their tongue? Go through the structure of the scene and speak aloud what you do not say.

5. Go through the text and consider the types of thought (e.g. reflections, plans, daydreams, questions and so forth). Register if each thought is in the past, present or future.

Text work

The following exercises refer to a scene which is taken from the BBC programme *The White Queen*.[1] To provide some context, here is some fundamental information about the scene:

• Elizabeth Woodville is from the House of Lancaster.

• Anthony Woodville is her brother.

• Edward IV is the King of England and is from the House of York.

This scene is in 1464 and is set against the backdrop of the Wars of the Roses (1455–1485), a conflict over the right to the throne of England. Elizabeth is a widow with two small children, and her husband died in battle fighting to put a Lancastrian on the throne. She temporarily lives with her parents, children and siblings in the country. Anthony, along with her father, has also been fighting for the same cause. Since her husband's death, Elizabeth fears for the future of her children and believes a prophecy that she will one day be queen. When she hears

---

1   This scene has been reproduced with permission of Emma Frost and Company Television, Ltd. (Note: The formatting has been altered.)

that the young King Edward will be passing through land close to her home, she waits beside the road and catches his attention.

They meet, fall in love and secretly marry within a few days of meeting. Anthony is very suspicious of the king and feels his sister has been tricked into bed. He is confident that the marriage is not valid and that Elizabeth will be abandoned.

When the scene starts, it is the day after the wedding night. Elizabeth has just said goodbye to the king, who is about to go into battle. Anthony has been watching and waits to confront his sister. (Note: The asterisks are mine and indicate, in the main transition moments, a significant emotional change or turning point in the action.)

ANTHONY

You whore.

ELIZABETH jumps as ANTHONY steps from the shade.

ANTHONY (cont'd)

You have shamed our house and our name. And your dead husband who gave his life fighting that usurper.

ELIZABETH

No, Anthony.*

ANTHONY

Don't touch me.

She's shocked as he swats her away.

ELIZABETH

It isn't what you think!

ANTHONY

What? My eyes deceive me? This is an 'honorable' coupling.

ELIZABETH

This is honorable!*

Furious, she thrusts her left fist towards him. Then he sees the ring.

ELIZABETH (cont'd)

We are married!

ELIZABETH is triumphant. ANTHONY stares at the ring —
then crumples with sadness.

> ANTHONY
>
> Oh dear God, Elizabeth…he's fooled you.*

> ELIZABETH
>
> What?

> ANTHONY
>
> Oh my poor, dear sister…

ELIZABETH's POV.

> ANTHONY (cont'd)
>
> Let me guess, a secret wedding in our chapel? None
> of his family attended, Lord Warwick must not be
> told?

> ELIZABETH
>
> For now, but —

> ANTHONY
>
> Elizabeth think. This is a man who is King of
> England. He will marry a princess, not some
> commoner from the camp of his enemy he found
> begging by the roadside!

> ELIZABETH
>
> He is married to me now!

> ANTHONY
>
> (hates to hurt her but)
> You are not married, Elizabeth. You've been tricked.
> It was a pretend service.*

> ELIZABETH
>
> There were witnesses.

> ANTHONY
>
> Who?

> ELIZABETH
>
> Mother!
> (off his look, triumphant)
> And a priest!

ANTHONY

Which priest?

ELIZABETH

I… I don't know.

ANTHONY

He's tricked you with a pretend priest to get you into
bed. He's done it before and he has a bastard son.
(ELIZABETH reels.)
He is Warwick's puppet, Elizabeth.
Without him Edward could never have claimed the
throne. Warwick is the Kingmaker, and you can be
very sure he will make the Queen as well.

ELIZABETH

You are wrong. Edward is King! He does not have to
do what Warwick tells him.*
(but she's tearful)
You are wrong!

But her protests are so loud because she fears he is right.

EXERCISE: SURVEYING THE SCENE

Having read the scene a few times, make a list of points which could affect
the character prior to the start of and during the scene. There are essentially
two elements: what your character is reacting to in their immediate or
distant past and what is happening in the present. This could translate into
images, memories, questions, conversations, observations of the immediate
environment, the reactions of the other people in the scene and so forth.

Here is an example using the character of Elizabeth and what she could
bring into the scene from her immediate past:

- sadness of her husband going to war

- memories of her wedding and the time she has spent with Edward

- images of the future life she may share with her husband.

As Edward has just left for battle, there may fleeting images of her dead
husband on the battlefield, her father fighting for the Lancastrians, Edward in
battle and the possible consequences.

This is what Elizabeth could bring into the scene from her present:

- what she sees, hears and/or smells such as the woods, fields, sky and
so forth

- the last words Edward said to her
- fading sounds of the army moving away
- the voice of her brother
- questioning what Anthony is doing there, how long he has been watching her, what he has seen and why he is being so abrupt.

To give the scene some context there is always information which forms the starting state and gives direction to where attention is focused. The above work provides the foundation layer from which to start.

EXERCISE: FILLING THE TRANSITION MOMENTS

Do the following to fill the transition moments:

1. Identify the main transition moments in the scene where there is a significant emotional change or turning point in the action (see asterisks above). In these moments there is likely to be a busier thought track. These moments could be realisations, and have strong emotional consequences, or when a decision is made. The implication is that feelings and emotions heighten, a result of the stakes. An example is when Elizabeth first takes Anthony's accusations seriously:

ANTHONY

Oh dear God, Elizabeth…he's fooled you.

ELIZABETH

What?

ANTHONY

Oh my poor, dear sister…

Her thought track could take her in many directions and consists of questions and realisations such as: Is it possible for Edward to trick me? No, he said he loved me. He told me not to tell anyone. Why did he say that?

2. Take the transition moments and write or improvise possible questions, statements or facts she may be thinking.

3. Create the possible visual images which may arise for the character. This could be a memory from the past or future.

EXERCISE: DESCRIBING THE PICTURE

Either to yourself or someone else, describe the scene as if it was a still picture; this could include the location, what the people around you look like, the objects, the colours, textures and the spatial dimensions. Any aspect of this visual picture could appear in your thought track.

EXERCISE: SPEAKING OUT LOUD

Speak all your thoughts out loud, including what is spoken but also the transition thoughts and observations between the lines. Make the journey from the spoken text to the next line, making sense of how the text has arisen in terms of the connecting thoughts.

EXERCISE: OBSERVING THE RHYTHM OF THOUGHTS

Each thought will have a specific quality which is linked to the character's immediate need. In a situation where a character needs to come up with a solution they may *thrash* out some idea. If they question their actions to someone, they may *beat* themselves up.

Select a quality for the exchange, noting when this changes, which will affect the tempo and feel of the dialogue.

EXERCISE: STORYBOARD

Create a series of pictures that accompany your thoughts as if they were a single shot from a film, showing the angles and perspectives of what you see.

Conclusion

A script needs to be excavated in order for the potential layers to be accessed and for you to add your own creative slant. The rigour is a discipline which will proffer rich rewards and come more automatically with practice and experimentation. There are many approaches, and it is my suggestion that you find the process that suits the role, but change things up from time to time and welcome new ways.

Chapter 14

INTERROGATING SIGNIFICANT MOMENTS OF ACTION
Finding the shifts

Introduction

A text is composed of moments of action, each of which takes the character on a journey. Regardless of the length of a scene, there will be instances that are more significant than others, which instigate emotional shifts when the character is taken closer to or further away from their goal.

As we noted in Part 1, nothing remains static inside the body; it is a changing landscape which actively responds to some stimulus or other, be that hearing a noise, stepping into the rain, being told that a friend has died, deciding to leave a job and so forth. Identifying these larger, more significant moments provides markers in the story, turning points.

Here are a series of exercises that focus on identifying these transition points. The overall approach is to be sensitive to the felt senses and tune in to the changes. A significant shift can feel like you are losing command of time, as if things are speeding up or slowing down, when more is packed into what could be only a few seconds. More questions are posed, sharp images flash by, conversations are recalled, emotions flood back and the body is searching for past events that make sense of the present. This tells us that these peaks need attention, to be filled with past memories and future consequences.

EXERCISE: CHARTING THE ENERGETIC MOVEMENT OF A SCENE

Do this exercise as follows:

1. In pairs, speak your text and pass a tennis ball between you. Allow the pace and rhythm to reflect the mood of what is being spoken.

2. Repeat the above but focus on the level of force you apply to the action. Notice how this changes from moment to moment; on some lines you may automatically pass the ball with increased velocity.

3. Repeat and focus on what you want to do to the other person. You may want to provoke them, which may mean you dash the ball at them, or flirt, so a softer and lighter quality may be applied.

4. Identify any moments when it feels like more is happening when the pace and emotions build. The transition points tend to be those where the bigger questions are posed, decisions are made and realisations felt. By attending to the rhythm of the scene, it is easier to discover them.

EXERCISE: PUTTING SOMETHING BEHIND A MOMENT

There is always a lot more going on than what is actually spoken. To identify and create some of these potential murmurings, pose some questions around your text. You will find that particularly at significant moments your thoughts are more active. The questions you ask yourself may be:

*   How do I feel about the person to whom I am speaking?

*   What do I want to say to them?

*   Why am I saying these particular words?

*   If I could say what I feel, what would I say?

*   What have they done in the past to create the reaction I currently feel?

*   What do I like or dislike about the person(s) in my company?

*   What would I rather be doing right now?

When you can stop posing the questions, then you may have investigated the moment. The answers are actively dancing around inside you and will stimulate other reactions and feelings.

EXERCISE: CREATING IMAGES

Once you have recognised the key moments, it is useful to work with images. Pictures of the events leading up to the moment, memories, related incidents or what you would like to achieve are good starting points. Then do the following:

- Speak the text and see what pictures arise; this may be the other character, the setting, specific objects and so forth.

- Speak the text again and begin to add sensory possibilities around the images that arise by reflecting on the colours, sounds, smells and textures.

- Watch the scene being played out as if you are watching it on a big screen. Notice how the characters move and interact. Focus on the moments you have identified as the significant shifts, and notice what the characters do.

- Rerun the scene and create several alternative versions. This will offer options of how to play the scene.

EXERCISE: JEWEL MOMENTS

Michael Chekhov used the term 'jewel moments' or 'jewellery' to describe the potential instances in the text that can be elevated. The moment could be a turning point in the journey of the scene, or it may reveal a clue about the character's feelings or desires which are not verbally expressed. Jewel moments are integrated fully into the stream of action but may have distinct qualities and could be marked by time, rhythm and structure in that there is a beginning, middle and end to the action.

I use Chekhov's idea to define movement and to explore how objects can be used to contribute to the story. This is especially good on screen when the camera may be drawn to a subtle and specific action an actor is doing with, say, their hands, eyes or feet:

1. Select a section in the scene which you identify as a transition point.

2. Find a personal prop that is appropriate for the moment. You may be about to smoke a cigarette, or blow your nose, or sniff into a handkerchief, or there could be an action that is mentioned in the scene such as reading or eating. Whilst working through the moment, experiment with how you use the prop, gradually allowing it to express how you are feeling. If there is a moment of frustration, maybe you will hurl the object or twist it till it breaks.

3. Discover a beginning, middle and end to your action. The beginning reflects your objective; once this bubbles inside, infuse the object with how you are feeling and take this into action. The climatic point, the middle, would express the want in action. End with a clear moment when you sustain it, which may indicate if you have reached your objective or are about to try another tactic.

4. Continue to work with the tempo of the action until it appears slightly suspended as a moment of action before you move on to the next moment.

EXERCISE: VITALITY OF THE MOMENT

This exercise helps to access and stimulate feelings through imagining and activating the dynamic quality of the action:

1. Select an image that focuses on the feelings that go with a transition moment, such as *It is like...*

   - getting pushed out of a plane

   - being slapped in the face

   - being squeezed till there is no air left inside

   - having all your blood drained away

   - being torn apart

   - being pulled in four directions

   - swallowing shards of glass

   - getting punched in the stomach

   - being crushed by a boulder

   - walking on glass or thin ice or hot coals.

Now do the following:

2. Close your eyes and place the image inside your body.

3. Create a sequence of movement which expresses the image. Consider the tempo, direction, force and quality. Start the movement internally – that is, this action may not be visible. Observe what happens to your breathing, as it will change as you continue with the sequence.

4. Allow the movement to inform outer action; for example, a twisting shape may result in your legs being wrapped around each other. Being pulled apart may result is your limbs appearing disjointed. You do not have to exaggerate the posture; just allow it to emerge.

EXERCISE: BEATS OF ACTION

A text is composed of a sequence of many beats, some of which last longer than others. A beat can be a thought or a moment between spoken text. When you first encounter a text, there may be a tendency for beats to glide into each other without full recognition of the changes. This tends to lead to generalisations and missed opportunities for detail and subtleties.

Try doing the following sequence:

1. Read your text, noting the changes in thought, reaction, literal action and behaviour.

2. Read your text out loud and have a brief pause at the end of each thought.

3. Identify whether or not there is another thought before you speak the next line. (If there *is* another thought, it is a beat. There may be a few thoughts between each line. They are connecting thoughts, like links.)

4. Decide which thoughts are more loaded, when there is more at stake. These thoughts require attention. They travel and therefore could also have more beats.

To clarify, a beat is not a unit; a unit may have many beats. Working through beats is really important in finding the detail of the text. It also tells you where the character's attention is in any moment. I compare this process to a musical score, where clearly the notes keep changing to create the overall piece. Actors sometimes rush through or fail to identify the possibilities behind the thoughts.

EXERCISE: SHAKE THE LINES OUT

This exercise is a way of engaging your whole body:

1. Stand in wu chi position (see Figure 4.1).

2. Start a gentle shake from your feet. All of your body should be involved in the action.

3. Begin to speak your text, allowing the quality and speed of the shake to alter according to what is being said. It may become more vigorous as the exchange gets heated, or it may change in tempo with each thought.

4. Reflect on the parts of the text you felt the need to change in force or if the movement encouraged stronger feelings. These are likely to be the transition points.

Conclusion

These are a few ways of noticing how a scene moves and changes. It is certain that no character feels the same at the end of the scene as they did at the start. Recognising the shifts often requires investigation as some are not obvious; they are a way of creating a journey and finding detail. As key moments represent emotional changes, feeling your way through the scene is the best way to detect them.

Chapter 15

OBSERVATIONAL STUDIES
Looking for detail

Introduction

Observing yourself and other people in real-life situations is very valuable and, in some instances, is an essential tool. One of the aims of observing is to bring an accuracy and precision to the playing of an action, to make it authentic: to create an embodied ease which comes automatically so you are familiar with what you are doing. Using smoking as an example, it is often easy to spot the awkwardness of a non-smoker attempting to enjoy holding a cigarette or blowing smoke circles from their mouth. If you have been doing something for a number of years, you will have your own ritual attached, which will include how you hold the object, the length of time given to each stage and the quality of the action; it will all be effortless.

One of the challenges and exciting aspects of acting is that you are likely to encounter actions that are new to you, that you need to make look real. The occupation of a character is one such consideration, as habitual patterns and routines are affected and shaped by how you earn your living. The demands have a physical impact on the condition and composition of a body. A trained chef handles food in a very specific way, as there is a dynamic and tempo attached to every action. The hands of a manual labourer have been shaped by the repetition of lifting, digging and heaving heavy loads.

What you spend your time doing will imply status, class, education, morality and so forth. There are also social and cultural associations attached: a doctor is often viewed as intelligent, capable, heroic; an artist possibly hedonistic, unpredictable, rule-breaking; a teacher bossy, ordered, powerful. These perceptions will affect behaviour, gait and minute gestures.

Observation also inspires creative options. It's useful to become a collector of sequences and watch how different people flavour their actions with intricate details. This may include walks, gestures with the hands, feet, lips or eyes, or the enactment of specific tasks like holding a fork, making a bed, taking off a coat and so forth. It also potentially extends movement vocabulary and enriches your own physical range, extending your emotional and imaginative expression, and brings depth to your work.

For what are you looking?

Once you begin to observe other people, it is fascinating to see just how differently we all move and what particular shapes and structural forms reveal about an individual. When specifically observing, it's good to know what you are looking for, such as:

- how people behave in a specific environment; this could be a workplace, home or social context

- the language used by the individuals being studied such as specific phrases, jargon, formal or informal speech, the rhythm, tone, clarity of speech, particular etiquette and so forth

- body action, including weight transference, centre, balance, qualities of movement, the direction of energy and spatial use

- rituals and rites, routines and habits.

EXERCISE: BODY PARTS

Choose different locations, such as your work environment, a cafe, a bar, the train station or the street, and observe the following:

- walking

- facial expressions

- hands and feet

- gestures with the head.

Pay attention to the distribution of weight through the feet and body, the level of force in actions and gestures, the overall rhythm of movement. Once you have made your observations, spend some time physically doing the actions, exploring how they feel different from how you use your own body. It is most productive to adopt the observed movements for a sustained period to really assess how affected your body is. It is likely that sensations, feelings and emotions will change, bringing either ease or discomfort. Breathing is usually immediately altered by even the smallest change in body structure, and this provides real insight into inner functioning as thoughts and breathing are intrinsically linked.

Observing situations

As a means of sharpening your observation skills, pick a theme to study and visit the appropriate locations to gather a range of observations. Possible themes are:

- departures

- greetings

- couples in restaurants

- smokers outside of bars

- sports fans watching a game

- entering into rooms.

Notice sequences and rituals associated with the scenarios, the cultural differences in terms of touch, expression and spatial use, as well as gender and gesture. Do men greet people differently than women? What does their entrance into a public space say about an individual?

Practise changing how you greet or say goodbye to people. Deliberately use your body in a new way and observe how you are received by others.

Routines

Observe any particular routines that are attached to the occupation of your character, such as:

- a teacher preparing for a class

- a chef chopping up vegetables

- a hairdresser drying hair

- a priest giving communion

- a carpenter cutting or chopping wood.

Whatever skills you are required to undertake, it is inevitable that practice is required. Make a list of activities that your character can do well and integrate this into your own routine. Experiment with how the actions are executed, considering tempo, space, rhythm and the movement quality.

Rituals

Rituals are a significant part of social and political structure as demonstrated in religious ceremonies, wedding, funerals, state openings and large sporting events. Attached to each event is a series of actions which are executed in a particular way and in a prescribed order. We all have various rituals and routines that are integrated into our lives, be that not walking under ladders or making the sign of a cross when in need of hope. Here are a list of instances where each of us, possibly on an unconscious level, is likely to follow a routine:

1. preparing to go out socially

2. getting up in the morning

3. going to bed

4. eating meals in family groups

5. cleaning a house

6. preparing to cook

7. putting on make-up

8. washing and bathing

9. responding to news (good or bad)

10. reading a newspaper.

Decide on a series of rituals that are important to your character. Explore how the character may execute the action and notice the care that could be taken at each stage of the ritual. This could inform you about characteristics such as if they are ordered, regimented, spontaneous, chaotic, controlled and so forth. It also enables you to consider how expressive they may be (e.g. do they like to experiment, are they overly routine-driven or are they playful?).

Conclusion

The reason that some actors spend long periods of time observing and participating in actions relevant to the life of the character is to be believable for the audience and themselves. Observing people is fascinating and provides a rich source of ideas for action and behaviour. The idea is not to imitate but rather to notice nuances and qualities, and where space, time and form can be used for character definition.

HOW

Finding ways to create action

Introduction

We each have personalised ways, behavioural patterns that are influenced by a number of factors such as age, gender, culture, fashion, image, personal ability, as well as mental and physical state. To give an example, it is very apparent that Juliet enters a room in a different way to her nurse. Apart from the obvious facts, such as status and age, she has her own distinct quality of energy, driven by her desires, which affects everything she does and how she does it.

HOW is not what you are doing, but the execution of the action. Inherent in how something is done is the manipulation of:

- time

- force

- space

- direction.

When you do something the action takes place over a length of time and has a speed or tempo. You pick an object up from the floor and it could take 2 or 10 seconds. This action will have a particular force, also known as effort or quality. The velocity or level of exertion attached to the action is linked to your intent. An example would be that if someone wishes to exit a room because they are really late for work, their movement is likely to be quick, direct and unsustained but sharp.

Spatial use is the next consideration, not only how much space is occupied but also the proxemic use and the implementation of the action. A wave goodbye can be tight to the body or can swish across your head like a sail. Direction also reveals intentions; for example, if a person moves forwards or away or hovers in limbo, a subtle message is conveyed. If you desperately want something, you will move towards the stimulus, and if you are repelled, you will move away. States of confusion tend to result in hesitation, an indecisive movement. The four factors, time, force, space and direction, are driven by intention – that is, what a person may want to do at any particular time.

Rudolf Laban and Michael Chekhov

Rudolf Laban created a comprehensive movement vocabulary for actors and dancers through a series of what are known as 'efforts' and the categories of space, weight, time and flow. He developed his work in the first part of the twentieth century, including a period at Dartington in 1936 where he crossed paths with Michael Chekhov. The language is similar, with Chekhov exploring what he called 'archetypal gestures' as a stimulant for waking up energy and the development of sensitivity. There is a slight difference in the words, but they share the aim of inspiring a range of movement possibilities which can be used in the exploration of how to execute action. Laban's eight efforts are:

1. wringing

2. pushing

3. flicking

4. dabbing

5. slashing

6. gliding

7. thrusting

8. floating.

Chekhov's archetypal gestures are:

- thrusting

- stretching

- beating

- throwing

- lifting

- holding

- digging

- pushing

- tossing.

Chekhov also incorporated musical terminology, notably staccato and legato, into his fundamental work on the qualities of movement.

Both techniques are valuable for extending expressive potential and exploring a character's physicality. As psycho-physical tools they are the articulation of wants and drives, and lead to precise choices as to how an action is executed.

How you make your choices

The given circumstances will provide you with the clues to, and subtleties of, the behaviour of your character, and it is up to you to creatively interpret this information. A good starting point is to identify what makes the character's actions different from your own. They may be bolder, more assertive and direct than you. Such observations are energetic and will slightly shade all actions. It is like adding a colour palette with varying shades to your performance.

HOW is directly linked to intention, often referred to as want, need or objective. Action choices come as a result of what we are looking for; it is instinctive to keep trying to achieve what we want and to apply different strategies in this pursuit. What is at stake at any given moment will also influence the strength and therefore the force of the action. The two are directly related and determine how you arrive at your score of action.

What should you notice? These four elements are fundamental:

- the intensity of each moment

- the urgency of the action

- how you feel about your situation

- what your environment contributes to how you feel.

EXERCISE: MOVEMENT DIRECTION

This is simply a reminder that we instinctively move our body in different directions: upwards, downwards, forwards, backwards, left side and right side.

When we communicate we rarely stand totally still, as according to what we want at any one time we move in a specific direction. Early in rehearsals I often find actors just stand still and fail to activate the momentary wants of the characters, or clutter the action with movement which does not seem appropriate for the text.

From a standing position, such as wu chi, take yourself through the six directions and see what impulses arise. As a development of this, let's specifically apply it to intention. Lenard Petit has applied these directions to six clear wants: give, take, stand your ground, yield, reject or give.

It is almost automatic to move in one of the following ways when you execute these actions:

- **reject** – backwards
- **yield** – side to side
- **want** – forwards
- **take** – usually a move **outwards then towards the body**
- **stand one's ground** – downwards
- **give** – forwards and slightly up.

Apply these six gestures to a piece of text, reflecting in every moment the action you are doing. For example, when Juliet says, 'O Romeo, Romeo, wherefore art thou Romeo?' this line could be a want or a give – that is, she wants Romeo's attention or she is giving him her love, so her movement could be forwards with a slight variance between the two intentions. This is a good way of discovering action and activating the body.

EXERCISE: STACCATO AND LEGATO

Staccato and legato are musical terms, and as they have contrasting qualities, they are good as a starting point to train the body to be receptive to the varying tones of movement.

Perform this exercise in the following manner:

1. Create a sequence which uses all six planes of movement: forwards, backwards, upwards, downwards, right side and left side. It can be an abstract routine or be based on an action, such as tidying up your bedroom or watching a sporting event on television.

2. Repeat the sequence in a staccato rhythm for a minimum of 2–3 minutes. Become aware of initiating the movement from the lower dantien, which is under your belly button.

3. Change the rhythm to legato. Notice which parts of your body you find difficult to move in this quality; it is usually the legs as unless you are a frequent mover, there is often less dexterity and control. Repeat the sequence for a minimum of 2 or 3 minutes.

4. Observe how each quality affected feeling.

5. Continue with the routine, but alternate by doing one round of the sequence in staccato and one in legato. In between, place a brief pause, where externally you are still, and internally feel the direction of your energy.

6. Then blend the two qualities – one part of the sequence could be staccato and the other legato.

EXERCISE: PLAYING WITH FORCE

This very simple exercise can be done in pairs or individually. Get a tennis-size ball and throw it up, applying a specific level of force (e.g. lightly, gently, softly, firmly, aggressively). Allow all of your body to receive and adapt to the selected force, letting the quality of the force affect your reaction.

Alternatively, you can throw the ball against a wall, applying a specific level of force or, in a pair, pass the ball between you as if you are having a conversation. After a while, stop throwing the ball but imagine that it is still being passed between you. You may find that the cycle of exchange and energy between you is heightened.

The result of regular practice is improved coordination and range of movement.

EXERCISE: MOVING BEFORE YOU MOVE

This exercise is based on the principle that energy is moving in you, through you, and beyond into the space that surrounds you. (Chapter 5 provides an explanation of the movement of energy in the body and the human energy field.) Based on this idea, there is always an energetic part of you moving in front of your actual body. If you shake someone's hand, your energy field has reached the person before your hand. All around your body, heat particles swirl and filter into the environment. (This concept is explored by Lenard Petit in *The Michael Chekhov Handbook*; Petit 2010.)

Imagine that you have an additional arm which hovers over your actual arm. To explore this, your action is simply to raise your arm above your head, but imagine that your imaginary arm moves before your real one. Once it is above your head, let it descend, closely followed by the real arm. Repeat this action with both arms a few times. Then do the same experiment with your head. Observe what happens to the weight of your movement; often there is more density to the action.

EXERCISE: EXPANDING BEYOND YOURSELF

Practise this exercise according to the following steps:

1. Stand in wu chi position (see Figure 4.1).

2. Connect to your breathing, sinking slightly upon inhalation and rising upon exhalation.

3. Take your attention to your back, and as you exhale imagine that heat is moving out of your body into the back space.

4. Do the same with the front, both sides and above your head. You are larger than you are in person.

5. Move around, at first slowly, and then adopt your usual pace and try to retain a sense of taking up more space. Connect into your electromagnetic field.

Applying this concept to the action of a scene, you could consider:

- how you enter the space

- how much space you take up

- the proximity between you and the other people

- how your body is positioned in relation to other people: towards, away, twisted and so forth

- the expanse of your action.

Imagine that each action begins before your actual movement and that your energy contributes to the mood and feelings in the space.

EXERCISE: HOW YOU EXPERIENCE THE WORLD

How we experience the world is affected by several givens, including culture, attitude, social/world view, gender, age, class and so forth. An example is that I have virtually always lived in a city, so I feel comfortable walking in crowded places and along streets that are blocked with traffic. The soundtrack is familiar to me, so I hardly notice it. If I go to the countryside, the environment is more alien. The quiet and stillness at first causes unease, but after a while I adapt and begin to observe that city life speeds up my mental and physiological processes. In a calmer state I am more aware of nature, sounds and smells, and look with different eyes.

The environment is one aspect of how you experience the world. Try this exercise:

1. Imagine that you are walking along a road. Take yourself on a journey which may last a few minutes. Here are things you could notice: colours, sounds, smells, objects, posters, people, faces, clothes, weather, your thoughts and your emotions.

2. Question why you notice a particular object. I look at the advertisements in the train station, but I am sure not everyone does. What we notice says a lot about us, our relationship to the environment and how we view the world.

3. Create a series of short, imaginative wanderings which place your character in a specific environment. As you navigate your way, decide where their attention may be, which of the senses are most alert and what your character would notice. Observe the sensations and feelings that crop up.

Here are some suggestions for further exploration:

- The character may be on a very busy street, such as Oxford Street or Fifth Avenue, and they are late for a meeting and have to cross several streets, pass a train station with people spilling out, and there is also a demonstration under way. What impact would this have on their feelings and sensations?

- They are at a train station at night, it's empty, they want to get home and an announcement is made that there is a delay due to a person being under a train. What would the character's actions be? Would they speak to others, leave or become affected by the announcement?

- It is the morning and they are waiting in an office for a job interview. There are a lot of people milling around, all doing various activities. Telephone conversations are being had, photocopies are being made and other candidates are also seated waiting for their turn to be interviewed. Imagine how your character would respond: would they talk to others, retreat inside themselves, notice the room or rehearse their answers to possible questions?

Apply this exercise to the script on which you are working and relate it to the locations of the scenes. Such musings help to fill out the world and explore and/or make choices regarding behaviour.

EXERCISE: IMAGINARY EYES

Imagine that you can change the aperture of your eyes like you can that of a camera lens. This one action would affect the amount of stimuli which you are able to notice and absorb:

- Narrow
  This would be almost tunnel vision. You see one thing and scrutinise it. This may be a face, or an article you are reading. It is inflexible and precise. Extend this concept to the personal opinions you hold; for example, you are not able to see both sides of an argument, there is a rigidity to your perspective and so forth. A narrow focus can also be internal and introspective.

- Medium

    You would be able to take in several layers of stimuli, such as a group of people in a restaurant, the background music, the clothes people are wearing, the taste of the wine and the smell of the food. There is more ease to how you communicate. You are able to travel between an internal and external focus.

- Wide

    At this range the scene is broad and the stimuli extensive. You would be aware of a large landscape, the breadth of colours, sounds, temperature, bodies – it may be overwhelming. To permanently live with a wide-lens focus could lead to saturation of stimuli, which would overexcite the body.

It is usual to alternate between the three lenses. Explore what it is like to stay with one for up to 15 minutes. Observe how this affects both your mental and physiological processes. Apply this concept to your character and you will notice that it starts to dictate what they notice, which in turn affects their actions. It may be that your character is more introspective and rarely adopts a wide range, or that they are outwards facing and spend little time reflecting and having inner conversations.

Conclusion

HOW is crucial to creating interesting action and making physical choices. As soon as you understand why you are doing something, HOW should be the next consideration. It is useful to ask the question 'What sort of a person does…?' and then ask how they do what they do. This is essential for movement, action and filling the life of your character. Clearly, how you do something changes with your thoughts and the stakes, and this affects not only the quality of the movement but informs us of the central behavioural traits of the character.

Chapter 17

AUDITIONS

Getting the job

Introduction

Auditions are strange but necessary events for all involved. Everyone in the process has something to gain and something to lose in relation to their future. It is fairly obvious what these are: the director wants the actors closest to their imaginative version of the role; the casting director wants to source the most talented and appropriate actors; the agents want their actors to work; and the actors want a job. That is the surface and most transparent level of activity. The undercurrents of the personal dynamic of selecting anyone for a job are usually more complex. This is because we all carry a multitude of perspectives, opinions, prejudices, tastes and agendas largely based on our personal history and experiences.

How to approach an audition

It's best to see auditions as meetings of like-minded people, opportunities to show your talent and share creative ideas. I experience many actors who become overly stressed and anxious, as if they are facing prosecution. With this in mind, it is beneficial to know your patterns of behaviour and how you can cope with the circumstances under which an audition is conducted. Understanding your patterns is the first step.

How we affect each other

A valuable fact to remember with any encounter is that we affect each other by our presence. As soon as you walk into a room, you change the dynamic: your energy contributes to the mood and reveals what you are truly experiencing, and it cannot lie. Read the room and adapt as necessary.

First impressions

First impressions often stick. This is recognised in the 'thin-slicing methodology', a term developed by psychologist Frank Bernien who identified that it is usual that the first thing you observe in a new encounter tends to stay with you to such an extent that you would always look for the exact initial reaction and tend to disregard other behaviour. So if someone was slightly awkward, you expect and look for this behaviour on other occasions when you meet. The significant thing here is that it's beneficial to consider the impact you would like to have on others.

How to open up to the experience

Opening up to the experience of auditions and job interviews can be difficult, largely because we know we are being judged and time is often short. The auditioner can quickly spot what they want: the first minute of a speech or scene, or 5 or 10 minutes of a workshop, are crucial for making an impact. In particular, the following points are relevant:

- how receptive the person is to the environment and others in it
- if they make eye contact, actively listen and are generally responsive
- the ability to create a detailed journey having made clear and interesting choices
- the level of interest in the project.

Any of these factors may lead to a more inquisitive response and get you through to the next round.

Developing audition skills

What you can do to acquire the skills to successfully audition is twofold: first, you can work on yourself, and second, you can work on your creative interpretation of the audition material. There are many exercises in the first part of this book which contribute to gaining somatic awareness, but specifically the exercises below may help.

EXERCISE: GESTURES OF OPENNESS

When we read bodies, we are more likely to want to engage with someone who is open than a person with an internal focus. The key places in the body to be aware of are the feet, pelvis, the chest around the diaphragm, the shoulder girdle and the head. As previously discussed, ground, centre and balance are crucial. The position of the limbs is also a factor: if the pelvis or groin is too open, it appears too sexual; if the shoulders are too far back, it appears cocky and arrogant.

Consider the following:

1. Walking into a room is revealing, as is how you shake a hand, how buoyant you are, the pace with which you enter and how you sit on a chair. You should practise having an open body which is alive and interested, with your attention on the person who speaks at any one time.

2. How you sit is important for communication and your own receptivity. Collapsing or being too rigid is not helpful, so find the right level of ease and attentiveness. Even when sitting, being centred and connected will help you to be more present.

3. Breathing is the key to ease and feeling more in tune with yourself. Should you begin to lose focus, connect to your breathing and control the rhythm. If you tighten up, imagine that you are melting the stiffness with your breathing.

EXERCISE: HOLDING THE SPACE

To hold a space implies that you are confident, comfortable and in control. There are a number of things you can do to immediately achieve this, including grounding and centring. This provides internal ease, energetic alertness and heightened presence. To do this exercise, follow these steps:

1. Stand in wu chi position (see Figure 4.1).

2. Drop your weight downwards. Feel the ground. Tune in to your lower dantien.

3. Observe your breath. Notice the depth and range of the expansion.

4. Begin to increase the length of time you inhale and the time for the breath to move through the diaphragm, allowing the abdomen to expand.

5. Be sure that your shoulders are down and your joints unlocked, and check that you are not holding in the buttocks or thighs.

6. Imagine that you are breathing beyond your body. Take your attention to above your head and believe that you are a foot or more taller. Move to the sides of the body and imagine that your body touches the walls of the room. Observe your back and breathe into your ribs, and get a strong sense that you are expanding outwards behind you.

7. Select a spot in the room to walk to, start to walk and imagine that you reach the spot at least a foot before you actually do.

EXERCISE: WHAT DO I DO?

List your usual behavioural responses to auditions, what happens to you physically before and during the event. Notice which of the following are familiar:

- Your breathing becomes shallow.
- You hold in your abdomen and tighten around your diaphragm.
- You have the sensation of flutters in your stomach.
- You lock your knees.
- You lock in your pelvis.
- You feel sick.
- You stiffen up when you walk into the room.
- Your voice goes high-pitched.
- Your mouth gets dry.
- You forget your text.
- You hear your own voice when you speak the text.
- You find it hard to reply to questions.
- You don't ask any questions.
- You close yourself off, fold your arms and legs, tightening and becoming rigid.
- You tell long stories about your journey.
- You open up and become very talkative.
- You dominate the conversation.
- You storm into the room.
- You creep into the room.

- You slink into the room.

- You know what the director asks you to do, but you don't do it.

- Your breath gets tight.

Having considered what happens to you, set goals to try other behaviours. The following exercise will help to bring immediate changes.

EXERCISE: MAKING THE CHOICE

To undo your usual response, there are four strategies that will make an immediate change to how your body feels and how you are received:

1. Locate your centre.

2. Breathe – send your breath to your centre.

3. Ground – feel the weight under your feet and unlock any joints.

4. Balance – bring your weight slightly forwards onto the balls of your feet and soften.

EXERCISE: BODY AUDIT

Do an audit of your body whilst you are waiting for the audition and make any necessary adjustments. See the above suggestions. The adjustments will involve working with your breathing and posture, so you may choose not to sit; rather, it may suit you to find somewhere to stand away from other people. Notice if what you have been doing is unhelpful and make a choice to try another way of being.

Preparation of audition material

Preparation is vital when it comes to audition. As long as you have fully prepared, you have done yourself justice. It is necessary to address the following:

- General points

    - Respond to the reader by listening and reacting.

    - Do not fix reactions.

    - Be prepared to be flexible.

    - Take direction, listen closely to what has been requested and be able to make different choices or adjust your interpretation.

- Areas of preparation

  - Get the facts.

  - Read the whole script.

  - Learn the given circumstances.

  - Decide how your chracter wants to affect the other person.

  - Sharpen your interpretation of the text and have an angle.

  - Ask yourself what you, in particular, bring to the role.

  - Know the journey of the scene. What happens to change you?

  - Register the significant shifts.

  - Know the key moments of transition and do something with them.

- Research

  - Ask yourself with what do you need to be familiar (e.g. an accent, a skill, a reference).

  - What experiential or factual information is needed?

- The journey

  - What has gone before?

  - What is your starting state?

  - What has changed by the end of the scene?

- Rhythm

  - Identify the tempo.

  - Pay attention to how the tempo changes throughout the scene.

Self-tapes

The same level of preparation applies to self-tapes, which are frequently how auditions are conducted in the early stages. The bonus of doing a tape is that you can do several versions and assess your work as you go along.

Conclusion

A crucial point to consider in auditions is to read the room and know how to adapt to the dynamic, remembering that you can change the feel by how you are engaging and listening. If you have fully prepared, considered clear choices and imagined potential ways to play the scenes, you have done the work and the decisions lie in how the producers and directors see the character. Being adaptable and able to respond to direction is the other vital consideration. So listen to direction and clarify as necessary.

Chapter 18

FULL-SCRIPT PROJECT FOR THE SCREEN

Preparing for the shoot

Introduction

This chapter outlines a process for preparing a role from a full-length screenplay, and charts the journey from the first read to the shoot. There are some examples taken from the script *Anna Karenina* written by Tom Stoppard to serve as ideas of how to apply the exercises. The focus is very much about exploration and creating possibilities which may shape the final performance.

I have chosen a screen project primarily as it is largely the responsibility of the actor to prepare in this medium. In most screen contexts time constraints mean less rehearsals, especially in commercial television where the turnaround is so quick. It is not unusual for contact with the other actors to be very brief and perhaps to only run the scene two or three times before you shoot. Therefore, to be fully prepared in what you can creatively bring, yet able to be spontaneous and adapt to direction, is beneficial. Preparation is a fundamental necessity and essentially offers the freedom to play and find a depth. The intention of this work is not to set and make final choices, but to develop the resources to discover possibilities.

The process is organised into stages which function as a guide; it can, of course, be jumbled up, but I have found that a structure helps. Clearly, after a while, all the stages fuse together to add layers and texture. There is no set time to spend at each stage, and you may just try a few of the exercises before dipping into the next stage; it is a matter of building blocks.

Screen preparation can be quite solo, so I have adapted a few exercises that may usually be executed in pairs or groups so they can be explored by an individual.

Stage one: first encounters

The first impressions of a script are created very quickly, as it is a time when ideas are lightly registered and images are textured with colours, sounds and smells. Your vision of the script will naturally be influenced by the places you have been, landscapes you have seen and the experiences through which you have lived. Interpretation is therefore shaded by you and your history. It is valuable in the early stages of the process to avoid making too many fixed decisions but to allow the script to move you – to be inquisitive about what you are able to create beyond the words and identify the distinctions between your world and that of the characters.

EXERCISE: **WHAT TO NOTICE**

Having read the script, jot down any first impressions or observations of:

- sounds
- colours
- smells
- textures
- the mood and tone of the story.

EXERCISE: **CREATING A PICTURE**

Using any materials you have, make a collage of the overall landscape of the script. This may be using paints or crayons or cutting up photos from magazines. The purpose is to express the themes, metaphors and feelings, rather than focus on an end product.

EXERCISE: **SOUNDSCAPE**

Sound has a profound impact on the stimulation of the senses, so start to gather pieces of music or sounds that evoke a sensory response. It may be that you pick a piece for each scene, or for a specific moment or for the starting state. Gradually create a sound scape for the whole script, one which follows the story.

EXERCISE: KEEPING THE PICTURE MOVING – TUNING IN TO THE WORLD

Images naturally arise as a backdrop to our lives, as we are constantly making our own movies where the action indulges our fantasies and desires. Before we meet someone, we have often already established a visual impression of their appearance and vocal quality, and mentally written the conversations we may have.

This exercise builds on your imagination, sharpens it and directs it towards forming your choices. Perform it as follows:

1. Find a comfortable position and close your eyes – that is, shut off any external stimulus which may be distracting.

2. Direct your gaze to an imaginary blank scene and see an image of your character.

3. After 4–5 seconds, allow your attention to drift towards the opening moment of the script.

4. Create your own version of the script as if you are watching a film, and notice colours, sounds, specific objects, the atmosphere and what the character does.

Having explored the opening sequence, you can apply the same process to other moments or full scenes. It does not matter if you jump from one part of the story to another or if the images are sequential – the aim is to build a virtual world and imaginatively expand beyond the descriptions on the page.

As a variation of this exercise, listen to a piece of music from your soundtrack whilst creating the images on an imaginary screen. The images and music not only guide you into the world but trigger sensations and emotions. It is instinctive to start to imaginatively meander around the actions of your character and see pictures of how they are in their world. At this stage it is useful to just allow those images to float and pass, rather than let them linger. Keep the pictures moving to discover possibilities.

Stage two: story and character

This stage involves excavating another layer of meaning, the focus of which is the story. To fully understand a narrative there must be engagement on a mental, sensory and somatic level. In that the story has lived through the bodies of the characters, the importance of experiential discovery is fundamental to grasping the imaginative situation. Building on the initial perceptions of the first stage, the work becomes more of an excavation which carefully disturbs the surface underneath the words.

Story

Discovering and interpreting the story involves registering the events and perceiving how they have affected your character. It is impossible to understand the present moment without grasping some information about what has gone before. The story will contain all you need to know; the crucial skill is to notice the clues.

Begin with the overall arc and a key question: what is the story?

EXERCISE: THE OUTLINE

Spend 10 minutes writing a succinct outline of the story from memory. It may be useful to write it in bullet points. Note the following: when, where, who, the crucial events/turning points and the conclusion. Then return to the text to see if you have missed any key points, and add them.

EXERCISE: WHAT IS THE STORY?

Jot down what the story is about in a succinct sentence. Two examples using the same work are:

- Anna Karenina is a story about the struggle against societal conventions.

- Anna Karenina is a story about cause and effect and living with the consequences of your actions.

This exercise will require reflection on the heart of what is actually being conveyed and will provide clarity. In addition, jot down themes that are intertwined into the narrative; these will directly relate to the story.

EXERCISE: CREATE A TIMELINE

Create a timeline of events in order to orientate yourself through the narrative structure. It may seem obvious, but it is easy to miss the period of time over which the story occurs in terms of hours, days, months, years and decades. Clearly this is vital to your character's actions given that we change as we respond to the circumstances in each moment.

Go through each scene noting 'when' and 'where'. It could be that the script is not linear and you may need to grasp the chronology of events. There may be jumps in time, so consider the chronological context for each scene, which may be hours, days, months, years and decades.

Even if a few hours have elapsed between scenes, it is interesting to consider what has happened during this time. How has your character spent their time? To move stories on in most scripts, we may not be dealing with real time, so jumps are common.

Character

The clues to the character will be woven into the text – some will be apparent and easy to find, others will need creative interpretation. The given circumstances provide the basic facts, the context and backdrop for the life. From this information you can begin to decipher the traits and actions that drive the needs.

EXERCISE: GIVEN CIRCUMSTANCES

Understanding the given circumstances is fundamental to being able to imaginatively immerse yourself in the story. To help with the rigour of observing the details, divide the given circumstances into categories of information:

- Personal – biographical facts such as age, family, relationships, occupation, education, likes, dislikes, what they know, attitudes, morals, ambitions, drives, goals, and so forth.

- External – the world, when, where, any reference to specific events that impact on the characters, dominant cultural considerations such as religion, political leadership, class, fashion, pastimes.

This information provides the foundation from which to work and will feed your choices.

EXERCISE: FAMILY/FRIENDSHIP TREES

This exercise is carried out as follows:

1. Create a family tree that identifies the relationships of the immediate family.

2. Write an alternative version that examines friends and relationships.

3. Map out how the central characters know each other.

EXERCISE: CHARACTER TRAITS

Traits emerge from what a person does; they describe behaviour. It is useful to discover all of the many sides to the character: the light, the not so light and the dark. It is easy to select the more noticeable qualities. The following exercises encourage you to find a range of qualities in the character and look for moments when you can bring detail to your work. Consider the following categories:

Table 18.1 Character traits

Sensory[a]	Behavioural[b]	Emotional[c]	Qualities[d]
Hot	Manipulative	Passionate	Ambitious
Cold	Calculated	Humorous	Adventurous
Frosty	Assertive	Cheerful	Sincere
Warm	Polite	Friendly	Genuine
Icy	Independent	Considerate	Loyal
Gentle	Disciplined	Loving	Intuitive
Soft	Conscientious	Scary	Gregarious
Cool	Confident	Aggressive	Quiet
Chilly	Meticulous	Stern	Earnest
Glistening	Efficient	Angry	Independent
Radiant	Open-minded	Sour	Optimistic
Sparkling	Logical	Envious	Honest
Colourless	Accepting	Joyful	Focused
Faded	Decisive	Bitter	Careful
Coarse	Realistic	Jealous	Organised

[a] Other words for sensory are: creepy, shiny, flashy, fluffy, fuzzy, gritty, prickly, bitter, nauseating, refreshing, sharp, sweet, spicy and so forth.
[b] Other words for emotional are: sad, anxious, jolly, annoyed, anxious, selfish, excitable and so forth.
[c] Other words for behavioural are: sarcastic, narcissistic, sardonic, mysterious, foolish, obnoxious, disgruntled, irritable, alarmed, startled, secretive, cautious, calculated, remorseful, resentful, purposeful, defensive, generous, diligent, cautious, decisive and so forth.
[d] Other words for qualities are: light, heavy, social, serene, strong, bold, brave, gentle and so forth.

Now follow these steps to do this exercise:

1. Identify the behaviour of your character based on your first impressions – that is, what they do in the story to themselves and to others. Write a list of words that describe the behaviour. (Use the table for suggestions.)

2. Allow these words to translate into dominant traits which inform both how action is executed and what a person does in response to events. An example is Karenin in *Anna Karenina* who is a government minister, logical, organised, efficient, focused, realistic and careful – almost the

antithesis of his wife, Anna, who is adventurous, passionate, loving and gregarious. The two descriptions imply very different physical qualities. As you explore the main traits, allow the words you have selected to influence your actions. If you are a logical person, how does that influence how you live your day? Before you go out, you may plan ahead, organise your belongings, wear the right clothes for the weather, carry objects you may need (e.g. a pen, diary, hankie) and so forth. Notice if this changes your actions and reactions.

Visualise some of the scenes being played out, with your selected traits influencing how the scene is enacted.

3. All human beings have many dimensions and sets of behaviours. Karenin softens when he is with his son and may become more playful. But his overall somatic pattern may be to hold in, contain and execute action in a controlled fashion. The public and private persona will be varied and, of course, affect physical choices. Having selected words that you feel describe your character, allow any images of your character to emerge and see them doing something such as looking for a glove they have mislaid or shopping for a new outfit. Experiment with the words so as to notice, for example, if you can bring a difference between 'organised' and 'efficient' to the action.

4. Give yourself a practical problem to solve which is a challenge for your character. Possible actions could be:

   • ironing a shirt

   • sewing on a button

   • doing the accounts for your household

   • writing a letter which reveals an action of which you are not proud.

   It does not matter if the activity is not likely of your character, as the purpose is for you to explore how they do things. It you are meticulous, you would be precise about the stitches whilst sewing, or you would get rid of every crease when ironing.

5. Take a scene and look for the moments when you can apply your list of words. When does Anna Karenina show her independence and how does this affect her actions? There may be one slight moment which can give you the opportunity to reveal a glimmer of that personality trait.

EXERCISE: PRIVATE MOMENT/PUBLIC MOMENT

We all behave differently in private than in public. When being watched in public, you may become more conscious of what you are doing, which ignites the level of energetic vibrancy. Spend 5–10 minutes doing one of the following activities in character as if you are in a private space:

- eating dinner
- making breakfast
- reading a book
- writing a letter
- watching television
- singing a song
- exercising
- painting your nails
- getting dressed.

If you have the opportunity, repeat the activity whilst being watched. This could be in a rehearsal if you ask someone to watch you. Observe how you are affected. Try to retain ease in what you do, as the tendency is to perform when being watched.

EXERCISE: BEHAVIOUR LIST

Draw up a list of words that describe the behaviour of your character in a scene. In the scene when Anna returns from a ball where she has publicly flirted with Vronsky, this could read: Karenin reflects, questions, suggests, warns, manipulates and threatens.

Once you have identified the chain of behaviour in detail, it can act as a score of action for the scene, a guide which brings a journey. It will be made clear that the character is not the same at the end of the scene, as they have been on a journey.

Objectives: wants, drives, needs and goals

It is beneficial to take an exploratory approach towards identifying the objectives behind behaviour and action. Making decisions too early can lead to fixing ideas before the whole picture is surveyed. Objectives, aims and wants seem to mean the same thing in that they imply there is a specific target and the behaviour is working towards achieving this; however, this may not be the case. A 'want' could be a desire or an ambition, which is more of a fantasy, but a 'need' is something that a person may not be able to live without, a matter of survival. In a similar way, a 'drive' appears to be direct and fuelled with strength and determination. The words are interchangeable according to the mental power behind the impetus and what is at stake.

A need seems more urgent and precise, as though you are dependent on the outcome. Needs provide real focus. What is clear is that at any moment we either move closer to or further away from achieving what we want or need.

EXERCISE: THE DRIVE

Here you can explore whether a drive feels different to a want. Consider how the drive of the character translates into the direction of movement. Create a moving sequence which symbolises the drive of the character for the whole story.

Describe your drive in a short sentence, such as 'Anna Karenina could want or need to be loved and passionately adored.' She is therefore driven to seek attention and love. Her movement is likely to be forwards and open, a bit like a peacock on show. As you do the sequence, discover how your breath contributes to the strength of the drive:

1. Select a scene and visualise the action. Notice how your character executes their drive, and pay attention to the tempo, spatial use and force.

2. Create a visual image of what your character would like to ultimately achieve in their life. Fill the image with details such as colour, sound, smells and physical action. It does not have to be a still image. This can be kept as a reminder of what rests behind the action of the story, and the image is there to reacquaint yourself with this when needed.

EXERCISE: THROUGHLINE OF ACTION

What does your character do in the scene? Go through each scene and write at the top of your script:

- where, when, why and what you want
- what you do in the scene (can be written as bullet points)
- facts regarding your starting state, such as relevant action that informs the immediate situation.

This is especially useful when shooting out of sequence, as this information acts as an immediate reminder.

EXERCISE: MOOD BOARD

A mood board is a creative way of exploring the expressive potential of a scene. You can draw on several aspects such as themes, drives, objects of importance, environment, atmosphere, sound, light, smells, tastes and textures. It allows for you to have an abstract or symbolic interpretation. Try to avoid thinking or planning too much to allow for a more spontaneous response to unfold. Using any materials that come to hand, start with images, colours, shapes and textures.

Stage three: the bigger picture

This stage focuses on discovery through research, imaginative play and engaging with what Michael Chekhov calls the 'higher ego'. This implies moving beyond the text to find potentially new stimuli for the action, which may be based on the accuracy of period or your imaginative resources.

The world and factual investigation

We are a product of the times in which we live and carry with us the traces of the dominant ideologies, cultural trends, attitudes and fashions. The research that is being suggested at this stage of the process of working on a script is very specific to the narrative. It is a way to understand the experiences and behaviour of the historical period and obtain a grasp of what it may be like to be in the shoes of the individual you are to play.

There are different types of tasks that can be undertaken such as:

- factual (e.g. reading)

- observational (e.g. watching documentaries, films or people doing relevant activities)

- experiential (i.e. doing)

- sensory (e.g. listening to music or an interview, watching a performance, looking at art).

Headings for research

Do a spidergram or jot down any topic headings such as:

- the period (when and where the action takes place)

- social climate, which includes the dominant ideologies, politics, government, organisation of society, laws, social reforms, democratic rights, gender issues relating to equality and so forth

- significant events of the period (e.g. wars, natural disasters, political events)

- social organisation (e.g. class, family structure, cultural groups, wealth, religion)

- occupations (e.g. pay, workers' rights, the organisation in the workplace)

- discoveries (e.g. inventions, science, medicine, astrology)

- education (e.g. access to education, the curriculum, qualifications)

- transport (e.g. travel daily and opportunities to see the world)

- geography and locations relevant to the story

- fashion (e.g. clothes, style, hair, make-up)

- art (e.g. theatre, music, dance)

- social pastimes (e.g. games, sports, children's activities)

- food and nutrition

- the home (e.g. facilities, design, gadgets, colours, routines, rituals, style, design).

Guidelines for research

It is important to be specific regarding where your attention is directed during this phase of exploration. It is very easy to get distracted and wander into territories that are interesting but not especially relevant to your particular task. Prior to embarking on the contextual research, identify what you need to know and what will enhance your understanding.

Among the questions you could ask would be: what would my character know about the world based on their class, education, age, interests, gender, culture, religion and attitude? If they are not likely to know the names of the cabinet ministers in government, don't bother finding them out.

If it's not in the text

The text will capture the world of the story, but it is unlikely to make reference to every detail of the period unless it is specifically relevant to the action. It is the actor's responsibility to bring life to the environment and discover possibilities such as etiquette or personal taste. An example could be period drama, such as *Downtown Abbey*, in which the art direction and location provide the actors with a realistic setting but do not necessarily provide them with the more personal choices. If you consider your own experience of the world in which you live, it is filled with details and routines that reflect your personality and lifestyle. Looking beyond the text is the creative challenge for actors, and to immerse yourself in the imaginative situation means knowing what to do in any event. Adding layers beyond the text is a combination of imagination and research.

Experiential research

Experiential research could potentially involve two main types of activity: observation and participation. Active observation implies that you are doing more than noticing: you are intentionally watching an activity, which may stimulate specific feelings and emotions in a similar way a film might. Participation involves actively doing an activity to gain realistic insight into the life of the character. Clearly there are limitations as to what can be safely done in an acting context, but through doing whatever is reasonably possible, the levels of immersion into the world of the character increases. It also stimulates the imagination and sensory stimulation. Essentially the objective of experiential research is to grasp an authentic interpretation of behaviour or a specific physical activity. It could also potentially offer a physiological understanding of what it feels like to be in those circumstances from the perspective of the participant. Although you carry your own perceptions and physical potentialities, which means you are always working from *your* interpretation, experiencing becomes beneficial as you place yourself in the given circumstances.

This can provide several insights into inner and outer tempo, muscularity and the natural energetic pulse of a person who does a particular job or lives a specific lifestyle. An example would be how someone who has a sedentary job, such as sitting at a reception desk all day, will clearly have an inner pulse different from that of a manual labourer. What we do and how we do it formulates the choreography of our life, and therefore it makes sense to obtain some understanding of what informs our actions.

Observations

It is useful to observe activities which are specific to the text, such as particular occupations where accuracy is required for a believable performance. Generally watching people in everyday situations that are relevant is helpful for making choices.

Useful ideas for making physical choices could include observing walking, how people use their hands, eating, drinking, laughing, relationship to etiquette, eating, dressing, couples in restaurants, people waiting at train stations, people saying goodbye or greeting each other and so forth.

Notice how the activity is executed with attention to time, rhythm, quality, spatial relationships, physical pose and breathing.

Participation

When deciding on the activities that may be useful, pose the following questions:

- What do I know how to do that is relevant to the story?

- Is there a specific skill required for the text?

Identify from the text or from historical and factual research the activities in which your character is likely to participate. This may be sewing, writing poetry, doing magic tricks or reading science fiction. Discover the specific details that are relevant to the time and attempt to master the level of skill you feel is appropriate to the character.

What we select to do as pastimes can become a part of physical vocabulary and a means of how your character expresses elements of their personality, an example being that those who dance and partake in physical activity will obviously have bodies that are different from those who are less active.

EXERCISE: LETTERS

Write a series of letters, texts or emails to one of the other characters with whom you have a relationship. This could be a lover, friend or member of your family.

EXERCISE: DAILY ROUTINE

We all have regular routines and ways of doing everyday things. These patterns have formed over time and are outer reflections of tempo, priorities, interests and personality. An example would be that one person may shower every morning, read the same newspaper and have the same breakfast every day, whereas others may have less order and live more chaotic or erratic lifestyles.

Based on either your research or imagination, sketch out a daily routine which is composed of actions that your character is likely to do, such as travel at approximately the same time each day, drink the same beverage, listen to specific music and so forth. You may decide that they have no routine or order, which offers a clue to their physicality or natural tempo.

EXERCISE: PHOTOGRAPHS

Create a photograph album of archive images from the period of the script. This is not meant to represent the photographs of your character but rather to offer some insight into the world of the story.

EXERCISE: GOING BACK IN TIME

This exercise works particularly well on a text that is not contemporary. It is an imaginative journey back in time to begin to observe and consider the impact our environment and society have on our body and how we move through the world. Perform it in the following manner:

1. Walk, or visualise yourself walking, in your own environment. Reflect on how you live your life – that is, the core influences, demands, tasks and activities you choose to do or are expected to do as a result of your responsibilities. This may include: occupation, pastimes, daily routines, self-image in terms of fashion and how you want to be viewed, class, culture, religion, the environment where you live and pressures you face regarding money, personal relationships and responsibilities. Allow these factors to impact on the tempo and direction of your walk. This may alter your speed and the movement pattern.

2. As a symbolic representation of your life, adopt the shape and direction in which you move; this may mean you walk in a straight line, in chaotic circles or zigzags.

3. When you feel ready, take yourself back in time – this jump could be 1 or 10 years – and then repeat the sequence. Imaginatively explore how you experience the world as you move. Does the tempo and quality of movement change? An example is that in the first decade of the twenty-first century, depending on where you live, the level of external awareness and sense of danger has generally increased, and this could have been due to events such as the 9/11 terrorist attacks.

4. Continue to repeat the sequence until you reach the decade or year in which your story is set.

5. Reflect on how the context of the story impacts on your bodily experience (e.g. a body in the twenty-first century is different from one of 1900). We are shaped by the world around us in very subtle ways. Historical accuracy is vital to believability.

Stage four: soma

Having spent time investigating the world of the story, the discoveries will already be working on your imagination and feelings concerning the trajectory of your character. The process of embodiment depends on how you are able to let the information you gather simmer and stimulate your whole being.

EXERCISE: SOMATOGRAM

See Chapter 2 for the exercise steps.

EXERCISE: IMAGINARY BODY

This exercise was created by Michael Chekhov but I have slightly adapted it. The intention is to encourage the actor to visualise the body of the character and imagine several options. Initially anything is possible – they can be fatter, taller, prettier than you. It is a useful exercise for early on in the process, to stimulate ideas and activate feelings.

1. Close your eyes. Place yourself in a landscape.

2. In the distance see a figure walking towards you. This is your character.

3. Observe how the character walks – in particular notice the overall shape of their body, the rhythm of their movement, how they place their feet on the ground and the space they take up.

4. Gradually the character gets closer to you and stands in front of you. Take a closer look at their face – do they frown, smile, wince? Are the features soft, open and relaxed, fraught with anxiety? What is the story of this face? Look into their eyes – is the focus soft, dense, piercing, alarming, fearful? Scan their whole body and notice every detail, from the length of their fingers to the shape of their muscles.

5. The character does a gesture towards you and says something. What is the quality of their voice? Is it smooth and resonant or raspy, high pitched or soft and seductive?

6. The character turns and walks away – watch them go, making more observations. When they have disappeared, take a step forward as if you are stepping into their shoes and adopt the movement patterns you have just observed. Walk for a while, experiencing what it feels like to see the world through their eyes.

This sequence can be repeated several times, so you imagine many options and experiment with different ways of moving. There may just be one small idea that comes from this exercise, such as that the person's breath is quick or they look down more than you do. It is beneficial not to have set ideas but to experience and see what comes.

EXERCISE: BREATHING AND ACTION

When a process is led by your body, all of your senses will begin to quickly engage and an embodied relationship to the material world will emerge. Because the majority of us spend a lot of time functioning through the thinking part of our body, it is easy to rely on this. This exercise aims to lessen that tendency and encourage trust in the body to offer suggestions and engage playfully with possibilities.

Michael Chekhov's work on gesture is the initial starting place for this series of exercises. Chekhov was a firm believer in training the body to be a tuned resource capable of moving beyond the text to fully and imaginatively express the complexity of the characters.

Start by following the 'Imaginary body' exercise above. Once you have a strong visual sense of your character, follow the next exercise:

1. Begin with the breath and the natural rhythm of expansion and contraction. Taking your attention to your ribcage and diaphragm, observe the timings of your natural breathing cycle. Is your inhalation longer than your exhalation?

2. Recall the image you had of your character. Reflect on the shape of your character, with particular attention on breathing and how this corresponds to their shape. It is likely that a rigid person may take in less breath and a less boundaried person may have an easier breathing rhythm. There may be relevant factors specific to the period in which the story is set; for example, the use of corsets dramatically affects the intake of breath.

3. Once you have made some choices regarding the breathing, try to retain this rhythm for 3–4 minutes. Do you notice any new sensations?

4. Speak the text out loud and reflect on how the thought processes relate to controlling your breathing. Is there a pattern?

5. Explore subtle actions that go with the pattern of breathing. An example is that a sigh is followed by a downwards collapse of the body. A large intake of breath opens you and means you occupy more space. Quick, sharp breaths are accompanied by a rise in your shoulders and often muscular tightness.

The simplest of actions are initiated through the state of one's breathing, and it is the starting point of discoveries regarding rhythm and the internal tempo of thought.

Memory bank

History is difficult to convey believably if you have not actually lived through the event. This is particularly true of relationships: when a couple have spent an extensive amount of time together there is an inherent resonance of all that has gone on between them. The same is true of siblings or a parent–child bond: past exchanges are present in a vibrational resonance. Factual and experiential research can always contribute to the cultivation of a physical understanding of a situation and the past but the creation of active memories contributes to an embodied experience.

Creating memories is a way of filling your story with a past and expanding the backstory. This is something that we automatically do in our imagination: it is usual to create images, and fantasise. When working on a story you can do the same with the character, taking them on a journey to move beyond the text and fill in the key events, those mentioned in the text and others that form the backdrop to your character's life.

There are a few ways of creating memories. You can improvise around the events of the story to create a lived experience, or you can undertake experiential research and gain practical experience of whatever is appropriate for the situation, or you can create your own memories. As explained in Chapter 6, your body stores memories – they live within you. The memory-bank exercises (see Chapter 20) are a way of formulating a somatic history to be drawn upon when required. Creating memory is a way of putting something behind the text.

Selecting the memories

The text will guide you as to which part of the story needs a vivid past. If there are references to specific events of which the character has been a part, it would be valuable to explore those either as improvisations or as a memory which you imagine. An example from *Anna Karenina* is that Karenin would be very familiar with government offices. He would have extensive experience of speaking at public meetings and being able to create a logical and well-prepared argument. There may be a very specific act or bill that he was responsible for which may have stayed in his memory. Creating this history of speaking at meetings, persuading and arguing his stance, will provide the character with substance and identity. The way in which he commands himself in his working life forms a large part of his identity.

EXERCISE: THE RELATIONSHIP AS A DANCE

Select any central relationship that your character may have in the story – this could even be a short scene with a fleeting exchange – and reflect on the dynamic of the exchange. Primarily, identify the dominant tempo, which will be indicated by the language or specific instructions. Does your character have any patterns of behaviour? It is usual for there to be a particular dynamic in any relationship, and this expresses a variety of information such as who you are to each other and how you feel in the other's presence. Clearly, professional relationships differ from those of lovers or siblings, and this is expressed in what you say and what you do. Do you touch, move into personal space, withdraw, tighten or open?

Relationship dynamics may involve heated or explosive moments, or instances when there is soft and flowing ease. Reflect on how the mood and physicality of the scene can be interpreted as a dance. Start with the direction and tempo of the responses. Does it feel like the action is back and forth like a pull and push, or side to side possessing no real direction, or circular and repetitious, or chaotic?

Either in your imagination or by practically doing the sequences, explore the qualities in which you feel your character moves. This could be passionate, seductive, soft, tender, sharp, forceful and so forth. It is also interesting to find possible polarities in the action, such as tender and forceful or fiery and calm. Create a short sequence that suggests the dynamic of the relationship. Consider the following:

- tempo
- direction
- quality
- dynamic.

Whilst working on the scenes you may recognise potential patterns which shape the behaviour of the relationship. Elements of your dance could be integrated at the early stages of work as a potential movement score.

EXERCISE: THE GAME

This exercise is an imaginative way to observe the physical interplay between the characters. It is about noticing the games that are being played. Perform it as follows:

1. Select any scene and read it, focusing on what you do and what is being done to you. Imagine that this exchange is a game and use the dynamic and the characters' intentions to identify whether it is more of a mental or physical game. It could be chess, backgammon, poker, snakes and ladders, draughts or tennis, boxing, basketball, hockey and so forth. Whatever you select should contain the rhythm and level of excitement of the scene.

2. Go through the scene imagining that you are playing the game. Syncopate the action and verbal text to the pace of the game, which may require pauses and suspended moments during which you calculate your next move.

3. Play your scene again and see where there are opportunities to use elements of the game. This does not mean to literally start playing chess but rather to explore, using the tempo or physical direction, what you discovered when playing the game.

Archetypes

In archetypes we recognise behaviour; it is as if there is already a physical score available to use as a resource from which to start work. The benefits of working with archetypes is to stimulate your work imaginatively and discover interesting ways to realise the action.

As Lenard Petit outlines in his book on Michael Chekhov (Petit 2010), in order to recognise the archetype it is necessary to know the actions of your character. What we first assume may not be the case, or we may select the most obvious type which leads to stereotypical choices. Petit gives the example of Romeo, who could easily be identified as a Lover, but with a more intuitive interrogation his actions are foolish.

The difficulty of this work is sometimes it is hard to select an archetype; or it is challenging to fit the actions of the character to one type. A solution is to explore with several archetypes and also to recognise that there may be elements of a few types within one character. Here are some examples:

Queen, King, Prince, Princess, Devil, Virgin, Witch, Innocent, Orphan, Hero, Heroine, Fool, Trickster, Mother, Father, Child, Wanderer, Warrior, Jester, Sage, Lover, Artist, Ruler, Leader, Elder, Hermit, Hunter, Bully, Martyr, Tyrant, Dreamer, Hedonist, Judge, Temptress, Loner, Wizard, Revolutionary, Villain, Victim, Everyman/woman, Orphan, Nerd, Geek, Femme fatale, Adulterer, Seductress.

EXERCISE: CHOOSING THE ARCHETYPE

To help you choose an archetype, try the following exercise:

1. Write a list of what your character does in the story. This provides you with a list of actions. For example, Anna Karenina does the following:

   1) She leaves her home to see her brother and sister-in-law.

   2) She meets Vronsky on the train.

   3) She attends the ball where Vronsky is likely to be.

   4) She flirts with Vronsky.

   5) She diverts Vronsky away from Kitty, to whom he was to propose.

   6) She falls in love with Vronsky.

   7) She confesses to Karenin.

   8) She puts off leaving after she has been forgiven by Karenin.

   9) She asks for a divorce.

   10) She give up society life and her son and moves in with Vronsky.

   11) She kills herself when her relationship with Vronsky declines.

   The list of behaviour will translate into a recognisable character type. Looking at Anna Karenina, she could be a Seductress, Temptress, Femme Fatal or even a Fool. Another example is that of a Bully who could be identified by his or her use of brute force, mental manipulation, and generally controlling behaviour. A Leader will make decisions, take control of situations, direct the course of action, speak out and possibly control, direct and influence what happens.

2. Close your eyes and imagine your character doing the action of the scene you have selected.

3. Observe the qualities that emerge. How dynamic or forceful is the action? Is the character playful and childlike? Are they sharp and serious?

4. Notice the dominant direction of the action. Is the character usually making quick decisions? Do they initiate the ideas and action in the scenes? Do they reject and withdraw from situations? Are they indecisive and chaotic in their choices? Do they appear to do very little? Reflect on your observations and allow a moving image to develop which is informed by the dominant direction of their actions.

5. Consider what archetype may fit the behaviour you have imagined.

EXERCISE: WORKING WITH THE ARCHETYPE

Once you have selected an archetype, allow the following to inform your work:

- energetic quality

- recognizable actions

- gestures and mannerisms

- tempo.

If you need ideas for how to create and explore action for the archetype, look at images, watch films, and consider props and costumes. Examples are that Harry Potter could be the Everyman or Orphan, Forest Gump the Innocent and Lara Croft (as well as Katniss Everdeen from *The Hunger Games*) the Heroine.

The option with this exercise is to either use one type for the whole story or a type for one scene. Anna Karenina is alternately the Child, Mother, Victim and Fool. Exploring each scene with a different type will offer ideas and different ways of using the body. To that end, do the following:

1. Close your eyes and create a moving image of your selected type. Notice the overall shape of the body and how they move.

2. Select a scene from the story and visualise this archetype as the character acting through the scene. Notice how the execution of the action changes as a result of the type.

3. Take what is the essential energetic quality of the type and play your scene imbuing the action with the archetype. This could be dynamic if you are a Warrior, or soft and gentle if a Child.

Alternatively, you can do this:

1. Allow the image of the archetype to emerge.

2. Create a gesture which incorporates the whole body, adjusting your weight, centre and balance. Stay in this position for 2–3 minutes and see what images and sensations appear. The posture is likely to stimulate new feelings and impulses.

3. Using this gesture as a starting point, select a scene and devise a little non-verbal sequence which is composed of some of the actual and potential actions of your character. This may include an entrance into a public space, greeting someone, eating or drinking. Explore how this body executes the action.

It is not intended for this work on archetypes to set your choices but rather for it to be a means of exploring options and shifting away from what is familiar to you.

Element work

The Elements are often used as a metaphor for emotional expression. 'Fiery' describes an angry or explosive temperament, earth is associated with calmness and control, air with confusion and potential chaos and water has an unpredictability from sadness to stormy in nature.

It is the distinctly tangible qualities of the Elements which makes them useful for the stimulation of the imagination and senses. As discussed in Chapter 7, the Elements form a central role in Traditional Chinese Medicine (TCM) and are considered to be directly related to health and human expression. The belief that the elements are integrated within the fibres of your body, affect the flow of qi or energy, impact the regulation of feelings and emotions, and interplay with the changes in the environment makes them valuable to consider in our work.

Working with the Elements is useful for:

- stimulating your imagination

- selecting a quality of movement

- activating the senses and emotions

- creating an overall mood for a scene

- creating a temperament for a character.

EXERCISE: ASSOCIATIONS

Select an Element that you feel may relate to the traits and behaviour of your character. Make a list of quality words that you associate with this Element. Examples of such words are:

- fire: simmer, blaze, explode, burn, hiss

- water: trickle, flow, wave, burst, gush, thrash

- air: bluster, breeze, blow, gust, float

- earth: dissolve, dry up, crack

- metal: bend, bubble, solidify.

Use these words as stimuli for your character's inner actions and reactions. Karenin may simmer inside at the news of gossip concerning Anna's flirting with Vronsky. Lady Macbeth may burn with irritation at Macbeth's inability to follow through on their plans to murder Malcolm.

Now follow these steps:

1. Draw up the list of words that relate to the Element.

2. Select which specific words you may associate with a particular scene or moment.

3. If the character's actions are chaotic and unpredictable the word could be 'bluster', which is associated with air or metal. Create a visual image, which may affect movement, breath and vocal quality.

4. Allow your breath to take on the quality of the word. How would your breath hiss or steam or burst?

5. Imagine the quality of the word travelling through your body.

6. Go through the scene or a specific moment and allow this image to inform your action.

Elements and character

Once you reflect on the potential metaphor of the Elements, it is possible to see how they relate to personality types. An obvious example is that a person whose behaviour is either explosive, dominant, volatile or passionate is likely to have a strong relationship to fire. If you begin to work with your upper body and explore gestures that are outward and expansive, a starting point for exploring the rhythm of the character will emerge. If you consider that the character's dominant Element is water, it is useful to explore movement that is downwards and flowing with various levels of force. Metal can be hard and solid but can also bend. This also will give you a clue about the physicality that matches the expressive tendencies. (See Chapter 7 for more on the Elements.)

Stage five: composition

Composition is a bringing together of all the stages of the work. It involves a return to the text to work for more precision, not to fix choices but to rigorously notice the key transitions and momentary changes.

Having excavated the surrounding context and how this affects the character somatically, a refocus on what is spoken can often feel alien, as if the language is separate from the body. Language arises from the fullness of the internal life and the need to communicate; it is not the first stage in the process of communication. Very often when the language is prioritised, without consideration or investigation of how the whole body experiences the imaginative situation, there can be a physical disconnectedness. By this I mean the actor is somehow in a transitional place between the thoughts of themselves, which may be associated with fully comprehending what is being said, and the thoughts of the character; or the actor may be challenged by the situation and what is required of it. An example would be a set of circumstances that demand venturing into the future: if it is difficult for the imaginary events to be fully cultivated, it will be impossible for the actor to somatically experience and surrender to the situation. A liminal space from the actor's reality into embodying the imaginative world will exist. With a full immersion of the circumstances, the somatic experience will set up the cultivation of the spoken word. This is the work of this stage of the process.

EXERCISE: WHERE IS YOUR ATTENTION?

It is the natural rhythm of the mind to continually shift from one stimulus to another. Our attention is never static even when in a state of calmness and rest. Thoughts arise, develop and fade. The peak of the thought will obviously depend on how much we have invested in it or what is at stake. An example would be a thought like *I have not called my mother today*. I now have a choice as to whether to invest in this thought and become concerned that my mother will worry or that she will be upset by my negligence, or I can let it go. This is a choice, we can navigate our mind, and if this is true of us in our everyday existence it is true of a fictional character.

There are a few stages to this exercise.

1. Read the scene and observe the following: Is the thought directed to yourself or someone else? Energetically, is it internally focused or projected outwards? In other words, are you sharing it with others?

2. How does the thought translate into words? As a question, a statement, a fact or an observation? (Each of these possibilities has a different quality.)

3. Before the words are spoken, identify where the attention of the character is. When Karenin tells Anna that he has waited up for her after she stayed at a function they had both attended, there is a complex series of thoughts leading to this statement. His attention could have been on imagining Anna talking to her lover, hearing the carriage, opening the door, back to Anna eloping, and then fade. The peak of the thought will obviously depend on how much internal and external focus he has as he responds to his imagination and the actual action in the real space. (This is all before he asks her where she has been.) To give a thought any depth you need to give it history, as there will always be a history.

4. The text will be the ultimate guide, but your imagination and the given circumstances of the character will add to this. Looking at the text, does the punctuation imply that the character is inquisitive? Are there lots of questions? This may tell you that their attention moves quickly – at a sound you hear, at the appearance of the person to whom you are speaking and upon recalling a memory.

5. How much are you investing in the thought? This will affect the level of attention.

EXERCISE: PRIVATE, SOCIAL OR PUBLIC SPACES

This is similar to the circles of concentration, which Stanislavsky included in his early work. It is intended to guide the actor towards identifying where they direct their attention and learn to be precise about energetic focus.

Private is directed internally and includes moments of self-reflection, imaginative journeys, memories, past thoughts which have perhaps not been expressed to anyone else and connecting thoughts which are not verbalised. Known as subtext or internal monologue, they are a vital component of truthful performance. What is actually spoken is always supported by the substance of our experiences of life.

Social refers to communication with another person or a small group. It is when we want to convey our thoughts, feelings and desires, and reach others. It can be intimate or opened to a larger space, but it is always confined spatially and the boundaries end with those to whom we are speaking.

Public implies that the individual has an outwards focus and is taking in either a large number of people or a more expansive space. A whole room would be public, as would delivering a presentation at a conference or looking at a landscape.

In most instances it is obvious when you are communicating at a private, social or public level, as the body automatically adjusts. The benefit of being precise about this when acting is that it sharpens the focus and guides the actor with regards to where to direct their energy. On screen this is very noticeable.

Perform this exercise as follows:

1. As you read through a scene, observe if your focus is directed inwardly (private), towards a particular person or object (social), or outwardly to take in a larger landscape or a group of people.

2. Experiment with swapping the focus so that you can see how the body is affected when you send what you identify as a private thought outwards as a public one. It is likely that your senses and the depth of feeling will be affected. Internal moments will lose intensity when they become social.

3. Notice how often you switch between the three spaces. It can be very quickly, especially when you are in conversation. It is important to

observe that even if you are chatting, there will be moments, even if they are for a fraction of a second, when you travel inwards into a private space. Identifying how your thoughts travel will give your performance texture and provide an interior complexity which is natural to human communication.

EXERCISE: FINDING THE STARTING STATE

The beginnings of scenes require intense focus as you will need to capture the history of the story. The starting state for a scene contains the history of the particular moment. It will remind you of the set of circumstances that has led up to this moment and requires that you allow these events to cultivate the depth of feeling and sensation appropriate to the start of the journey.

The purpose of this exercise is to experience different ways to set up the starting state:

1. Prepare the first few moments as if there is a state of heightened anxiety in a scene, and observe the quality of the energy in your body. Which muscles and joints are tightening? What is happening to your breath?

2. Repeat the exercise but register how you feel. What is the level of excitation in your body?

3. The third time, take time to centre and ground and identify with your current feelings, and allow the circumstances of the scene to drop into your body. Breathe into the starting state and then consider the moments of action. Observe how that felt.

4. What has gone on before is clearly the stimulation for the starting state. Decide where your attention is. This could be on something someone said, an action you have done or an image of what you have seen that has affected you. Drawing on the work of the memory-bank exercises (see Chapter 20), decide on the relevant memories that are on the surface, those that trigger the feelings associated with the action of the scene.

5. Create an image of your goal, what you want to achieve in the scene. Decide on your first tactic as to how you can achieve this. Apply the stakes; in other words, how much you need or want to succeed.

EXERCISE: AS IF

'As if' exercises are personal imaginative replacements which help with immersing yourself in the situation. There are various versions of the exercise, which derives from Stanislavsky's 'magic if'. I find that it is useful for accessing the starting state and discovering specific moments. I suggest a personal experience which is not related exactly to the event of the scene.

This exercise calls for the following steps:

1. Get clear as to the action of the scene, such as two people struggling to connect to each other.

2. Think of a comparison event that stimulates the same feeling. In this instance the scene may be about separation, and a potential 'as if' is like the first time a child's mother leaves him or her at the school gates.

3. Allow the selected event to stir in you, and then start the scene.

Conclusion

It is important to find a process that works for you. I have outlined the potential stages in which you can pick and choose the exercises that suit the needs of the script and enable you to develop a detailed performance prior to shooting. Being inquisitive is part of an actor's job. The more rigorously and imaginatively you delve into the world of the character, the more immersed you will be. Making choices that are fully steeped in the contextual information brings not only a layer of authenticity but also an array of options for making interesting choices. Marking a clear process which takes you on a journey into unfamiliar territory is both stimulating and necessary. There is no avoiding the work if you want to fully inhabit the character.

Chapter 19

LESS IS MORE
An energetic interpretation

Introduction

'Less is more' is a phrase that is commonly used by acting teachers, directors and performers. The instruction implies that the force of either verbal or emotional expression is out of sync with either a potentially realistic or an aesthetic portrayal of the circumstances, so the acting is visible.

Despite what appears to be relatively clear, I have found that the instruction can cause confusion. Actors can feel that by 'doing less' there may not be a depth of feeling or emotion, or that there is not enough action created. This is a common experience for those who have worked more in theatre and begin to make the transition to screen work where subtlety and the balance of energy is crucial.

Actors often do too much when they are not able to fully inhabit their role or they have not committed to choices that reflect the given circumstances. Anxiety and nerves can also contribute, as by attempting to hide what could be the actor's truth – their anxiety – the acting becomes heightened. A clear indication that an actor is not connected on a sensational or an emotional level to what is being said is when they 'push' – usually forwards with the upper part of the body leading.

How do you know when you are pushing?

It may not be obvious to you that you are pushing. Here are the most usual signs:

- The direction of movement is forwards and led by your upper region.

- The relationship between the head and spine is out of sync.

- The vocal quality becomes strained and often high in tone.

- There is a lack of genuine feeling and emotion appropriate to the dramatic moment.

- A disconnection is experienced resulting in not being able to feel your whole body.

Of what are you asked to do less?

You are being asked to change your energy, to find the right level of emotional expression, which means you are experiencing genuine feelings. If you are not able to feel your way through a scene, it is difficult to judge how much energy you would naturally exert, in which case it is likely that you rely on behaviour you know or have observed, such as when you are angry you shout and rage, or when recalling a sad memory you cry. When there is no real felt sense of the situation, gestures and cluttered actions tend to emerge and the work is performative.

Doing what is needed

Starting from cultivating a felt response, which stimulates sensations and establishes the foundation for genuine emotion, is the way to stay connected. The instruction could easily be 'do more' but of the right kind of activity. Placing your focus on the inside of your body through tuning in to what senses are stimulated is the place from which to start and to which to return.

EXERCISE: BALANCING AND TUNING IN

Developing a pattern of always checking how you feel is a good starting place. This will enable you to acknowledge and build from your own emotional state and register how far you need to travel to reach the starting place of the scene. To do this, take the following steps:

1. Stand in wu chi position (see Figure 4.1).

2. Observe your breath.

3. Notice any sensations and feelings that crop up.

4. Breathe into any areas of your body that feel tight.

5. Begin to drop into the circumstances of the scene. Follow what your body wants to do.

EXERCISE: ASKING THE RIGHT QUESTIONS

Asking the right questions about a scene is key to accessing the right level of feeling and discovering the emotional pitch. Questions should focus on helping you to make choices about the stakes. Interrogating how, why and what creates the response to the stimulus that provides action.

Pay attention to the descriptions in the instructions, which will provide clues as to how a character responds. An example would be: 'Peter hurries, distraught.' The word 'distraught' is very specific and offers a guide to the emotional starting point of the scene. Playing with the levels of how distraught the character is may be a good place to start. How one person experiences being distraught is very different from another – the interpretation is up to the actor.

Examples of relevant questions are:

- How much does [person] care about [other person]?
- What would [person] like to do to [other person]?
- Is this behaviour new to your character?
- Where else in the story does this behaviour emerge?
- What do you feel like when [a particular thing happens]?
- What may the character lose or gain in this moment?
- What would both feel like?
- How would you feel in a similar situation?

EXERCISE: FEELING THE TEXT

This exercise aims to encourage listening and feeling:

1. Sit back to back and speak the text with no attempt to dramatise it. Repeat this a few times, placing your attention on what is spoken and allowing yourself time to cultivate a felt response before you reply.

2. Stand up and face your partner. Maintain eye contact and speak the text. If you have an urge to move and gesture, do so but only if the feelings arise.

3. If there are any sections of the text in which you are not able to create a felt response, repeat the specific line until you are able to discover the emphasis that stimulates a feeling. Try placing the emphasis on different words. Cultivate a feeling before you speak.

4. Continue to go through the text and gradually begin to add any action as it organically arises, allowing it to come from the urge to move.

EXERCISE: TUNING IN TO FIND THE BALANCE

Tuning in to the situation requires some focus on how it will move you and the character. Starting by observing yourself is important because you acknowledge how you are feeling before the circumstances of the scene begin to affect you. Having done that, read the scene and notice your own reactions to the events and how they are different from those of the character. Articulating the difference between your responses and your character's responses provides a trajectory, an angle from which to shift – even if it is simply that she or he is more anxious than you would ever get, or that you would never challenge someone in that way. It is an indication of the energetic expression which may or may not be familiar to you. The unfamiliar requires more excavation as you will need to invite sensations into your body that, from choice, you may not have felt before.

This exercise is carried out as follows:

1. Identify the points of action of the scene. What does your character do and potentially how do they do it? Pay attention to the descriptions in the text which can be used as a guide rather than rigidly followed. Examples of such descriptions are:

    • He enters furiously.

    • He assertively challenges.

    • He withdraws and excuses his behaviour.

    • He defends his actions strongly.

2. Imagine that your character is executing each point of action.

3. Repeat the visualisation and focus on the quality of your breathing. There is a totally different level of force between entering furiously and assertively challenging. This should stimulate the feelings of the action.

4. Having got a felt sense of the internal expression, begin to action the points and play with the exertion you express.

5. Concentrate on trying to *feel* your way through the journey rather than think.

Conclusion

Finding the right balance of what you do becomes more instinctive as your experience grows. Taking the time to tune in to how your body feels and gaining a command over your own responses to being watched and judged, which tends to sabotage immersion, is also crucial. 'Less is more' is really about being precise and clear, as all action is justified if it is truthful and embodied.

Chapter 20

THE MEMORY BANK
Putting something behind the text

Introduction

The objective of this sequence of exercises is not to replicate your own memories, but to draw on them as a platform from which to work. There is nothing as complex or as interesting as you, and if you reflect on yourself, it is easy to recognise that you are composed of many layers, like an ageing rock. This work acknowledges that the present is inextricably linked with history, and encourages the creation of a detailed past which is filled with subtlety and substance.

The act of remembering is a form of reconstruction, as each memory is based on your lived experience. It is impossible for every detail of an event to be identically recalled or for your body to reach the same levels of sensation. Any feelings and emotions that emerge are coloured by other factors, such as your present circumstances, how the story has been fictionalised over the passage of time and your current physiological state. As you age, the structure of your body changes, which affects the speed of how it functions, a consequence of which is that the accuracy of your memory changes. So when revisiting a happening from childhood, it is more of a series of fragments with blurred edges.

The memory-bank exercises have several uses and have been developed to work with the senses and imagination. The memories that are being created are those of the character – they are not necessarily your own – though they may automatically be governed by what you have experienced in your life and your terms of reference. To work beyond what is familiar is vital for any artist, and the strategies are very much connected with discovery and establishing a lived experience which is unfamiliar.

What do the memory-bank exercises do?

The exercises work on several levels with an overall aim of creating a richer inner life. They place the narrative into a context that offers depth and sensory resonance, and also do the following:

- aim to create a past for the character which is experienced and embodied

- establish a starting point for every scene

- identify the similarities and differences between you and the character

- expand both inquisitiveness and a curiosity for detail.

Components of the memory bank

Acquaintance

This stage of the process concerns becoming acquainted with what knowledge and memories your character may have stored. This could be images, smells or sounds associated with the environment in which they live. Or more concrete events may have been described in the text, such as an encounter with another person, so building up a clear account of the meeting could provide clues as to feelings and action.

EXERCISE: ONE-MINUTE FLASHBACKS

This exercise comprises the following steps:

1. Close your eyes and let your mind wander over your life. Over a minute, see where you travel and which instances flash up. How much of your life did you see in that minute? Observe the speed with which the images moved and how many different pictures you saw or voices you heard.

2. Repeat the same sequence but apply it to the character. What images pop up? Do you see faces or places or hear sounds? What smells and tastes float into your awareness? Observe the tempo and the number of images that you experienced. (My guess is that it is less than when you recalled your own memories.)

3. As a means of getting to know your character, repeat the same exercise with more specific situations. This will involve imaginative embellishment, as you are extending beyond the descriptions of the text. When creating a backstory, specificity is needed, so discover

what you need to know and allow your imagination to guide you. Choose relevant moments in the story and build on what is written as a way of expanding the dramatic moment. An example would be that the location is a field but there is no description of what this field looks like, so you create it. Then perhaps recall other events that have happened in that same place.

Try creating the following situations for your character:

- a memory from a significant moment that they encountered yesterday
- a recent disagreement they had with someone
- the last time they did something outrageous
- how they obtained an object that is important to them
- the first time they visited the place where they currently live
- the last conversation they had with a close relation
- when they last went for a job interview and how they felt about the results
- when they last felt uncomfortable (what were the physical sensations?)
- an incident where they had to stand their ground
- a significant life-changing decision which brought a change of direction
- a conversation they recently had with one of the important people in their life.

The world

Working with your semantic memory, which includes what you know about the world in which you live, contextualises who you are and accounts for the actions and decisions made. We are not always conscious of how the environment in which we live dictates and contributes to the person we are. My mother was very conscious of how much things such as groceries cost, as she grew up during the Second World War and post-war period when most items were rationed and in short supply. I am less conscious of cost, and my son has no interest or knowledge whatsoever of the prices of anything. This is a small example of how the times in which we live shade our levels of observation and what is prioritised. Small factors such as this affect behaviour and the actions we do. In this instance it is reflected in my son's impulsiveness and my more reserved instinct when it comes to most factors in life.

When developing a role, research should be an immediate activity. Deciphering the background contextual information is a primary route of enquiry. If the story is set in House of Tudor times, naturally you need to comprehend the period in order to bring the character to life and allow the text to make sense to you. In theory, research should automatically sift into your consciousness and affect your imagination and choices. To further embed and build an inhabited storehouse of lived experiences, this stage of the memory-bank work concerns selecting relevant events and creating real memories.

There are two categories of memories to explore: one that concerns the procedural (motor skills, things you know how to do), and one that deals with the episodic memory (autobiographical experiences, events, times and places). (See Chapter 6 for more details on the construction of memory.) In both instances the suggestion is that the events and skills have passed into the character's long-term memory, so they are remembered and have an effect on the actions taken. It is the long-term memory that will have a lasting impact, and it will be automatic for the senses and fragments of pictures to be triggered by what is recalled.

The general environment

Drawing on the factual research you may have done, the next set of recollections concern the overall world in which the story is set. The aim is to create a personalised relationship to the period and encourage the absorption of general and factual knowledge into your episodic memory. There are some events that cannot be authentically improvised in action for logistical and practical reasons, but they *can* be imagined and therefore shifted into your lived experience.

The process involves the creation of memories. The guidelines are that each memory must have:

- a beginning, a middle and an end

- something that affects you

- an intention behind the action.

Allow your understanding of the character to determine how they would react in this situation.

To create a rich event, follow these steps:

1. Decide the event for which you are going to create a memory.

2. Let your imagination wander over possible stories.

3. Once you have selected a specific story, be specific about what happens, where it is, who is there and how you react.

4. Repeat the sequence in your imagination several times and add to the detail things such as colours, sounds, objects and smells.

5. Register the feelings and emotions that emerge.

6. Repeat the sequence, paying attention to sensations and where they are felt.

Examples of possible situations include:

- a memory of what is heard on the news or read in the newspaper

- a memory of going on a form of transport

- a memory of shopping for a specific item of clothing

- a memory of a large social event that you attended

- a memory of a significant world event of which you hear, of which you are a part or which you watch happening

- a memory of listening to a piece of music in a social setting.

EXERCISE: PERSONALISED STORIES

Perform this exercise in the following manner:

1. Make a list of the relevant events that you believe are significant for your character (including actual instances from the script or those that are mentioned in the dialogue). Be specific, as it is easy to go off track. An example would be that if the story is set in a war zone, it is likely that you will have a memory of explosions or siren warning sounds. This would also affect the physical levels of alertness, which would somehow be revealed by action and reaction.

2. Develop concrete stories about these event, which will be based on the factual knowledge that you have accrued, your observations about the character and your imagination. The following list of questions will provide a way deeper into the exercise, starting with the obvious points of enquiry. Begin with a situation that involves interaction with at least one other person. Answer the questions as the character:

1) When? (Include the year, season, month, day and time.)

2) What were you doing there and what was the purpose of the event?

3) Why did you go there? What did you want to achieve as a result?

4) Where are you? What do you see? Observe the people, clothing, the objects they have with them, the objects in the space and the colour scheme.

5) What are you and those around you doing? What happens in this space?

6) What are the smells? Take a moment to inhale them.

7) What can you hear? Tune in to the sounds in the space and then those beyond it. Be specific about the tone and pitch, and observe what this does to you.

8) Place yourself in the space. What do you do? Take yourself through a sequence of actions.

9) What do you want to say to anyone in the space who is not part of the dialogue?

10) What do you say? What is said in response?

11) Allow your attention to travel to something, such as an object. Be very curious about it. Notice specific details regarding shape, texture, colour and so forth.

12) Identify the key points of this event.

13) Did you achieve what you wanted to do? If not, what prevented this?

14) How did you feel at the end of the encounter?

There are two perspectives from which to create memories, as if you are living through them (participant), or as an outsider (observer) when the character watches the events happen. Each perspective will proffer varied results on how much feelings and emotions are stimulated. Experiment from both perspectives to see which version stimulates the strongest sensations.

Creating the footprints

Creating the footprints is a means of shaping the habits and routines that give the character their traits and an element of predictability. They help to explore the cognitive processing which indicates what is likely to occur when a person is in a certain situation, and for choices to be made regarding the routines that form the central characteristics.

EXERCISE: DAILY ROUTINES

Write a list of factors that define an average day for the character. Begin with the structural considerations such as work or family commitments. The routines may revolve around dressing, washing, eating, cleaning, the order of how they approach their work and so forth.

EXERCISE: GOALS AND ACTION

Consider a goal that is important to your character. This may be to attract a romantic partner or to be recognised for a particular skill. What actions are necessary for the achievement of this goal that may form part of a routine? Is it important for the person to be perceived as attractive? Would this mean serious attention to clothes, hair and make-up? How would this be integrated into the daily routine? What are the smaller actions that this choice could stimulate? This may include looking in the mirror or checking how you smell.

EXERCISE: HABITUAL THOUGHTS

Does your character have unspoken thoughts which are repeated regularly? Do these thoughts reflect personal goals, beliefs systems or how they see themselves (which is etched into their past because they have repeatedly been a part of their thought track)? Examples of such thoughts are:

- I am not good enough.
- I look unattractive.
- I am not doing what I want to do in life.

Decide what such thoughts may be. Relate the thoughts to goals. A person may be competitive, which could lead them to be judgemental of others. They may believe that they are inferior to others, which could result in thoughts of self-doubt. We all have thought habits that are difficult to eradicate, as they form a layer of our inner life and a part of our thought track. Considering what thought habits a character may possess is just one more layer.

Conclusion

The memory bank is a way of filling the backstory and creating embodied history. Knowing your character as well as you know yourself is never going to be totally possible, but putting yourself in their shoes will get you closer.

Chapter 21

THE STARTING STATE
Working with what has gone before

Introduction

The starting state is the accumulation of how the events of the story have activated the body. What has been felt and emotionally expressed before the beginning moment of a scene is fundamental to the portrayal of the events. To access the undercurrents of any action, there is more than just the present moment: there are also the attachments, patterns, associations and the vibrancy of the moment.

When scenes are shot out of sequence and there are a limited number of rehearsals, screen performances especially require a deepened receptivity to a starting state. Although there is the opportunity to have multiple takes, accessing the intensity of where a moment actually commences sets a tone for what is to follow. Whatever is spoken is always many beats away from being the first thought, so tracking back is hugely important.

A three-point process

It seems to me that the journey from you to the immediate story is a three-point process:

1. Establish a focused state.
   The first stage concerns you and requires listening to what is happening and noticing where your attention is. This will enable you to create a distance from irrelevant factors and establish the appropriate working state.

2. Tune in to the relevant circumstances and character facts. The considerations are:

- immediate (when, who, why, doing what)

- context (broader picture of the world of the story, e.g. Mars is different from 1920s Paris)

- personal (attitudes and behaviour: what you do and why you respond in that way; what you want to achieve).

3. Allow the events to move you.
   Surrender to the significant facts of the story (e.g. I no longer enjoy the company of the person with whom I live and I need to escape). What does this feel like to be in such a dilemma?

Below are a series of exercises that can take you through these three stages.

EXERCISE: ESTABLISHING A FOCUSED STATE

This is a period when you tune in to thoughts, sensations, feelings and emotions with the intention of clearing irrelevant distractions:

1. Sitting or standing, close your eyes and take your attention to your breathing. Notice the movement, rhythm and sensations.

2. Beginning with your feet and moving upwards, observe your joints and unlock them, if necessary, as you travel towards your head.

3. Connecting breathing and movement, slightly sink upon inhalation and rise upon exhalation.

4. Place your weight more onto the balls of your feet and imagine that your weight is dropping through the floor.

5. Observe any feelings that arise and any places in your body where you may feel restricted or tight. Using intention, send your breath to those areas, as if your breath is loosening them.

6. Remain standing or sitting for a few moments, just staying with your breathing and any sensations or feelings that crop up.

EXERCISE: TUNING IN TO THE CIRCUMSTANCES

This exercise begins with an assessment of where the story is at present. To determine this, address the following:

1. What has just happened? Write the relevant action points leading to this moment.

2. Attach an image to each point.

3. In the few moments prior to the start of the scene, in character have a conversation with yourself about the immediate circumstances. Register what you feel about them. What concerns you? What do you want to do about that concern? How are you going to do it?

4. Have a rewind of the events that have led you to this moment. Allow the images you created to emerge.

5. Cultivate the need to speak by weighing your options in this moment. If you are in a court case, you can confess or fabricate. You hear someone breaking into your house and you can hide or face the intruder. Go for the choice that corresponds with the dialogue, but be sure to ponder around your options.

6. Place your attention on your breathing and allow it to steer you into the starting moment.

EXERCISE: BEING MOVED BY THE EVENTS

Images provoke strong sensations and activate the felt sense. Select some photographs that are either personal and part of your history or ones that you have collected as a part of the character's past, or visual images that reflect the mood and feelings associated with the starting state. Take time to look through them. This is a very simple activity that will stimulate feelings and sensations; these may come from anywhere – your past or the story. Allow yourself to be moved.

Selecting relevant memories
EXERCISE: SELECTING THE MEMORIES

To select the memories, follow this process:

1. Focus on the events that have a significant impact on the circumstances of the scene. If the scene is about resolving a conflict, it may be that you could recall the last conversation or interaction you had with the appropriate individuals. Trace the origins of the conflict so you have a lived history of the event, even if it resides in your imagination. This will establish feelings and give a context to the action.

   The memories you decide to create are dependent on the story of the scene, so be selective and make them relevant to the feelings of the starting state.

2. Make a list of the potential important events that have an impact on the scene. The clues are in the text. If it is mentioned that the

character smuggles drugs through a border crossing and is now being examined for this, it's useful to have an account of the experience.

3. When you invent a memory, pay attention to: when, where, who, why, what happened, what was said and what the outcome was of the encounter or what the implications are.

The memories put a layer of action behind the words; they are like the fabric of the story.

EXERCISE: AS IF (A VARIATION)

Here is a slightly different take on the 'As if' exercise (see Chapter 18) as developed in Stanislavsky's 'magic if'. The intentions are the same: to stimulate a response which may emerge as a sensation, a feeling or an emotion. It establishes a connection to the dilemma of the character.

Take the essence of the scene and imagine an active event to which the sensation could be compared, such as:

*   jumping off a diving board
*   swimming in deep water
*   drowning in a piranha-infested pond
*   being smothered by a pillow
*   crying a river of tears
*   walking up a rugged and steep mountain
*   being hit in the stomach with a huge slab of wood
*   walking on a tightrope across the Grand Canyon.

Let this moving image work on you and see if it stimulates any changes in your felt senses.

EXERCISE: MUSIC AND MOOD

Find a piece of music that expresses the mood of the scene. Listen and allow your felt senses to just respond.

Conclusion

The three-point process of accessing the starting state is really useful as a way into a scene, a journey from your reality into the imaginative world which needs to be real for you. Channelling focus comes easier with practice and could take 3 or 30 minutes depending on how easy it is to concentrate. Having a method that works for you is important for the depth of feeling and how present you are to others and the environment. It's good to begin before the beginning.

Chapter 22

REBALANCING
Working to enhance the felt senses

Introduction

In daily life it is unlikely that you consciously place yourself in situations that cause heightened levels of arousal. Each of us has our own cycle of response, and our nervous system has a tempo which usually copes with the levels of stress that we place on it. Instances such as being late for an appointment or becoming worried about an interview may stimulate a change in your anxiety levels, but generally it is unlikely that you deliberately take yourself too far beyond what is familiar.

There are times when acting requires that you travel beyond what is familiar to you. It is usual for plots to require twists and turns to make them interesting, with the characters being placed in high-stakes situations. The mundane routines of the average individual are not necessarily stimulating enough to draw an audience.

To a certain extent each of us has a pattern of physiological expression based on daily routine and habitual behaviour; however, for actors their work will create deviations. Action that requires entrance into heightened states will automatically create and demand a change in how the body functions, and what is often overlooked is that emotional expression also triggers immense activity and fluctuation of neurotransmitters.

Although acting is responding to imaginary circumstances, just entering into the *belief* of an event will stimulate physiological activity. This is especially manifested when there is the need to repeat performances, be that in a nightly show or for multiple takes on set. Susana Bloch uses the term 'emotional hangover' to describe the effects of repeatedly playing intense emotional states. This emphasises the lingering effects of adrenaline or epinephrine, which will have swamped and seeped through every cell in your body.

Rebalancing is like a cooling down after physical exercise. It is a means through which you can take time to steady yourself and balance your system – a personal moment of transition from the unreal to your own reality. Sometimes you will find that you naturally do one of the exercises below, especially regulating your breath control and shaking off tension. In the times when your bodily systems have taken a battering, adopting a specific routine will support a return to stability – that is, it will rebalance you and, on a long-term basis, bring calm and ease to how you function.

The following set of exercises can be used in a sequence or on their own according to what is needed. Shifting away from an experience that has demanded a high level of emotional expression can leave you feeling high or low.

EXERCISE: TAKING A MOMENT

Take a moment to register what you feel. Observe your breathing, any sensations, feelings, your posture and your balance, and then do the following:

1. Stand in wu chi position (see Figure 4.1).

2. Connect to your breathing pattern. Place your hand on your abdomen and feel the rise and fall of your breath.

3. Adjust whatever is required (e.g. you may need to slow your breathing and extend it).

EXERCISE: CLEARING

Most methods of qigong have a set of clearing exercises which aim to declutter and calm the mind as well as assist with detoxification of the body. In elemental qigong they consist of gentle moving sequences where the hands loosely trace along the meridian channels or where the qi is guided in a specific direction through brush-stroke-type movements. The notion of clearing at the end of practice is integral to the discipline, as throughout the exercises a cleansing process occurs whereby toxins are released from the organs, breath and bloodstream. Such toxins may be slowing up the flow of qi or affecting the direction of the movement in which it flows.

Clearing is a natural way of bringing energetic flow and encourages a calm and open state. Perform it as follows:

1. Stand in wu chi position (see Figure 4.1).

2. Place your hands in front of your abdomen with palms up.

3. As you inhale, slightly sink and open your arms so they are in line with your pelvis, and keeping your palms up, float them until they reach the height of your head.

4. As you exhale rise and take your hands down the front of your body until they reach your pelvis.

5. Try to synchronise the length of your breathing cycle with the movement sequence.

You can also trace the meridian channels by placing the palm of one of your hands about an inch above the skin and moving it along the pathway of specific meridian channels (see Figure 7.1). Alternatively, making contact with your skin through brisk brushing movements will also stimulate qi flow. Furthermore, tapping along the meridian channels is another means of awakening or resetting the nervous system.

EXERCISE: WORKING WITH BREATHING

The regulation of your breathing will allow you to switch from a reactive place to one of control. Experiment with breathing in and out through either your nose or mouth. To do this, follow these steps:

1. Breathe in and out for a specific count. Begin with four and then gradually increase the count and the tempo of the exhalation.

2. Imagine that you are breathing in through the balls of your feet and breathing out through your palms.

3. Place your hand on your diaphragm and consciously slow down the rise and fall of your chest.

4. As you breathe in slightly sink, and rise as you breathe out. Use your hands to remind you of the direction with your palms facing down as you sink and up as you rise.

5. Ask someone to place their hands on your shoulders to encourage intercostal breathing, so that your ribcage extends outwards rather than rises.

EXERCISE: ENGAGING THE VAGUS NERVE

This exercise is carried out in two steps:

1. Place the fingers of both hands into the indentation between your neck and head (vertebrae C1 and C2).

2. Put your attention on your breath, extend your exhalation and imagine tracing the path of the vagus nerve all the way into your body (see Figure 8.4). It passes through all the major organs and activates the parasympathetic nervous system. The effect will be to calm and usually leads to a feeling of being connected.

Conclusion

The complexity of the body means that the work of the performer does not end with the performance. The effects of what has been lived through linger in the body. Rebalancing is a way of training your body to be adaptable – it brings an awareness of how we are changed by experiences and resets the clock so you can return to your own comfortable patterns whilst registering what feels new.

Chapter 23

MAKING CHOICES
Finding creative options

Introduction

Each day we make thousands of choices, most being automatic and routine but others having more significant consequences. As we make decisions, value judgements are attached which weigh the risk or reward. To spend a little or a lot of money on a particular type of clothing or to challenge someone's behaviour after an inappropriate comment has ramifications which may or may not be of high stakes for your immediate or long-term future. Whatever the outcome, our choices are where our past, present and future collide; they are made to satisfy immediate needs, which are anchored in personal goals set over a lifetime. Psychologist William Glasser (1925–2013) believed that choices fall into one or more of the following categories:

- survival

- love

- belonging

- power

- freedom and fun.

The implication is that all action is motivated by what could be considered to be fairly primal needs, which are so deeply rooted that there is little conscious awareness of them. Glasser further divided behaviour into four components: thinking, acting (doing), feeling and physiology. This is similar to Rudolf Steiner's concept, later adopted by Michael Chekhov, of action, feeling and thinking. Glasser (1998) explains that all behaviour is chosen with control over thinking and doing, through which we have the ability to change feeling and physiology. This seems a clear and useful explanation to apply to acting. The process looks like this: there are thoughts about something, which arise for reasons linked to the past or future, and the thoughts lead to a decision or choice to take action, which results in a change in feelings within the body.

What is a choice?

Making a choice is a mental activity involving different parts of the brain; it concerns decision-making, leading to a specific course of action. As Glasser suggests, the specific results have significant effects on the feelings, sensations and emotions that may arise. They instigate internal action and reaction and trigger the impetus to fuel the drive of each moment. Damasio (2012) says that emotion is needed to consciously make choices. His studies have identified that choices do not exclusively derive from facts and logic but from stored emotions which connect to our past. This would explain feelings that steer a decision, a sort of knowing which is unconsciously drawn upon, when the body senses something is right or wrong.

Is a choice the objective?

Choices are clearly connected to objectives (goals, drives, wants), but they are the playing out, the physical realisation, in action. Playing out choices concerns how we do things, which is of course informed by the need for and the purpose of the action. It is important to remember that if there is a choice, there are alternatives; it is the process of selection of the options, as opposed to a decision, which is when the course of action has been decided. The stage when actors usually make choices is during preparation, when the whole story is being considered. What keeps a performance alive is when choices remain available, so decisions are not necessarily made, the alternatives are always present and there is active thought during the performance.

In classes and rehearsals I often experience a level of confusion over choices, as an actor may have a clear objective and believe that they have made an active choice but they may stand relatively still or rigid and solely deliver the lines, in a monosyllabic tone, with little substance behind them, as if the words do all the work. The creative interpretation at the disposal of the actor is the perusal of options.

The text indicates the choices made, but to keep the story alive it is interesting to always consider what else is possible. If an action is to open the front door, it is interesting if for a brief second the character considers not opening it. This adds layers to the internal processes.

What is the 'right' choice?

There is not necessarily a 'right' choice, but there are ones that are obvious and draw on stereotypical perceptions, such as a traumatic situation that involves screaming and crying hysterically, or anger that involves violent outbursts. This may actually be true in some instances, but it may also be an assumption. The character profile, past actions and given circumstances provide the factors that indicate whether one choice would be made over another. What is vital is that the actor make sense of the choices written in the text and those they create from their own interpretation. Playing a set of behaviours that have not surfaced at all in the narrative would make no sense even if they were interesting.

Can we make more than one choice?

The questions that often arise are: Is there a governing choice in a scene? Are there many choices? I advise that there is one dominate objective which guides the choices.

We are continually making choices, so although there may be a central decision based on need in a scene, such as Romeo needs to see Juliet so he makes the choice to climb into her garden, as the scene progresses moment by moment other choices arise. Is it safe to get closer? Should he risk getting caught? Should he take this risk? Should he speak to her or make himself known? All of these options are guided by his goal, which is to win Juliet's heart.

The level of commitment to a choice is determined by the level of need, which provides the level of urgency. When an actor is unclear about any aspect of the action, it is noticeable and the work is generalised and under-energised. Reasons for this could be that the thought and intentions are not clear enough. Without the reason, there is no definite action. Consider that every choice you make is a collaborative experience between mind and body. The mind may know that the situation should stimulate certain feelings and emotions and intend to fully carry them out, be it to shout, scream or sob, but if the real need is not played out, confusion arises, words are empty and the body indicates 'dis-ease'.

Prior to a choice being made, there are alternatives which can be weighed; it is a mistake to believe that the words appear without musings and internal conversations. Social scientist Albert Schutz (1899–1959) suggested that action as conscious behaviour appears as a plan, the motives having two factors: 'because' (i.e. something has happened in the person's history) and 'in order to' (what is going to happen in the future). This highlights that action is always moving forwards to put the plan into action.

The process of the actor

Let's look at the process through which an actor journeys. There is a script which contains a series of thoughts behind which is a driving objective, a goal. The goal (thoughts) stimulates feelings and physiological activity which may drive the urgency, which becomes a need. The actor weighs the options available and makes a choice as to how to reach the need.

The text provides the words, and the actor makes it their own by interpreting and understanding what is behind the thoughts and overall situation. This is achieved by adding images and memories – all the unspoken thoughts that connect to the character's immediate need.

EXERCISE: PREPARATION FOR MAKING CHOICES

The choice about how to play a scene comes after the fundamental information has been absorbed as this will govern the action and the choices. Initially, answer these key questions:

- Where, when, what, who and why.
- What is the story of the scene?
- What is happening?
- What is the objective of your character?
- How can they reach it?
- Where are the key moments when their needs increase or decrease?
- What are the options in each moment?

Without this initial work, choices do not become apparent.

EXERCISE: CHOOSING HOW TO PLAY A SCENE

A scene can be played many ways depending on the angle you decide to prioritise. Returning to the example of Romeo, a possible angle is to make him worried about the risk of getting caught in the Capulets' garden, or an alternative is to play the scene as if he is certain he could overcome any challenges, and he would therefore be bolder in his action.

- Working from the given circumstances, consider the options for your character. Could he or she be more or less concerned about the situation?

- What are the stakes? What could the character lose or gain?

- Consider playing the scene where you alter the importance of the stakes. If there is no danger to Romeo in the garden, this changes his actions. He does not have to hide or be at all worried.

- What is the ideal outcome? Draw up a list of ways that the character may consider to reach the outcome. It is not necessary to stick to the text, but be clear about the goal. Play versions of the scene.

- Return to the text, but feel that the options you considered are alive.

It is useful to play with options and assess what feels right. Then, remain *awake* to the possibilities that arise as you move through the scene.

EXERCISE: WHAT'S THE GAME?

It is interesting to play action as if it is a game, as if there are strategies to help you win. What determines the action is the type of game you are playing. Hide and seek is different from chess, which is calculated and thought driven. To win, your character decides on the plan of action, which may mean choosing to be playful, defensive, combative, determined, provocative, ruthless and so forth. Try this exercise:

1. Decide on your strategy.

2. Select a game which you can secretly play to achieve your goal.

3. You do not actually have to play the game whilst moving through the scene, but have it behind your action. So if you are playing chess, you would focus on thought. If it's tag, you may move around and possibly add actions which are quick and light. If it's a competitive ball game, you may be assertive and bold in your interaction.

4. Each time you go through the scene, change the game and see how that affects your choices.

EXERCISE: GOING AGAINST THE OBVIOUS

There will be an obvious way of playing a scene, and this is based on stereotypes and what you may have experienced. To move away from the obvious, try other options which may even go against the action. For example:

- What is the most obvious way to play the scene? A scenario with a mother mourning her child is clearly a tragedy, but what happens if it is played with humour?

- List opposite ways.

- Play the least likely options.

It is surprising what comes from this exercise. None of the options may feel right, but it is the exploring that is important, and small moments may be influenced.

EXERCISE: CHOICES AND THE EYES

Sharpening an awareness of what the eyes reveal is really valuable, especially for the screen actor, where we have intimate access to what is being thought. The eyes reveal thoughts, they make us available or not to others, convey emotion and indicate general health and mental state. Ultimately they present the truth of what is being experienced and indicate where a person's attention is.

In screen performance the thinking is apparent, and as thoughts have journeys, it is important to be able to have access to them. The way to achieve this is to be active and on thought, really clear about where you place your attention and what you are thinking. Trace back the origin of the potential thought and gauge the stakes attached to it.

It is interesting to compare the eyes to an aperture of a camera, where we choose what we want in the photograph. It is good to be reminded that the eyes create action and reveal what a person wants to achieve.

Select a scene and work through the following points:

1. Consider if you are reflecting, informing, questioning, imagining, confessing, challenging and so forth, as each of these is a different action and has a particular quality and direction of focus.

2. What is the energetic quality attached to the action? Is it linked to your intention? Is it soft, heavy, light, floaty, direct, indirect, dense or something else?

3. Notice the direction of focus. Is it inwards, outwards, left, right, upwards, downwards, sending energy in or radiating energy out?

Tips for the eyes on screen

On camera there are some choices that are needed which may feel unnatural, such as finding an eye line to suit the position of the camera. Similarly, you may be asked to cheat, for example, when the position of your body may not be natural to the situation, such as not looking at the person to whom you are talking. This is for the shot construction. In these instances you need to make the position make sense to you and look at ease. For example, you could do the following:

- Notice the position and/or angle of your head.

- Know what you are communicating through your eyes.

- Practise different ways of using your eyes.

- Keep your thinking active.

- Avoid relying solely on the eyes to communicate as this will disconnect you from your body.

EXERCISE: PRACTISE ON CAMERA

A way to notice what you do with your eyes is to film yourself. With that in mind, do the following:

1. Position yourself so the camera has access to you.
2. Find an eye line on either side of the camera.
3. Experiment with where you choose to place your attention: past, present or future?

Below are some scenarios that can be used for practice.

Listening situations

The first scenario requires listening and responding to what you hear:

- a phone message which gives you news regarding an application or the result of a hospital test

- a discussion at a dinner party with people you do not know very well regarding a topic about which you have a strong opinion

- sitting at a desk constructing a letter or email to inform someone that you plan to leave a relationship

- on a train on your way to an important meeting.

Talking situations

Now imagine yourself in these talking situations or, if you have someone to work with, improvise these situations:

- explaining the story of *Hamlet* to a friend

- confessing to lying about an incident to a partner

- giving a speech to a conference (on a topic with which you feel comfortable)

- explaining your innocence in court regarding something of which you have been accused

- telling a group of people about what you want to achieve in life.

'Playing back' and noticing yourself

'Play back' and notice:

- the movement of your eyes

- what happens when you are in the past, present or future

- the intensity and quality emerging through your eyes.

Repeat the situation and change your eye movement, reflecting on the difference and the impact. Then experiment with the following actions: search, select, shift, sustain, shut, flash, twinkle, glisten, hypnotise, dart and dance. Finally, change the force and timing of how you direct your eyes whilst sustaining and holding the act of looking.

We create action with our eyes and convey meaning, especially text that is not actually spoken. Exploring making conscious choices and creating action will change the intensity you generate and have a significant impact on your performance.

Conclusion

Choices are vital for how a story is told, as they affect:

- feelings and emotions

- inner tempo (i.e. speed of thoughts)

- movement

- vocal tone

- action

- reaction

- spatial use

- relationships (i.e. how they are defined)

- clarity and precision in a performance.

When you explore a scene you are surveying possibilities, but in performance you make the choices as you play the moments. Preparation is not decision-making but rather surveying what *could* happen.

The ideas that I have presented throughout this book all originate from my own experiences of working with actors. The questions, obstacles, solutions and breakthroughs are grounded in practice. The ongoing theme is the willingness to look around for options and additions to your work, as they may be found in territories that you least expect (in my case, biology and physics).

There are many excellent techniques available to actors, and the approach you choose will depend on the type of actor you want to be. I am interested in the transformative performer who identifies the distinctions between themselves and the character, and imaginatively immerses themselves in the fictional world. Our body is continually changing; nothing is static, and what seems habitual and routine can be mistaken for being identical and mere repetition. But this is not the case: every thought and action, even if you rehearse it, is new because the movement of substances in your body is continually shifting. Different amounts of neurotransmitters are swirling around, the heart is pumping and millions of cells are darting back and forth: like a river, the internal life never stops flowing.

Studies in neuroscience inform us that although the brain lays down neural pathways, it also has the capacity to keep producing new ones. So doing things in a different way brings a changing landscape. In this sense, transformation is inevitable when you perform, but the extent to which you can experience far away from your own baseline depends on how you work.

My suggestion is that you embrace holistic training, avoid prioritising the thinking part of your body, engage in working with the energy systems and embark on new ways to get to your destination, which for most actors is embodied performance.

I firmly believe that, like musicians and dancers, actors need to fine-tune their instrument and keep looking at various ways of working.

Embracing different approaches is fundamental to growth as a creative artist. Attend classes, set goals, learn new skills and read up on other disciplines. Keep ideas moving forwards, experiment, blend concepts, take risks and see what happens.

REFERENCES

Chapter 1

Hackney, P. (2002) *Making Connections: Total Body Integration*. New York, NY. Routledge.
Keleman, S. (1985) *Emotional Anatomy*. Berkeley, CA: Center Press.
Lakoff, G. and Johnson, M. (2003) *Metaphors We Live By*. Chicago, IL: University of Chicago Press.
Levine, P. (1997) *Walking the Tiger: Healing Trauma*. Berkeley, CA: North Atlantic Books.

Further reading

Boston, J. and Cook, R. (eds) (2009) *Breath in Action: The Art of Breath in Vocal and Holistic Practice*. London: Jessica Kingsley Publishers.
Keleman, S. (1987) *Embodying Experience: Forming a Personal Life*. Berkeley, CA: Center Press.
MacDonald, M. (2013) *Simple Step-by-Step Alexander Technique: Regain Your Natural Poise and Alleviate Stress*. Leicestershire: Lorenze Books.
Merlin, B. (2007) *The Stanislavsky Toolkit*. London: Nick Hern Books.
Stern, D. (2010) *Forms of Vitality: Exploring Dynamic Experience in Psychology, the Arts, Psychotherapy and Development*. Oxford: Oxford University Press.

Chapter 2

Downing, J.H. (1996) 'Establishing a discipline plan in elementary physical education.' *Journal of Physical Education, Recreation and Dance 67*, 25–30.
Dychtwald, K. (1977) *Bodymind*. New York, NY: Tarcher Penguin.
Hackney, P. (2002) *Making Connections. Total Body Integration Through Bartenieff Fundamentals*. New York, NY: Routledge.
Keleman, S. (1981) *Your Body Speaks Its Mind*. Berkeley, CA: Center Press.
Keleman, S. (1987) *Embodying Experience: Forming a Personal Life*. Berkeley, CA: Center Press.
Keleman, S. (1999) *Emotional Anatomy*. Berkeley, CA: Center Press.
Sheldrake, R. (2011) *The Presence of the Past: Morphic Resonance and the Habits of Nature*. London: Icon Books.
Tiffin, J. and McCormick, E. (1971) *Attitude and Motivation*. London: HMSO.
Weiss, H. (2009) 'The use of mindfulness in psychodynamic and body oriented psychology.' *Hakomi Forum* 22. Available at www.hakomiinstitute.com/Forum/Issue22/04ArtMindfulness.pdf, accessed on 17 May 2016.

Further reading

Ekman, P. (2003) *Emotions Revealed*. New York, NY: St Martins Griffin.
Johnson, D.H. (1995) *Breath, Bone and Gesture*. Berkeley, CA: North Atlantic Books.
Levine, P. (1997) *Walking the Tiger*. Berkeley, CA: North Atlantic Books.

Chapter 3

Blair, R. (2008) *The Actor, Image, and Action. Acting and Cognitive Neuroscience.* New York, NY: Routledge.
Csikszentmihalyi, M. (2002) *Flow: The Classic Work on How to Achieve Happiness.* London: Rider.
Gendlin, E. (1981) *Focusing* (revised). New York, NY: Bantam.
Gray, H. (1918) *Anatomy of the Human Body.* Philadelphia, PA: Lea and Febiger (20th edn, thoroughly revised and re-edited by W.H. Lewis).
Harter, J. (ed.) (2005) *Old-Time Anatomical Illustrations.* New York, NY: Dover Publications.
Kemp, R. (2012) *Embodied Acting: What Neuroscience Tells Us About Performance.* New York, NY: Routledge.
Levine, P.A. (1997) *Walking the Tiger.* Berkeley, CA: North Atlantic Books.

Further reading

Boston, J. and Cook, R. (2009) *Breath in Action: The Art of Breath in Vocal and Holistic Practice.* London: Jessica Kingsley Publishers.
Corwin, H. (2012) *Evolving the Actor's Neutral Body. Structural Integration 40,* 1, 37–40.
Keleman, S. (1981) *Your Body Speaks Its Mind.* Berkeley, CA: Center Press.

Chapter 4

Eden, D. (2008) *Energy Medicine: Balancing Your Body's Energy for Optimal Health, Joy and Vitality.* London: Piatkus.
Heckler, R. (1984) *The Anatomy of Change: A Way to Move Through Life's Transitions.* Berkeley, CA: North Atlantic Books.
Mitchell, T. (1998) *Movement from Person to Actor to Character.* Lanham, MD: Scarecrow Press.
Oschman, J. (2000) *Energy Medicine: The Scientific Basis.* London: Churchill Livingstone.
Snow, J. (2012) *Movement Training for Actors.* London: Methuen.
Sullivan, C. (1990) *The Actor Moves.* London: McFarland.
Wang, M., Lamers, R.J., Korthout, H.A., van Nesselrooij, J.H. *et al.* (2005) 'Metabolomics in the context of systems biology: Bridging traditional Chinese medicine and molecular pharmacology.' *Phytotherapy Research 19,* 173–182.

Further reading

Allain, P. (2002) *The Theatre Practice of Tadashi Suzuki.* London: Methuen.
Barba, E. (1995) *The Paper Canoe: A Guide to Theatre Anthropology; the Secret Art of the Performer* (trans. R. Fowler). London: Routledge.
Bogart, A. and Landau, T. (2005) *The Viewpoints Book.* New York, NY: Theatre Communication Group.
Lavy, J. (2005) 'Theatrical Foundation of Grotowski's Total Act, Via Negativa, and Conjunctio Oppositorum.' *Journal of Religion and Theatre 4,* 2, 175–188.
Marshall, L. (2001) *The Body Speaks.* London: Methuen.
Merlin, B. (2001) *Beyond Stanislavsky.* London: Nick Hern Books.
Merlin, B. (2010) *Acting: The Basics.* New York, NY: Routledge.
Sermonti, G. (1995) 'The inadequacy of the molecular approach in biology.' *Frontier Perspectives 4,* 31–34.
Shumway-Cook, A. and Woollcott, M.H. (2001) *Motor Control: Theory and Practical Application.* Philadelphia, PA: Lippincott Williams & Wilkins.
Zarrilli, P.B. (2008) *Psychophysical Acting: An Intercultural Approach After Stanislavski.* London: Routledge.

Chapter 5

Chamberlain, F. (2003) *Michael Chekhov.* Routledge Performance Practitioners. London: Routledge.
Chekhov, M. (1991) *To the Actor.* New York, NY: Harper Perennial.
Chen, N. (2011) 'Qi in Asian Medicine.' In D. Mayor and M.S. Micozzi (eds) *Energy Medicine East and West.* Hong Kong: Churchill Livingstone/Elsevier.

Chuen, L.K. (2005) *Chi Kung: The Way of Energy.* London: GAIA.

Dale, C. (2009) *The Subtle Body: An Encyclopedia of Your Energetic Anatomy.* Louisville, CO: Sounds True Publishing.

Ergil, K. and Micozzi, M.S. (2011) 'Qi in China's Traditional Medicine: The Example of Tuina.' In D. Mayor and M.S. Micozzi (eds) *Energy Medicine East and West.* Hong Kong: Churchill Livingstone/ Elsevier.

Hamill, J. and Knutzen, K. (2009) *Biomechanical Basis of Human Movement* (3rd edn). Baltimore, MD: Wolters Kluwer/Lippincott Williams & Wilkins.

Kaptchuk, T. (2000) *Chinese Medicine: The Web That Has No Weaver.* London: Rider.

Lipton, B. (2005) *The Biology of Belief.* London: Hay House.

Low, C. (2011) 'Systems Theory: Tracking and Mapping Healing with Qi.' In D. Mayor and M.S. Micozzi (eds) *Energy Medicine East and West.* Hong Kong: Churchill Livingstone/Elsevier.

Marieb, E. (2009) *Essentials of Human Anatomy and Physiology.* San Francisco, CA: Pearson.

Mayor, D. and Micozzi, M.S. (2011) 'Themes of Qi and a Dozen Definitions: Content Analysis and Discussion.' In D. Mayor and M.S. Micozzi (eds) *Energy Medicine East and West.* Hong Kong: Churchill Livingstone/Elsevier.

Mróz, D. (2015) 'Cycles of Creation: Michael Chekhov and the Yinyang Waxing Cosmology.' In M.-C. Autant-Mathieu and Y. Emerson (eds) *The Routledge Companion to Michael Chekhov.* New York, NY: Routledge.

Nelson, L.A. and Schwartz, G.E. (2005) 'Human biofield and intention detection: Individual differences.' *Journal of Alternative and Complementary Medicine 11*, 1, 93–101.

Newman, T. (2011) 'Evidencing Energy: Experiences in Acupuncture and Therapeutic Bodywork (Zero Balancing).' In D. Mayor and M.S. Micozzi (eds) *Energy Medicine East and West.* Hong Kong: Churchill Livingstone/Elsevier.

Pert, C. (1997) *Molecules of Emotion.* London: Pocket Books.

Schwartz, G.E. and Simon, W.L. (2007) *The Energy Healing Experiments: Science Reveals our Natural Power to Heal.* New York, NY: Atria Books.

Stanislavsky, C. (1980) *An Actor Prepares.* London: Methuen.

Stronik, G. (1998) 'Principles of Cardiomagnetism.' In S.J. Williamson, M. Hoke, G. Stroink and M. Kotani (eds) *Advances in Biomagnetism.* New York, NY: Plenum Books.

Tiller, W.A. (1997) *Science and Human Transformation: Subtle Energies, Intentionality and Consciousness.* Walnut Creek, CA: Pavior.

Tiller, W.A. (1999) 'Subtle energies.' *Science and Medicine 6*, 3, 28.

Tiller, W.A. and Cook, W. (1974) 'Psychoenergetic Field Studies Using a Biomechanics Transducer.' Proceedings of New Horizons in Healing Symposium. Phoenix, AZ: ARE Clinic.

Further reading

Ashperger, C.A. (2008) *The Rhythm of Space and the Sound of Time.* Amsterdam: Rodopi.

Eden, D. (2008) *Energy Medicine: Balancing Your Body's Energy for Optimal Health, Joy and Vitality.* London: Piatkus.

Brahe, P. (2008) 'Beyond Michael Chekhov Technique: Continuing the Exploration Through Mask.' In A. Bartlow (ed.) *Handbook of Acting Techniques.* London: Nick Hern Books.

Juhan, D. (2003) *Job's Body: A Handbook for Bodywork.* New York, NY: Station Hill.

Mayor, D. and Micozzi, M.S. (eds) (2011) *Energy Medicine East and West.* Hong Kong: Churchill Livingstone/Elsevier.

Merlin, B. (2001) *Beyond Stanislavsky: The Psycho-physical Approach to Actor Training.* London: Nick Hern Books.

Wolford, L. and Schechner, R. (eds) (2001) *The Grotowski Sourcebook.* London: Routledge.

Zarrilli, P.B. (2008) *Psychophysical Acting: An Intercultural Approach After Stanislavsky.* London: Routledge.

Chapter 6

Alfreds, M. (2007) *Different Every Night.* London: Nick Hern Books.

Andrews-Hanna, J.R., Reidler, J.S., Sepulcre, J., Poulin, R. and Buckner, R.L. (2010) 'Functional-anatomic fractionation of the brain's default network.' *Neuron 65*, 4, 550–562.

Buchanan, T.W. (2007) 'Retrieval of emotional memories.' *Psychological Bulletin 133*, 5, 761–779.

Conway, M.A., Justice, L.V. and Morrison, C.M. (2014) 'Beliefs about autobiographical memory and why they matter.' *The Psychologist 27*, 502–505.

Conway, M.A. and Pleydell-Pearce, C.W. (2000) 'The construction of autobiographical memories in the self-memory system.' *Psychological Review 107*, 2, 261–288.

Damasio, A. (2012) *Self Comes to Mind: Constructing the Conscious Brain*. London: Vintage.

Edwards, R., Honeycutt, J.M. and Zagacki, K.S. (1988) 'Imagined interaction as an element of social cognition.' *Western Journal of Speech Communication 52*, 23–45.

Fernyhough, C. (2012) *Pieces of Light: The New Science of Memory*. London: Profile Books.

Fleming, N.D. (2001) *VARK: A Guide to Learning Styles*. Available at www.vark-learn.com, accessed on 20 May 2016.

Foster, J.K. (2009) *Memory: A Very Short Introduction*. Oxford: Oxford University Press.

Jacobs, J., Lega, B. and Anderson, C. (2012) 'Explaining how brain stimulation can evoke memories.' *Journal of Cognitive Neuroscience 24*, 3, 553–563.

Herz, R.S., Eliassen, J., Beland, S. and Souza, T. (2004) 'Neuroimaging evidence for the emotional potency of odor-evoked memory.' *Neuropsychologia 42*, 371–378.

Herz, R.S. and Schooler, J.W. (2002) 'A naturalistic study of autobiographical memories evoked by olfactory and visual cues: Testing the Proustian hypothesis.' *American Journal of Psychology 115*, 1, 21–32.

Honeycutt, J.M., Zagacki, K.S. and Edwards, R. (1989) 'Intrapersonal communication, social cognition and imagined interactions.' In C.V. Roberts and K.W. Watson (eds) *Intrapersonal Communication Processes: Original Essays*. New Orleans, LA: Spectra.

Knight, W.E. and Rickard, N.S. (2001) 'Relaxing music prevents stress-induced increases in subjective anxiety, systolic blood pressure, and heart rate in healthy males and females.' *Journal of Music Therapy 38*, 4, 254–272.

Krumhansl, C.L. and Zupnick, J. (2013) 'Cascading reminiscence bumps in popular music.' *Psychological Science 24*, 10, 2057–2068.

Leung, M.Y. and Fung, I. (2005) 'Enhancement of classroom facilities of primary schools and its impact on learning behaviours of students.' *Facilities 23*, 13/14, 585–594.

Manning, C.G. (2000) 'Imagination inflation with posttest delays: How long will it last?' Unpublished doctoral dissertation. Seattle, WA: University of Washington.

Mazzoni, G., Scoboria, A. and Harvey, L. (2010) 'Non-believed memories.' *Psychological Science 21*, 9, 1334–1340.

McIsaac, H.K. and Eich, E. (2004) 'Vantage point in traumatic memory.' *Psychological Science 15*, 4, 248–253.

Meisner, S. and Longwell, D. (1987) *Sanford Meisner on Acting*. Toronto: Vintage Books.

Nigro, G. and Neisser, U. (1983) 'Point of view in personal memories.' *Cognitive Psychology 15*, 4, 467–482.

Noice, H. (1991) 'The role of explanation and plan recognition in the learning of theatrical scripts.' *Cognitive Science 15*, 425–460.

Noice, H. (1992) 'Elaborative memory strategies of professional actors.' *Applied Cognitive Psychology 6*, 417-427.

Noice, T. and Noice, H. (1997) *The Nature of Expertise in Professional Acting: A Cognitive View*. Mahwah, NJ: Lawrence Erlbaum Associates.

Oschman, J.L. and Oschman, N.H. (1994a) 'Somatic recall, part 1: Soft tissue memory.' *Massage Therapy Journal 34*, 3, 36–45; 111–116.

Oschman, J.L. and Oschman, N.H. (1994b) 'Somatic recall, part 2: Soft tissue holography.' *Massage Therapy Journal 34*, 4, 66–67; 106–116.

Schine, J. (2010) *Movement, Memory and the Senses in Soundscape Studies*. Available at www.sensorystudies. org/sensorial-investigations/movement-memory-the-senses-in-soundscape-studies, accessed on 17 March 2016.

Schulkind, M.D., Rubin, D.C. and Hennis, L.K. (1999) 'Music, emotion, and autobiographical memory: They're playing your song.' *Memory and Cognition 27*, 948–955.

Sheldrake, R. (2011) *The Presence of the Past Morphic Resonance and the Habits of Nature* (2nd edn). London: Icon Books.

Spreng, R.N. and Levine, B. (2013) 'Doing what we imagine: Completion rates and frequency attributes of imagined future events one year after prospection.' *Memory 21*, 4, 458–466.

Spreng, R.N., Stevens, W.D., Chamberlain, J.P., Gilmore, A.W. and Schacter, D.L. (2010) 'Default network activity, coupled with the frontoparietal control network, supports goal-directed cognition.' *Neuroimage 31*, 303–317.

Stanislavsky, C. (1980) *An Actor Prepares*. London: Methuen.

Suddendorf, T. and Corballis, M.C. (2007) 'The evolution of foresight: What is mental time travel, and is it unique to humans?' *Behavioral and Brain Sciences 30*, 299–313.

Talavico, J., LaBar, K. and Rubin, D. (2004) 'Emotional intensity predicts autobiographical memory experience.' *Memory and Cognition 37*, 7, 1118–1132.

Thomas, A.K. and Loftus, E.F. (2002) 'Creating bizarre false memories through imagination.' *Memory and Cognition 30*, 423–431.

Tulving, E. (2000) *The New Cognitive Neurosciences* (2nd edn). Cambridge, MA: MIT Press.

Webster, G.D. and Weir, C.G. (2005) 'Emotional responses to music: Interactive effects of mode, texture, and tempo.' *Motivation and Emotion 29*, 19–39.

Willander, J. and Larsson, M. (2006) 'Smell your way back to childhood: Autobiographical odor memory.' *Psychonomic Bulletin and Review 13*, 240–244.

Further reading

Ho, C., Cheung, M.C. and Chan, A.S. (2003) 'Music training improves verbal but not visual memory: Cross-sectional and longitudinal explorations in children.' *Neuropsychology 17*, 3, 439–450.

Honeycutt, J. and Gotcher, J.M. (1990) 'Influence of Imagined Interactions on Communicative Outcomes: The Case of Forensic Competition.' In R.G. Kunzendorf (ed.) *Mental Imagery*. New York, NY: Springer Science and Business Media.

Marshall, L. (2001) *The Body Speaks*. London: Methuen.

Oschman, J. (2000) *Energy Medicine: The Scientific Basis*. London: Churchill Livingstone.

Seung, S. (2012) *Connectome: How the Brain's Wiring Makes Us Who We Are*. London: Allen Lane.

Chapter 7

Brewer, J.A., Worhunsky, P.D., Gray, J.R., Tang, Y.Y., Weber, J. and Kober, H. (2011) 'Meditation experience is associated with differences in default mode network activity and connectivity.' *Proceedings of the National Academy of Sciences of the United States of America 108*, 50, 20254–20259.

Caruso, A. (2005) *Sports Psychology Basics*. Ann Arbor, MI: Reedswain.

Dale, C. (2009) *The Subtle Body: An Encyclopedia of Your Energetic Anatomy*. Louisville, CO: Sounds True Publishing.

Ekman, P. (2010) *Emotions Revealed*. New York, NY: St Martin's Griffin.

Garza, D.L. and Feltz, D.L. (1998) 'Effects of selected mental practice techniques on performance ratings, self-efficacy, and state anxiety of competitive figure skaters.' *Sport Psychologist 12*, 1–15.

Hatzigeorgiadis, A., Zourbanos, N., Mpoumpaki, S. and Theodorakis, Y. (2009) 'Mechanisms underlying the self-talk–performance relationship: The effects of motivational self-talk on self-confidence and anxiety.' *Psychology of Sport and Exercise 10*, 186–192.

Humara, M.A. (1999) 'The Relationship Between Anxiety and Performance: A Cognitive-Behavioral Perspective.' *Athletic Insight 1*, 2.

Kabat-Zinn, J. (2003) 'Mindfulness-based interventions in context: Past, present and future.' *Clinical Psychology: Science and Practice 10*, 144–156.

Kaptchuk, T.J. (2000) *Chinese Medicine: The Web That Has No Weaver*. London: Rider.

Klocek, D. (2013) *Sacred Agriculture: The Alchemy of Biodynamics*. Herndon, VA: Lindisfarne Books.

Lensen, M. (2005) 'Feeling our emotions.' Interview with A. Damasio. *Scientific American 16*, 1, 14–15.

Oschman, J. (2009) *The Development of the Living Matrix Concept and Its Significance for Health and Healing*. Presented in collaboration with Nora H. Oschman Nature's Own Research Association, Dover, New Hampshire. Science of Healing Conference, Kings College, London, 13 March 2009.

Post, P.G. and Wrisberg, C.A. (2012) 'A phenomenological investigation of gymnasts' lived experience of imagery.' *Sport Psychologist 26*, 98–121.

Stefanini, P. (2011) 'Ki in Shatsu.' In D. Mayor and M.S. Micozzi (eds) *Energy Medicine East and West*. Hong Kong: Churchill Livingstone/Elsevier.

Sumner, J. (2009) *You Are How You Move*. London: Jessica Kingsley Publishers.

Thelwell, R.C. and Maynard, I.W. (2002) 'A triangulation of findings of three studies investigating repeatable good performance in professional cricketers.' *International Journal of Sport Psychology 33*, 247–268.

Thelwell, R.C. and Maynard, I.W. (2003) 'The effects of a mental skills package on "repeatable good performance" in cricketers.' *Psychology of Sport and Exercise 4*, 377–396.

Todd, D.A., Thatcher, R., McGuigan, M. and Thatcher, J. (2009) 'Effects of instructional and motivational self-talk on the vertical jump.' *Journal of Strength and Conditioning Research 23*, 196–202.

Weinberg, R.S. and Gould, D. (2011) *Foundations of Sport and Exercise Psychology*. Champaign, IL: Human Kinetics.

Further reading

Seung, S. (2012) *Connectome: How the Brain's Wiring Makes Us Who We Are*. London: Allen Lane.

Chapter 8

Beckett, C.A. (1997) 'Directing student attention during two-part dictation.' *Journal of Research in Music Education 45*, 4, 613–625.

Behnke, E. (1984) *World Without Opposite. Flesh of the World: A Carnal Introduction*. Felton, CA: California Center for Jean Gebser Studies.

Blair, R. (2008) *The Actor, Image, and Action: Acting and Cognitive Neuroscience*. New York, NY: Routledge.

Childre, D. and Martin, H. (2000) *The HeartMath Solution: The HeartMath Institute's Revolutionary Program for Engaging the Power of the Heart's Intelligence*. New York, NY: HarperOne.

Dharani, K. (2014) *The Biology of Thought*. London: Academic Press.

Ho, M.W. (2008) *The Rainbow and the Worm*. London: World Scientific Publishing.

Jarmey, C. (2008) *The Concise Book of Muscles*. Berkeley, CA: North Atlantic Books.

Kemp, R. (2012) *Embodied Acting: What Neuroscience Tells Us About Performance*. New York, NY: Routledge.

Levine, P. (1997) *Waking the Tiger*. North Berkeley, CA: Atlantic Books.

Marieb, E. (2009) *Essentials of Human Anatomy and Physiology*. San Francisco, CA: Pearson.

Marshall, L. (2002) *The Body Speaks*. London: Methuen.

McNeill, D. (1998) 'Speech and gesture integration.' In J.M. Iverson and S. Goldin-Meadow (eds) *The Nature and Functions of Gesture in Children's Communication*. New Directions for Child Development 79. San Francisco, CA: Jossey-Bass Inc. Publishers.

McNeill, D. (2005) *Gesture and Thought*. Chicago, IL: University of Chicago Press.

Merlin, B. (2001) *Beyond Stanislavsky: The Psycho-physical Approach to Actor Training*. London: Nick Hern Books.

Nielsen, J.A., Zielinski, B.A., Ferguson, M.A., Lainhart, J.E. and Anderson, J.S. (2013) 'An evaluation of the left-brain vs. right-brain hypothesis with resting state functional connectivity magnetic resonance imaging.' *PLoS ONE 8*, 8: e71275. doi: 10.1371/journal.pone.0071275

Oida, Y. and Marshall, L. (1997) *The Invisible Actor*. New York, NY: Methuen.

Oschman, J. (2000) *Energy Medicine: The Scientific Basis*. London: Churchill Livingstone.

Pinker, S. (1997) *How the Mind Works*. New York, NY: W.W. Norton.

Saladin, K. (2014) *Anatomy and Physiology: The Unity of Form and Function*. Columbus, OH: McGraw Hill Higher Education.

Shier, D.N., Butler, J.L. and Lewis, R. (2015) *Hole's Human Anatomy and Physiology*. Columbus, OH: McGraw Hill Higher Education.

Sperry, R.W. (1977) 'Reply to Professor Puccetti.' *Journal of Medicine and Philosophy 2*, 2, 145.

Watkins, A. (2011) 'The Electrical Heart: Energy in Cardiac Health and Disease.' In D. Mayor and M.S. Micozzi (eds) *Energy Medicine East and West*. Hong Kong: Churchill Livingstone/Elsevier.

Zarrilli, P.B. (2008) *Psychophysical Acting: An Intercultural Approach After Stanislavski*. London: Routledge.

Zatorre, R. and Beckett, C. (1989) 'Multiple coding strategies in the retention of musical tones by possessors of absolute pitch.' *Memory and Cognition 17*, 582–589.

Zatorre, R.J., Perry, D.W., Beckett, C.A., Westbury, C.F. and Evans, A.C. (1998) 'Functional anatomy of musical processing in listeners with absolute pitch and relative pitch.' *Proceedings of the National Academy of Sciences of the United States of America 95*, 3172–3177.

Further reading

Agnew, Z.C., McGettigan, C., Banks, C.B. and Scott, S.K. (2013) 'Articulatory movements modulate auditory responses to speech.' *Neuroimage 73*, 192–199.

Blandrine, G. (1993) *Anatomy of Movement.* Seattle, WA: Eastland Press.

Hornsby, J. (2004) 'Agency and Actions.' In H. Steward and J. Hyman (eds) *Agency and Action.* Cambridge: Cambridge University Press.

Levine, P. (2010) *In an Unspoken Voice: How the Body Releases Trauma and Restores Goodness.* Berkeley, CA: North Atlantic Books.

Liebman, M. (1986) *Neuroanatomy Made Easy and Understandable.* Rockville, MD: Aspen Publications.

Mayor, D. and Micozzi, M.S. (eds) (2011) *Energy Medicine East and West.* Hong Kong: Churchill Livingstone/Elsevier.

Nataraja, S. (2008) *The Blissful Brain.* London: Gaia Thinking.

Omar, R., Henley, S.M, Bartlett, J.W., Hailstone, J.C. *et al.* (2011) 'Structural neuroanatomy of music emotion recognition: Evidence from frontotemporal lobar degeneration.' *Neuroimage 56*, 1814–1821.

Chapter 9

Heckler, R. (1984) *The Anatomy of Change.* Berkeley, CA: North Atlantic Books.

Chapter 16

Petit, L. (2010) *The Michael Chekhov Handbook for the Actor.* New York, NY: Routledge.

Chapter 18

Petit, L. (2010) *The Michael Chekhov Handbook for the Actor.* New York, NY: Routledge.

Chapter 23

Damasio, A. (2012) *Self Comes to Mind: Constructing the Conscious Brain.* London: Vintage.

Glasser, W. (1998) *Choice Theory: A New Psychology of Personal Freedom.* New York: Harper Perennial.

SUBJECT INDEX

AUTHOR INDEX